Dear Diana,
lovely to meet you,
I hope you enjoyed your taste
of down under,
Best wishes

Where are the traditional craftsmen, the skilled and passionate individuals?
They are vanishing in a world of fast, overly simplified foods.

Good food takes time.

Technique is a means, and culinary artistry visually appetising,
but flavour is the only true hand to guide you.

Diana Kennedy
Sydney
1.X.11

Bécasse

JUSTIN NORTH

Recipes inspired by Australia's
great food producers

Photography by Steve Brown

hardie grant books
MELBOURNE · LONDON

To Mum and Dad:
Thank you for everything. Your unconditional love and
support are what I have thrived on for the past thirty years.

And to Raymond, a genius in the truest sense of the word.
You changed my life – your energy and constant search for
excellence will stay with me forever. You taught me to taste
and think – two of the greatest attributes a chef can ever have.

First published in 2006.

Reprinted in 2009 by
Hardie Grant Books
85 High Street
Prahran, Victoria 3181, Australia
www.hardiegrant.com.au

Cataloguing-in-Publication Data is available from the
National Library of Australia.

Photography by Steve Brown
Cover design by Pfisterer+Freeman
Internal design by
Cassandra Warner, Scribble Design and Pfisterer+Freeman
Typeset by Pauline Haas, bluerinse setting
Printed and bound in China by C&C Offset Printing Co., Ltd.

3 5 7 9 10 8 6 4 2

Foreword

Great love and great achievements often involve great risk. A decade ago, Justin North left behind all he knew and came to work for me. He spent nearly three years by my side and was one of the finest chefs to ever work at Le Manoir aux Quat' Saisons. And since he took that risk, Justin has gone from one achievement to the next. He rose quickly from commis to sous chef at Le Manoir and was voted employee of the year. Now, his restaurant in Sydney is a huge success, fully booked every night and the recipient of several awards. In his quest for perfection, Justin refuses to stand still and I am proud to introduce his latest achievement: this wonderful book.

The book *Bécasse* celebrates those who take great risks in the pursuit of excellence; people who go to extraordinary lengths for results; people who are not satisfied by the good but look for the great and, hardest of all, look to produce it every day. Justin does this at Bécasse, and his suppliers do the same on their farms, lakes, and on the open sea. The relationship with one's producers is the most important relationship a chef can have. One can't survive without the other, and each inspires the other to reach new heights. The best way to show respect for your producers is to treat their food with love and care, as Justin does.

If you are interested in food you will love this book. You will love it because good food is not about fashion but about research, quality and craft. Good food is starting with the perfect product, then having the skill and knowledge to get the best out of it, and the confidence to let it taste of itself or the talent to make it taste more of itself.

These recipes illustrate Justin's command of technique. Like so much good produce, skills are being lost in the kitchen through mass production and people who consider the 'in things' more important than the great things. It is vital that we support the tradition of using quality ingredients, to ensure the traditions of great cooking continue. Justin has put up his hand and said, 'I want to do this', and he does it with immense skill in his kitchen. With this book he can now reach further and inspire not only the people who work for him, but chefs and home cooks everywhere.

Justin came to me for inspiration from the old world, and is now blazing a trail in the new. Searching for the best from earth and sea is a battle I fight every day in Europe. It is a battle for committed craftsmen and women who love good food and great cooking. I'm happy to know that halfway around the world, my protégé and friend Justin North is doing the same. And I wish him well in his journey of discovery.

Raymond Blanc
UK, May 2006

Contents

Introduction

The seed of this book was planted five years ago. Having arrived in Australia after working in Europe – a continent with an abundance of extraordinary produce – I soon discovered the remarkable produce Australia has to offer. Incredible seafood, the freshest and most diverse selection of fruit and vegetables, and an increasingly high quality of meat, offal, poultry and game. I wanted to find a way to celebrate the produce and the producers, to give them the recognition and exposure they deserve.

I began talking to local suppliers to learn more about how they selected the products they sold me: the best fresh produce available in Australia. From those early conversations came meetings with farmers, businesspeople and cultivators. I started to travel on the days Bécasse was closed, and I loved what I saw and tasted.

From garden nurseries to the most technologically advanced processing plants, what these producers have in common is a steadfast commitment to excellence. Whether it's time spent researching their product abroad, or years of trial and error to perfect their recipe for livestock feed, in their own way each producer embodies what I want to express via my food in the restaurant: timeless depth of flavours through solid technique.

Once the basic idea for the project was in place I set about gathering a team of equally passionate people to turn the dream into a book. Together we travelled around Australia talking to producers, capturing the mood of the land, and recording it in an attempt to bring to life this unwavering commitment to truly superior food.

As a chef, it was a delight to learn more about each product, and it is with great pride that I serve each of them, season permitting, at Bécasse. Every story I heard was inspiring. Whether sharing a cup of tea with an octogenarian yabby farmer or discussing the finer points of humane, efficient slaughter of lambs, each experience in its own way strengthened my resolve to preserve these people's unique stories.

Plenty of heart has gone into the making of this book and, of course, a good deal of cooking and eating and I am confident that you wil be inspired by a breadth of produce that begs to be explored.

Justin North

May 2006

Notes from the chef

The recipes in this book are all from Bécasse, past and present. In creating them I wanted to bring out each product's unique qualities as well as demonstrate its versatility. Many of the recipes use secondary cuts of meat, and offal. I have taken this approach to show how great these often-overlooked cuts can be with the right technique/recipe. While offal might not be to everyone's taste, the point I want to make is that a whole animal can be used in cooking and can, when handled correctly, display an extraordinary breadth of flavour and texture.

Before you start on any dish, I ask you to read the recipe through several times. By doing this you will gain a sense of its scope and complexity, and hopefully see that elegant food should be prepared with patience and a respect for the ingredients.

Some dishes will take only a few minutes and others might take you a day or even longer. Where applicable I have offered a faster alternative, but creating good food takes time, and I know you will savour the experience.

There is a glossary of ingredients, and French culinary terms that I use throughout, on pages 285–6. I also keep a copy of *Larousse Gastronomique* within reach at all times. It's an amazingly comprehensive cookery encyclopedia, and a worthwhile investment for cooks of all abilities.

Although these recipes are the real thing, made the way we prepare them at the restaurant, they are only guidelines. Please use them as a base from which to experiment with other flavours and ingredients. Good cooking takes time and practice. So relax, enjoy and have fun!

Alcohol

I often add a splash of raw alcohol to freshen a finished sauce or soup; a good example is a drop of Madeira to finish a mushroom consommé. Red and white wine I tend to reduce, depending on the level of acidity required for a recipe – the more it reduces the more acidic it will become. A good quality wine can be used to freshen a sauce, but should only be boiled for a few seconds. This will kill the straight alcohol taste but retain its unique flavour. Cognac, Armagnac, dry sherry and the like should never be reduced as they will lose all flavour. If a fresh drop is too strong, boil for a second.

Braising

The comfort of a warming braise simply cannot be beaten. Once a cook has mastered the art of braising, a whole new world of cookery will open up – one that includes the amazing array of secondary cuts of meat that are so often overlooked. The slow cooking process breaks down the collagen and sinew in these tougher cuts, leaving you with a highly flavoured, meltingly tender dish.

There are three parts to a braise: marinating, browning and then slow-cooking the meat in an oven, covered with an aromatic, flavour-rich stock that becomes a sauce. A braise has such integrated flavours it becomes hard to tell where the meat ends and the sauce begins. A braise should never boil: just a gentle 'blip' on the surface will suffice.

Butter

Using unsalted butter gives you greater control over the salt level in your cooking.

Foaming with butter: This method is invaluable to the cuisinier's repertoire. Foaming is the caramelisation of meat, fish or vegetables by adding butter to the pan during the cooking process and heating the butter to a light, frothy 'beurre noisette', over a constant heat with regular basting.

Caramelising

I love to roast a piece of fish and then caramelise its skin until crisp and aromatic. Fish skin has a similar nature to that of chicken skin. Making small incisions in the skin with a sharp knife, slowly caramelise the fish and roast it, basting with foaming butter, lemon and all the pan juices. These are absorbed through the incisions.

Frothing sauces

There is the misconception that this technique is a trend simply for visual effect. When executed correctly, frothing aerates a sauce, emphasising its lightness while still getting intense flavour from a good, fragrant and tasty base.

Herbs

All herbs used in the recipes are fresh unless otherwise stated. If you use dried herbs I suggest drying them yourself – the flavour will be far superior.

Garlic

Always use fresh, new-season garlic – as garlic ages and dries it loses its flavour.

Meat

I recommend cooking meat from room temperature. This produces a more evenly cooked end result, as the heat is able to penetrate the meat almost instantly. As a general rule, and in most cases in this book, I rest meat for half the amount of time it has been cooked . This allows the meat to relax and the juices to be absorbed back into the meat, keeping it moist and tasty.

Oils

I refer to non-scented cooking oils throughout. Canola or grape-seed oil fit the bill perfectly. Grape-seed oil is almost totally neutral in flavour – ideal to take on robust flavours. I use extra-virgin olive oil for finishing foods and if any heat is required I use a second-pressed olive oil. Always buy your olive oil locally and as fresh as possible as this will have the purest taste.

Salt

When used correctly, salt is a trigger to release the full flavour of foods. Food should be seasoned with salt immediately before and after cooking. Too far in advance and the salt will penetrate the meat too much. Without salt just prior to cooking, the moisture in food is drawn to the surface which causes stewing in the pan. In cooking I use fine sea salt that doesn't contain any chemicals. To season raw food or to finish foods that do not require any further cooking I use fleur de sel (see page 8) as this salt has a clean, fresh taste.

Pepper

Peppercorns are berries from a climbing vine that ripens from green to red and then brown. They are harvested at various stages of maturity. I always cook with freshly ground white pepper straight from the mill – these are ripe peppercorns with the husks removed, which makes the pepper less spicy and, in my opinion, more suited to cooking. Black pepper is simply red peppercorns that are dried, which makes them a lot more pungent and spicy.

Vegetables

Vegetables should be cooked until the crunch has just gone but the resistance remains. No more and no less.

Salt

MURRAY RIVER GOURMET SALT

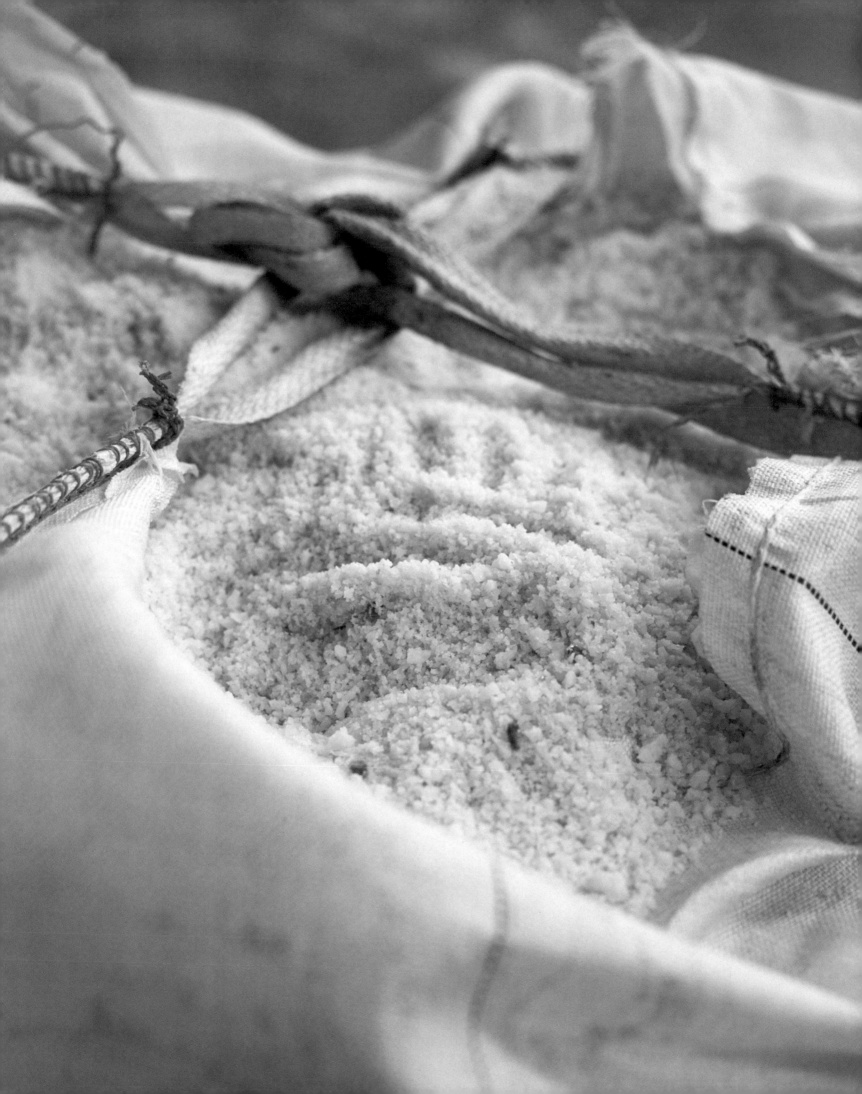

KINGS AND *conquerers*

Over the centuries, salt has been a valuable commodity. Traded thousands of years ago around the Mediterranean, wars were fought for salt, land ceded over it, and humans and animals alike have always depended upon it for survival. Salt has had a variety of uses.

Egyptians marinated olives in brine to make them edible; they also used salt for mummification. The naturally occurring salt in the soil along the Silk Road of China during Marco Polo's time served to preserve bodies that were buried there.

The ancient Roman government subsidised salt prices during its reign to ensure that plebeians could afford to buy it. They did this to shore up popular support when they needed it, according to author Mark Kurlansky whose book *Salt* charts the course of this essential mineral. Indeed, most Italian cities were established in close proximity to saltworks, starting with Rome and the saltworks at the mouth of the Tiber River.

Nowadays salt is often used when cooking green vegetables to retain their colour and flavour. Romans salted their raw green vegetables to counter the bitter taste they yielded, and this is the origin of the word 'salad', which means 'salted'. Salt also symbolised the binding of agreements in ancient Rome, so the absence of salt on a meal table would have been seen as unfriendly, even hostile.

The word 'soldier' is also a derivative of the word 'salt'. In centuries past soldiers were paid in salt (which, incidentally, is also the origin of the word 'salary'), which they would trade on the open market for other goods.

This seemingly innocuous substance has inspired passion and superstition for centuries and is an essential component of the human body. The identification of a salty taste triggers production of saliva and the gastric juices essential for digestion. This is perhaps salt's most important function, although it is rapidly eliminated by the body and must be replaced frequently.

OPPOSITE: The Mourquong Basin evaporation pan

Conventional belief that salt comes from the ocean seems to make sense, but in reality the ocean is not saline enough to produce salt in the quantities we use. Cheap table salt is mass-produced using a process far removed from the romantic idea of giant salt pans drying slowly under a desert sun. Salt water is heated to 290°C, which removes eighty-two of the eighty-four naturally occurring minerals found in sea water. Then chemical additives (aluminium compounds) are mixed in with the salt to prevent caking. It is far from a natural process, and perhaps adds to the reputation that salt has attracted in recent years as a robber of health.

The drying of salt water under the hot sun does happen, however, and sometimes in the most unlikely places. Its Mediterranean climate and fertile soil have made Mildura on the New South Wales and Victorian border (and about an hour's drive from the border of South Australia), a popular place to settle, and the agricultural centre has a permanent population of 65,000.

In Mildura, an ancient underground aquifer is used to bring us Murray River salt, a salt distinguished by its unique colour: the minerals from the inland sea give the salt flakes a pink tinge.

The underground source of saline water in Mildura is naturally occurring and has existed for thousands of years. Mining this water for commercial purposes is helping to solve Australia's considerable salinity problem. It is estimated that an area of earth the size of a football field is lost to creeping salinity in Australia every hour, making the earth impossible to farm, and eventually leading to creeping desert spaces across the continent.

BELOW: Alan Hutcheon of Murray River Gourmet Salt

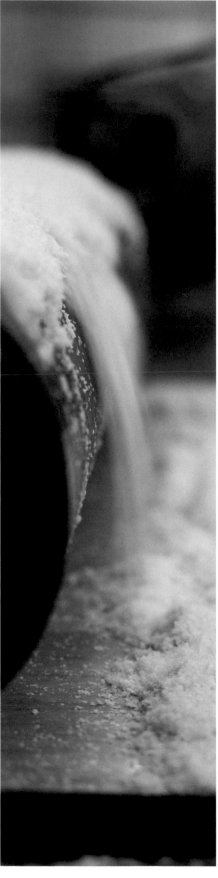

THE PATH OF THE *salt crystal*

The company SunSalt was established by Duncan and Jan Thomson in 1983 as a boutique offshoot from a commercial salt-production venture. The processing plant also produces magnesium sulphate (commonly known as Epsom salts) and cheaper industrial salts. SunSalt operates three evaporation pans: two in New South Wales and the other in north-west Victoria. We visited the Mourquong Basin, 13 kilometres from Mildura: a naturally occurring semi-circular salt basin, eight kilometres in diameter. The basin is a natural depression in elevated land, creating conditions perfect for salt production.

Brine is pumped from underground reservoirs 45 metres below the earth's surface, and diverted into the Mourquong Basin. It rises above the ground from the Parilla Aquifer, an ancient inland sea. Pumping the water out is part of the government-sponsored Buronga Salt Interception Scheme, in place to divert salty water from entering the Murray River system at Mildura.

This brine yields twice the salt content of sea water and is reddish brown. It travels through several man-made locks along a supply channel and into a giant salt pan. At this point, the water is rich in both magnesium and calcium. The area resembles a moonscape, the odd, low-growing salt bush the only vegetation. On higher ground, orange groves are abundant on the horizon. The Riverina district, of which Mildura is a part, is also famous for its citrus production.

The water travels through several canals before making its way to crystalliser ponds that have been laser-levelled. The laser-levelling creates a completely flat surface so that the salt water can dry in flat sheets that can be surface-scraped without mixing soil in with the salt. Facilitated by the depth of the pond, which helps enable sodium chloride crystals to form, the brine is evaporated by the sun. The area around Mildura coincidentally has extremely high evaporation rates (about 1.2 metres of water per year), which creates optimum conditions for the brine to crystallise.

The salt crystallises over the summer months and is then harvested, tractors pushing the salt into mounds that are metres high. It is transported to a nearby processing plant where the salt is slowly and gently passed beneath huge heating devices that dry it, though it does retain slight moisture. The crystals are sorted by size and are ready for sale.

FLEUR DE SEL

Fleur de sel is the salt that has the most romance about it: it is light, fine and fluffy, and this is actually the result of weather conditions on the salt pans. The name, meaning 'flower of the salt', originates from the village of Guerande, Brittany, where the salt was first discovered. The temperature in this region is milder than other parts of France. Atlantic currents run clearer. On warm breezy days without rain, a single day's evaporation of salt crust atop the salt pond is harvested by *artisan paludier* (craftsman salt harvesters) as the fleur de sel. It is the least salty, purest part of the saline. In Australia, this salt is harvested in much the same way when conditions are right, but they are rarely perfect for creating fleur de sel, which is why it is the most expensive type of harvested salt. It is usually the result of drifts of salt, driven by the wind, that accumulate on the edges of the salt pan.

PINK SALT

Pink salt was around in ancient Egyptian times, first harvested from a wadi (dry river bed) north-west of Cairo. Its colour was a result of the mineral-rich soils where the salt water originated.

The pink colour of Murray River salt comes from the rich mineral stores of the inland sea Parilla Aquifer. The salt is full of nutrients from the soil through which it is mined.

GOLDEN SALT

Like pink salt, the colour of golden salt is the result of residual minerals in the brine from which the salt is harvested. Potassium, iron, calcium and magnesium – substances not found in other salty waters used to make table salt – are present and unadulterated. The golden salt is unwashed, unrefined, and as a result it makes an excellent, highly flavoured garnish. The crystals of golden salt are harder than that of pink salt or fleur de sel due to the minerals present. The water that is used for harvesting salt is quite acidic, adding to the distinct colour of both pink and golden salts.

WET SALT

This salt is harvested while the concentrated, salty-sweet brine is still present in the crystals. When stockpiled, the salt dries and is leached, resulting in an intensified flavour in the salt crystals themselves. This occurs as a natural progression when the wet salt is exposed to the atmosphere. Because the wet salt is bulldozed into piles before it is completely dry (other salts are dried beforehand), it has a strong, salty flavour. At Bécasse I use wet salt for marinades as the moisture in the salt carries flavours further. The wet salt crystals are delicate and have similar flavours to fleur de sel and pink salt; fresh without being too strong.

AROMATIC CONFIT *salt*

100 g (3½ oz) wet salt
½ cinnamon stick
2 cloves garlic
4 sprigs thyme
1 sprig rosemary
1 small bay leaf
1 star anise
2 white peppercorns
4 coriander seeds

This is a wonderfully aromatic salt that we use to rub on the legs of poultry and game birds before making a confit.

Pound all ingredients together using a mortar and pestle to form a coarse, aromatic powder. Store in an airtight jar and refrigerate. Use within 2 weeks.

Makes around 110 g (3¾ oz)

These recipes are examples of salt mixes commonly used at Bécasse, and are intended to show the versatility of the various salts. Each recipe is based on 100 grams (3½ ounces) of salt; the remaining ingredients can be adjusted to your palate. Each has a shelf life of two weeks when stored in the refrigerator in an airtight jar.

CURING *salt*

100 g (3½ oz) wet salt
50 g (1¾ oz) sugar
2 cloves garlic
2 sprigs thyme
1 sprig rosemary
1 small bay leaf
6 juniper berries
2 white peppercorns

A very versatile salt mix that we use to cure various meats, especially beef and venison.

Pound all ingredients together using a mortar and pestle to form a coarse, aromatic powder. Store in an airtight jar and refrigerate. Use within 2 weeks.

Makes around 150 g (5 oz)

CITRUS *salt*

100 g (3½ oz) golden salt

30 g (1 oz) sugar

zest of 1 lime

zest of 1 orange

zest of 1 lemon

4 coriander seeds

2 white peppercorns

A wonderful salt that we use to cure and marinate whole raw fish, such as ocean trout and salmon.

Place the salt and sugar in a mortar. Zest the lime, orange and lemon over the mortar to capture the aromatic oils with the zest. Add the coriander seeds and peppercorns and pound all the ingredients together to form a coarse aromatic powder. Store in an airtight jar and refrigerate. Use within 2 weeks.

Makes around 130 g (4½ oz)

DRIED FISH *seasoning*

100 g (3½ oz) pink salt

8 sprigs lemon thyme

1 sprig rosemary

zest of 1 orange

zest of 1 lemon

freshly ground pepper

This is another salt that is perfect with all fish and seafood, especially Mediterranean-style dishes using red mullet, sea bream, snapper or John Dory. This is a dry seasoning salt, rather than a wet curing salt – just sprinkle it on before cooking.

Pick the leaves of thyme and rosemary and place them in a mixing bowl with the salt. Zest the orange and lemon over the bowl to capture the aromatic oils with the zest and stir well. Spread an even layer on a baking tray and dry in an oven set to its lowest temperature for 1–2 hours. Remove from the oven, tip the mixture into a bowl and rub together with your hands to release the flavours. Store in an airtight jar and refrigerate. Use within 2 weeks.

Makes around 110 g (3¾ oz)

DRIED PORCINI *salt*

100 g (3½ oz)) golden salt

20 g (²/₃ oz) dried porcini mushrooms

A wonderful earthy salt that we use to season poultry and game. It is also fantastic in fricassées and ragoûts.

Mix the salt and porcini mushrooms together then spread them in an even layer on a baking tray. Dry in an oven set to its lowest temperature for 1–2 hours. Remove from the oven, tip the mixture into a bowl and rub together with your hands to release the flavours. Store in an airtight jar and refrigerate. Use within 2 weeks.

Makes around 120 g (4 oz)

SEAWEED TEA *salt*

2 tablespoons crumbled
dried konbu seaweed

2 tablespoons crumbled
dried wakame seaweed

1 teaspoon Marco Polo tea

2 teaspoons sugar

freshly ground pepper

100 g (3½ oz) fleur de sel

This Japanese-inspired salt is especially good with marron, tuna and whiting. You can find the seaweeds in Chinatown or in the Asian section of most major supermarkets.

Place all ingredients except the salt in a spice blender and pulse to a medium-fine powder. Rub the mixture into the salt with your hands. Store in an airtight jar and refrigerate. Use within 2 weeks.

Makes around 110 g (3¾ oz)

CELERY *salt*

leaves from 1 bunch celery

100 g (3½ oz) fleur de sel

A versatile savoury salt that is particularly good with lamb, tuna and salads.

Blanch the celery leaves for 30 seconds in boiling water, then refresh in iced water. Dry in an oven set to its lowest temperature for 1–2 hours. Remove from the oven and crumble them into the salt. Store in an airtight jar and refrigerate. Use within 2 weeks.

Makes around 110 g (3¾ oz)

SMOKED CELERIAC *salt*

1 small celeriac
100 g (3½ oz) fleur de sel

Peel the celeriac and grate it finely. Put in a large airtight container and mix thoroughly with the salt. Refrigerate overnight to allow the flavours to meld and develop. Squeeze out the excess liquid, and tip into a smoker. Smoke for 30 minutes over hickory or oak, then dry in an oven set to its lowest temperature for 1–2 hours. Remove from the oven and rub the mixture well with your hands to release the flavours. Store in an airtight jar and refrigerate. Use within 2 weeks.

Makes around 130 g (4½ oz)

Mushroom

NOEL ARROLD

THE *tunnel*

In 1866, a railway tunnel was laboriously cut through a mountain separating the rural New South Wales towns of Mittagong and Bowral. In 1904, when Canberra was declared capital city of the newly federated Australia, a bigger railway line and tunnel were constructed near the site, to connect the nation's largest city (Sydney) and its new capital city. The original tunnel became obselete.

These days, the dimly lit 1866 tunnel houses more than a dozen varieties of exotic mushrooms, which are grown here year-round. Cooma-born doctor of microbiology, Noel Arrold, settled in Mittagong in 1979 and began the painstaking work of isolating mushroom strains and growing them in sterilised conditions both in the railway tunnel and his nearby laboratory.

Conditions in the tunnel are consistent, with temperatures hovering between 16 and 18°C all year round and a humidity level between 80 and 90 per cent. At certain points the 650-metre long tunnel is further than 50 metres under the ground. The tunnel is a warm cocoon: perfect for farming the mushrooms that prefer these conditions. In fact the climate is strikingly similar to those of mountainous regions of China, Korea and Japan where some of these mushroom strains grow wild.

Arrold has travelled far and wide researching exotic mushroom strains for the market in Australia. A recent trip involved travel to villages 60 kilometres from Lijiiang, near Tibet, to study the potential for importing exotic mushroom strains, which fetch up to A$3000 a kilogram on the Japanese market. In terrain similar to that of the Rocky Mountains, Arrold explains, entire families venture into the mountains to pick mushrooms.

Importing mushroom spores into Australia can only be done through approved laboratories and Arrold deals with laboratories and universities in France, Hong Kong and the United States. The Australian Quarantine and Inspection Service (AQIS) is currently reviewing the mushroom species approved for import into Australia and Arrold is hopeful they'll approve a further three or four species.

CULTIVATING *cultures*

Mushrooms are extremely fast-growing and Arrold's company, Li-Sun Exotic Mushrooms, produces 1500 kilograms of them every week.

Exotic mushrooms grow naturally on decaying trees in forests. In a controlled environment they are cultivated on sawdust or other plant materials such as straw or cottonseed. At Li-Sun the sawdust is mixed with wheat, rice bran, lime and gypsum, placed in bags or bottles and sterilised at 120°C for two hours to eliminate any organisms present. When the sawdust has cooled a pure culture of the mushroom is added and the bags or bottles incubated at 22°C. The incubation period is anywhere from three to ten weeks, depending on the species.

After this incubation period the crop is taken to the tunnel and the plastic bags removed to allow for cropping. The combination of watering the crop and the warm, humid conditions in the tunnel promotes growth and within five days mature mushrooms appear. The inoculated sawdust will continue to fruit for several weeks before the mushroom culture is exhausted.

Oyster and shimeji mushrooms are grown on pasteurised cottonseed hulls and wheat straw that has been steamed at 70°C. This mix goes into bags with holes punched in them through which the mushrooms will grow.

Staff move through the tunnel daily, picking mushrooms, watering the bags and soaking the sawdust blocks in water. Once the mushrooms are harvested they are returned to the laboratory where they are packaged and sent directly to produce markets around Australia.

The tunnel evokes distant childhood memories of demons and leprechauns emerging from the murky gloom.

SHIITAKE (*Lentinus edodes*)

Also known as the 'black forest mushroom', the shiitake has a pronounced meaty flavour. Its name is derived from the Japanese shii (oak) tree and records trace cultivation as far back as 1000 years. Used both fresh and dried, its active ingredient, lentinan, is a registered cancer treatment in Japan. It has also been proven to lower cholesterol. Cracked skin on the top of the mushroom indicates a fuller flavour.

OYSTER (*Pleurotus spp.*)

Its fluted, shell-like appearance coupled with a meaty flavour have made the oyster mushroom a favourite around the world. It is a great natural composter and has been credited with eliminating heavy metals from soils where it grows, especially in Eastern Europe. In Asia, oyster mushrooms are favoured for their medicinal properties believed to lower cholesterol and boost the immune system.

PINK OYSTER (*Pleurotus djamor*)

This light, delicately gilled mushroom is a strain from South America. It prefers a temperature of 28°C, although when grown at this temperature its shelf life is dramatically shortened. This mushroom is bitter when raw and best when lightly cooked, as prolonged cooking leaches its brilliant colour.

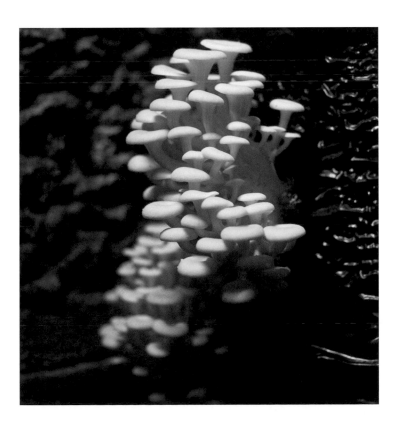

YELLOW OYSTER
(*Pleurotus cornucopiae*)

Yellow oysters grow in greater numbers than the pink oysters, but at a smaller size. The flavour is delicate and responds best to only light cooking; anything more and both flavour and colour are diminished. The sweet, slight straw and delicate nutty flavour when raw makes this a popular mushroom.

CHESTNUT *(Agrocybe aegerita)*

Also known as the 'black poplar mushroom', the chestnut mushroom grows in clusters on dead tree species in Europe. The flavour is mellow when young and the texture crunchy. The chestnut mushroom was one of the first mushrooms to be cultivated by man.

NAMEKO *(Pholiota nameko)*

Native to cool, mountainous regions in China and Japan, the nameko is one of Japan's most popular mushrooms. Its bright orange cap (which has a sticky fluid coating) contrasts a long white stem. The gelatinous coating dissolves during cooking, releasing a delicate, nutty flavour and aroma.

ENOKI (*Flammulina velvtipes*)

Also known as the 'golden needle mushroom', the enoki is grown in clusters and is easily distinguishable by its unique slim shape, long stems and pin-head cap. Trimming off the base is all the preparation required for enoki mushrooms; heating can too easily destroy the texture and taste. The Japanese developed a method of growing enoki mushrooms in chilled rooms where carbon dioxide levels are elevated and light exposure limited, and these conditions are replicated by Arrold at Li-Sun.

SHIMEJI (*Lyophyllum spp.*)

Highly versatile, the shimeji mushroom has an intense, sweet and nutty flavour coupled with a succulent texture. The firm-fleshed mushroom grows wild in Japan, flourishing on dead native Japanese trees. In Australia this species is different from the hon-shimeji or true shimeji as grown in Japan. It usually has a blue/grey cap and white stem, though colours range from woody brown to white.

MUSHROOMS *à la grecque*

20 ml (²/₃ fl oz) non-scented cooking oil

400 g (14 oz) mushrooms (a selection of Swiss brown, button, shiitake, shimiji, oyster, enoki, nameko, oyster and chestnut), wiped clean and cut into even-sized pieces

salt and freshly ground pepper

80 g (2³/₄ oz) butter

few drops lemon juice

MARINADE

60 ml (2 fl oz) virgin olive oil

1 large shallot, finely diced

2 cloves garlic, finely sliced

salt and freshly ground pepper

pinch of ground turmeric

1 bay leaf

4 sprigs thyme

100 ml (3¹/₂ fl oz) dry white wine

20 ml (²/₃ fl oz) white wine vinegar

150 ml (5 fl oz) White Chicken Stock (page 254)

4 sprigs tarragon

TO SERVE

40 Braised Baby Shallots (page 280)

24 baby red radishes, trimmed

24 parsley roots (optional), washed

1 cup baby lamb's lettuce leaves (mâche), snipped and washed

6 sprigs tarragon, leaves and flowers picked

6 sprigs thyme, leaves and flowers picked

A la grecque, meaning 'in the Greek style', is a French method that usually refers to vegetables (such as mushrooms or artichokes) and herbs cooked in olive oil, white wine and lemon juice or vinegar and served at room temperature.

In this recipe the mushrooms are briefly cooked, then left to marinate in the cooking liquor. Preparing both the mushrooms and the braised baby shallots a couple of days in advance, allows the flavours to develop. Two or three days will allow the flavours to reach their absolute peak – sublime.

TO PREPARE THE MUSHROOMS, heat a large frying pan over a high heat until almost smoking. Add half the oil and half the mushrooms and sauté quickly with a pinch of salt and pepper. Add the butter and heat to a nut-brown foam. Add the lemon juice then tip the mushrooms and cooking juices into a bowl. The whole process should be executed with speed and take no longer than a couple of minutes as mushrooms are delicate and will easily overcook.

Repeat with the remaining oil, mushrooms and butter, then transfer the bowl of mushrooms to a cool place and leave, uncovered, while you prepare the marinade.

TO MAKE THE MARINADE, heat a heavy-based saucepan over a medium heat, and add half the olive oil, the shallot, garlic and a pinch of salt and pepper. Sweat for 2 minutes, then add the turmeric and continue to sweat for a further 3 minutes until the shallots soft and transparent.

Add the bay leaf, thyme, wine and vinegar. Increase the heat and reduce the mixture quite rapidly by about half. Add the chicken stock and, once again, reduce the mixture quite rapidly by half.

Remove from the heat and whisk in the remaining olive oil, adjusting the seasoning and acidity if necessary. Add the tarragon sprigs and pour the mixture over the mushrooms. Cover immediately with cling film and leave at room temperature for 25 minutes to infuse before refrigerating until required, but at least overnight.

TO SERVE, put the mushrooms, braised shallots, radishes and parsley roots into a heavy-based saucepan and heat gently over a low heat until just warm. Check seasoning and acidity; you may want to add a drop of lemon juice to freshen slightly. Spoon onto warmed serving plates and sprinkle with the lamb's lettuce, herbs and flowers. Drizzle with any remaining marinade and serve immediately.

Serves 8 as an entrée or 4 as a main meal

MUSHROOM *risotto*

BASIC RISOTTO – BÉCASSE-STYLE

3 tablespoons extra-virgin olive oil

½ onion, finely diced

3 sprigs thyme

3 cloves garlic, roughly crushed

1 bay leaf

salt and freshly ground pepper

400 g (14 oz) Ferron Vialone Nano
risotto rice

100 ml (3½ fl oz) dry white wine

100 ml (3½ fl oz) Madeira

1.25 litres (2½ pints) Mushroom Stock
(page 254), kept simmering

MUSHROOMS

30 ml (1 fl oz) non-scented cooking oil

400 g (14 oz) mushrooms (a selection of
Swiss brown, button, shiitake, shimiji,
oyster, enoki, nameko, oyster and
chestnut), wiped clean and cut into
even-sized pieces

120 g (4 oz) cold butter, diced

30 ml (1 fl oz) Madeira

100 ml (3½ fl oz) Mushroom Stock,
(page 254), kept simmering

50 g (1¾ oz) freshly grated parmesan

3 tablespoons pure cream,
lightly whipped

3 tablespoons finely chopped herbs
(parsley, chervil, tarragon and chives)

salt and freshly ground pepper

few drops lemon juice

Risotto means 'individual to the fork'. For my risotto I always insist on using Ferron Vialoni Nano rice. It is a little more expensive than other brands, but definitely worth the investment as it gives a wonderful starchy creaminess to the dish, without breaking down.

Everybody has their own preferred way of making risotto. At Bécasse we use the traditional absorption recipe, but I am also including Gabriele Ferron's unique method (page 32) as it achieves a fantastic result.

TO MAKE THE BASIC RISOTTO, heat a large heavy-based saucepan over a medium heat. Add the oil, onion, thyme, garlic and bay leaf and season well with salt and pepper. Sweat gently for about 4 minutes until onion is soft and transparent.

Add the rice and cook over a medium heat for 2–3 minutes until well coated with oil. Add the wine and stir (using a wooden spoon) until it is almost completely absorbed. Pour in the Madeira and again stir until the liquid is absorbed.

Add about 100 ml (3½ fl oz) of the stock and stir over a gentle, constant heat until the liquid is almost completely absorbed. Continue in this way, adding the remaining stock in small amounts. It should take around 15 minutes.

The basic risotto can be prepared ahead of time to this stage. If you wish to finish the dish later, spread it out onto a shallow tray, cover and refrigerate for up to 2 days. Otherwise continue with your choice of ingredients.

TO PREPARE THE MUSHROOMS, heat a large saucepan over a medium–high heat. Add the oil and mushrooms and sauté briefly. Add 30 g (1 oz) of the butter and heat to a nut-brown foam. Baste the mushrooms until they are golden and caramelised.

Pour in the Madeira and simmer until reduced by half. Add to the basic risotto (as above) with the additional mushroom stock. Bring to a gentle simmer and cook for 2 minutes or until the risotto is cooked to your liking. Add the parmesan and remaining butter, and mix well. Gently fold in the cream and herbs. Season to taste and add the lemon juice. Serve immediately.

Serves 8 as an entrée

GABRIELE FERRON'S *basic risotto*

3 tablespoons extra-virgin olive oil

½ onion, peeled and finely diced

salt and freshly ground pepper

400 g (14 oz) Ferron Vialone Nano risotto rice

1 litre (2¼ pints) Mushroom Stock (page 254), kept simmering

TO MAKE THE BASIC RISOTTO, heat a large heavy-based saucepan over a medium heat. Add the oil and onion and season well with salt and pepper. Sweat onion gently for about 4 minutes until soft and transparent.

Add the rice and stir briefly until coated with oil. Pour in the hot stock, swirl it around gently and cover with a tight-fitting lid. Lower the heat and simmer gently for about 13 minutes. Remove the lid and stir well to release the gluten.

The basic risotto can be prepared ahead of time to this stage. If you wish to finish the dish later, spread it out onto a shallow tray, cover and refrigerate for up to 2 days. Otherwise continue with your choice of ingredients.

Finish the risotto with your choice of flavourings, such as mushrooms (page 31). Taste and adjust seasonings then serve.

Serves 8 as an entrée

TERRINE AND *mille feuille*
of Mushroom and Confit Celeriac

CONFIT CELERIAC

2 medium celeriac

1 litre (2¼ pints) Rendered Duck Fat
(page 274)

½ head garlic, cloves separated

3 sprigs thyme

1 bay leaf

salt and freshly ground pepper

MUSHROOM DUXELLES

300 g (10½ oz) Swiss brown mushrooms,
wiped clean and quartered

300 g (10½ oz) button mushrooms,
wiped clean and quartered

200 g (7 oz) shiitake mushrooms, wiped
clean and quartered

80 ml (2¾ fl oz) non-scented cooking oil

120 g (4 oz) unsalted butter

6 cloves garlic, roughly crushed

6 sprigs thyme

salt and freshly ground pepper

juice of ½ lemon

MILLE FEUILLE

16 slices confit celeriac

800 g (1 lb 8 oz) small, even-sized
mushrooms (a selection of shiitake,
shimiji, oyster, nameko and chestnut),
wiped clean

80 ml (2¾ fl oz) non-scented cooking oil

120 g (4 oz) unsalted butter

¼ cup flat-leaf parsley leaves, finely
shredded to a chiffonade

salt and freshly ground pepper

few drops lemon juice

TO SERVE

200 g (7 oz) Mushroom Purée (page 278)

At Bécasse we use a small hors d'oeuvres terrine mould to make the terrine, which is about 5 cm (2 in) high, 5.5 cm (2¼ in) wide and roughly 30 cm (12 in) long. Try to buy one with removable sides. The terrine is best made the day before to allow adequate pressing time.

The confit method of preparing food comes from the French term meaning 'to preserve'. It is a method of slow-cooking in fat (rendered pork, duck or goose) or an aromatic oil.

TO CONFIT THE CELERIAC, clean and peel the celeriac then use a sharp knife to cut into 2 mm slices. Put the rendered duck fat into a shallow braising dish and heat gently to about 75°C (165°F). Use the blade of a heavy knife or the palm of your hand to smash the garlic cloves roughly and add them to the duck fat with thyme and bay leaf and season to taste.

Add the celeriac slices, and cover with a piece of greaseproof paper, cut to fit the dish. Place a plate on top to keep the vegetables submerged in the fat. Cover the pan and cook at a very low even temperature, between 70–80°C (160–175°F) for around 30 minutes. Don't allow the fat to simmer – you should just see the odd bubble rising to the surface. Drain the celeriac, which should be tender but not mushy. Set aside 16 large slices of celeriac for the mille feuilles, reserving the rest for the terrine. Discard the aromatics and reserve the duck fat for another recipe.

TO MAKE THE MUSHROOM DUXELLES, heat a heavy-based frying pan over a high heat until smoking. Add a drizzle of the oil followed quickly by a large handful of the mushrooms. Sauté briefly until light and golden. Add a knob of butter to the pan and heat to a nut-brown foam. Add a clove of garlic and a sprig of thyme and season with salt and pepper. Caramelise for a few more seconds then add a drop of lemon juice. Tip into a colander to drain, reserving the fat for the terrine.

Repeat this procedure until all the ingredients are used. Only cook a large handful of mushrooms at a time – if you overcrowd the pan they will stew in their own juices, and end up pale and rubbery.

When all the mushrooms have been cooked and drained, tip them out onto a work surface and use a large sharp knife to chop to a coarse, rather chunky duxelles. Tip into a large bowl and season well.

continued …

TERRINE AND *mille feuille*

continued

TO ASSEMBLE THE TERRINE, double-line your mould with cling film, leaving a generous overhang. Arrange overlapping slices of celeriac over the bottom and up the sides of the mould. Spread a layer of mushroom duxelles on top and drizzle on a generous spoonful of the reserved mushroom pan juices. Press firmly into the mould. Continue to build the terrine with alternating layers of celeriac and mushroom duxelles, finishing with a layer of celeriac. Fold the cling film over the top and weigh down with a 1 kg (2 lb) weight. Refrigerate overnight.

TO PREPARE THE MILLE FEUILLE, trim the reserved celeriac slices to even-sized rectangles. Sauté the mushrooms in the oil and butter, following the method described above. Again, only cook a large handful of mushrooms at a time. When all the mushrooms have been cooked and drained, tip them into a mixing bowl, toss through the parsley and season with salt and pepper and a drop of lemon juice.

WHEN READY TO SERVE, gently warm through the mushroom purée. Unmould the terrine, remove the cling film and use a very sharp knife to cut it into 8 slices. Place a slice of terrine on each warm serving plate and spoon a little of the purée next to it. Assemble the mille feuille on each plate by stacking alternate layers of celeriac and sautéed mushrooms. Serve straightaway.

If you wish to serve the terrine hot, carefully pan-fry each slice over a medium heat in a little lightly foaming butter.

Serves 8 as an entrée

CHESTNUT MUSHROOM *raviolo*

with an Almond Nage

CHESTNUT MUSHROOM STUFFING

30 ml (1 fl oz) non-scented cooking oil

400 g (14 oz) chestnut mushrooms, cleaned and cut into quarters

60 g (2 oz) unsalted butter

2 cloves garlic, roughly crushed

3 sprigs thyme

1 bay leaf

salt and freshly ground pepper

few drops lemon juice

80 g (2¾ oz) shelled walnuts

20 ml (⅔ fl oz) walnut oil

RAVIOLI

250 g (9 oz) Pasta Dough (page 269), at room temperature

1 egg, lightly beaten with a little water to form an egg wash

plain flour for dusting

VEGETABLE GARNISH

½ tablespoon non-scented cooking oil

30 g (1 oz) unsalted butter

200 g (7 oz) chestnut mushrooms, cleaned

1 clove garlic, roughly crushed

salt and freshly ground pepper

few drops lemon juice

TO SERVE

250 ml (8¾ fl oz) Almond Nage (page 259)

200 g (7 oz) very fine baby green beans, trimmed

60 g (2 oz) flaked almonds, lightly toasted

Raviolo is a larger, individual version of the better-known ravioli and it is thought that both originated in Liguria as a means of using leftover foods. The original name, rabiole, means 'bits and pieces'.

TO PREPARE THE STUFFING, preheat the oven to 190°C (375°F). Heat a heavy-based frying pan over a high heat until smoking. Add the oil and then the mushrooms and sauté for a few seconds. Add the butter and heat to a nut-brown foam. Add the garlic and herbs and cook until everything is golden brown and caramelised. Season well and add a drop of fresh lemon juice. Remove from the heat and drain in a colander, reserving the pan juices.

Heat an oven-proof, heavy-based frying pan over a medium heat. Add the walnuts and walnut oil and toss briefly. Season with salt and pepper then place in oven, and roast for 8 minutes until the walnuts are golden, aromatic and crunchy. Drain in the colander with the mushrooms, reserving the oil with the pan juices.

When cool enough to handle, chop the mushrooms and walnuts with a large very sharp knife to achieve a coarse duxelles. Tip into a mixing bowl and add enough of the reserved pan juices and oil to form a moist stuffing. Season to taste and keep at room temperature while you prepare your pasta dough.

TO ASSEMBLE THE RAVIOLI, dust your work surface lightly with flour. Roll the pasta dough through a pasta machine, working down from the thickest setting to the finest setting to form a smooth, thin sheet. Lay the pasta sheet on your work surface and cut out 16 rounds using a 10 cm (4 in) cutter.

Spoon a mound of duxelles on 8 of the pasta rounds, leaving a border around the edge. Brush this lightly with the beaten egg and place the remaining 8 pasta rounds on top. Press the edges together to seal, making sure that the pasta is pressed against the filling and there are no air gaps. Place on a lightly floured tray and refrigerate while you prepare the vegetables.

TO PREPARE THE VEGETABLE GARNISH, heat a frying pan over a high heat until almost smoking. add the oil, followed by the butter and heat to a nut-brown foam. Add the mushrooms and garlic and caramelise until golden. Season with salt and pepper and a few drops of lemon juice.

continued …

continued

TO SERVE, bring a large pan of lightly salted water to the boil and add a teaspoon of oil. Keep at a gentle simmer ready to cook the pasta. At the same time, in a separate pan, heat the almond nage to a gentle simmer.

Add the ravioli to the pan of boiling water and cook for 2 minutes. Add the green beans to the pan and cook for a further 2 minutes, by which time the pasta should be warmed through and the beans just cooked. Tip into a colander to drain then pat dry with kitchen paper and season with salt and pepper.

Use a hand-blender to whisk the almond nage to a frothy foam for 10–15 seconds. Divide the beans between 8 warmed serving plates and scatter on the mushrooms. Place a raviolo on top and spoon on the foamy nage. Finally, sprinkle with toasted almonds and serve straightaway.

Serves 8 as an entrée or 4 as a main meal

Truffle

TIM TERRY

BLACK GOLD: *Tuber melanosporum*

In France, the country with which they are most associated, truffles enjoy a mythical reverence. Renowned gourmand Jean-Anthelme Brillat Savarin (1755–1826) praised the truffle as 'the jewel of French cooking; prized for its unique flavour and intoxicating aroma' and writer Alexandre Dumas (1802–70) hailed it as 'gastronome's holy of holies'. Ancient Greeks and Romans attributed benefits both aphrodisiac and therapeutic.

All this over a peculiar little fungus that grows underground. Yet the truffle remains a hugely expensive – not to mention popular – delicacy and culinary fascination. Centuries of tradition surround truffle-buying etiquette: buyers at a market cannot touch a truffle; they are permitted only to look and to smell. Such is the seductive delicacy of the fungi.

French folklore suggests that truffles are born of summer claps of thunder, and around the end of the nineteenth century, France was producing as much as 1000 tons of truffles annually. Over the next hundred years, however, its output fell dramatically, and wartime destruction, acid rain and the development of traditional truffle land for food production reduced the country's annual truffle harvest to 30 to 60 tons. All such tribulation pushed truffle prices well into the thousands of dollars per kilogram.

Before their harvest was a commercially lucrative enterprise, it was a simple passion for truffles that led to their proliferation through the forests of Europe. All animals, it seems, love truffles and, once sniffed out, the truffles would be dug up and eaten by pigs, snails, deer and rodents. By defecating somewhere else, the animal would effectively inoculate a new area with truffle spores.

French farmers also tried planting acorns in the hole from which a truffle had just been taken, in the hope that the elusive *T. melanosporum* fungus would attach itself to the roots of the sapling of the oak or hazelnut tree. Oak and hazelnut trees are the two main species known to host the *Tuber melanosporum* and the truffles are found near, but not attached to, the root systems of the trees, generally about 100 millimetres below ground level.

Relying on this method of proliferation, however, proved too uncertain and since the 1970s scientists have been working on ways to artificially produce the truffle.

THE TRUFFLES OF *Tasmania*

The two predominant truffle species that have captured the world's imagination are the White Italian Alba (*T. magnatum*) and the French Black Perigord (*T. melanosporum*). Truffle farms (known as 'trufferies') have been springing up all over Tasmania during the last few years, and now anyone can buy an inoculated tree infected with either the black or white truffle. The white truffle is grown on the roots of the poplar tree.

'The French said we couldn't grow wine, either,' laughs Tim Terry. Terry is a Tasmanian entrepreneur expanding his current business into producing truffles for the commercial market. While deep-sea fishing with a friend off Tasman Island years ago, a conversation about truffle farming planted the seed in Terry's mind. 'It had never been done before, as far as we knew, in the Southern Hemisphere,' he explains. 'I now know that that's because it's too bloody hard!'

That it's too hard hasn't stopped Terry, who grew Australia's first truffle in 1999, and has been running his truffle business for thirteen years. Terry formed Tasmanian Truffle Enterprises following the explosion of global interest in the potential for farming truffles in the Southern Hemisphere. 'I realised this could be a commercially viable industry,' he says. Producing truffles has taken Terry to France, for research

into farming methods, several times. It has also made him something of an expert in dog training.

Askrigg, Terry's 120-hectare property, houses some 19,000 trees over 33 hectares of cultivated plantation: 15,000 hazelnuts and 4000 oaks. The main house doubles as Terry's office, and on his desk sits Australia's first truffle, proudly cast in bronze.

With the help of a government grant, Terry has invested a great deal into monitoring conditions on his property. Probes in the ground measure rainfall and the depth of its penetration – an important factor influencing whether truffles will flourish. A truffle is almost always found, according to Terry, in the first 10 centimetres of earth around the base of a tree. Heavy rains at the wrong times adversely affect production, as truffles rot in the ground in excess moisture, or may not grow at all if the soil is too wet or cold.

Terry understands truffle faming better than anyone in Australia, but at the same time his confidence is riddled with the inconsistency of his truffle finds. 'I don't know why some trees consistently produce truffles and others don't,' Terry admits, pointing out a particular row of trees on his property that have produced more truffles than any other row, without any obvious feature that might contribute to their success.

TRUFFLE *hunters*

Truffles are harvested in winter as that is when they mature. Traditional truffle hunters have been female pigs, attracted by the aroma that resembles pigs' sexual hormones. Yet despite their indisputable prowess in tracking down truffles, sows also have a fondness for the valuable fungus. 'I have heard stories of pigs taking off their owner's fingers in the wrestle for a truffle,' cautions Terry, who has opted instead to train a young dog for the job.

'Dogs have a 21-day imprint period,' Terry explains, 'after which they'll remember something for life.' So every day for twenty-one days while training his springer spaniel, Hoover, Terry played increasingly complicated retrieval games. Using a film canister of cotton wool drizzled with truffle oil ('Canitruf' – a French product designed specifically for training dogs to find truffles) as bait, Terry would initially reward the dog to fetch and return the canister. The game graduated to the dog having to find canisters buried around the roots of trees where truffles were likely to be found. The process is not without fault, however, and dogs have 'about an hour's' concentration span, according to Terry, before they need a rest.

Mechanised detection systems have also proved successful in testing, with a pre-programmed automated 'nose' sniffing out truffle spore. The electronic nose was developed by Terry and Professor Bryn Hibbert of the chemosensory department at the University of New South Wales, but until Terry's plantations are large enough and commercially viable enough to complete the half-million-dollar machine, dogs are still the best means of truffle detection.

A machine can get close to the truffle, but can't pinpoint it exactly, which is why the last word remains with the human nose. 'It's a cold, wet occupation,' says Terry, who demonstrates the final stage: when the dog has sniffed out a potential truffle, Terry gets down on his knees and sniffs around the area. Truffle hunting is best at about 10 or 11 a.m. as a truffle's aroma needs the gentle heat of the day to sufficiently intensify for detection. A ripe truffle will emit such a strong scent it is distinguishable from just above the ground to the human nose. Gently prising the earth, care must be taken not to damage the truffle as it's being unearthed.

It's obvious that a truffle spore has inoculated the area around the roots of a tree by the presence of what's known as a *brulé*. Like the culinary version, *brulé* in this sense means 'burnt', and refers to the parched appearance of the circular area of soil around the base of the tree. The *brulé* generally expands to occupy the diameter of the tree's branch span, killing grass and any other plants living on it.

It is the *brulé* that has been a time-honoured indicator of the presence of a truffle fungi working beneath the ground, but the *brulé* simply means that the fungus is there and that it's active. It does not guarantee the presence of truffles beneath the soil's surface.

INTRODUCING THE *truffle spore*

Truffles don't actually grow on the tree roots; they develop near inoculated roots. The tree is a carrier or facilitator for the hyphae in the soil, the spider's web of spore development surrounding the roots of the trees around which truffles appear. It is within this web that truffles can develop.

Tim Terry leaves little to chance in his trufferie. In the inoculation process it is necessary to be clinical because, 'the last thing you want is the wrong fungus to establish itself around the roots of a tree,' he explains. Once another type of fungus has settled there, it is very difficult to introduce the truffle spores: this must be established early.

While Terry won't divulge all his secrets, he does give a rough guide to the inoculation process. The first step in this process is to collect the acorns and hazelnuts and sterilise them. From there they are germinated in a sterile medium. Terry uses an outside contractor to sterilise his potting mix, so that there is a trackable audit trail. Diligence in the sterilisation process is crucial. The trees have to be grown in near hospital-like conditions.

Only after young oak and hazelnut trees have grown to at least 5 centimetres is the truffle spore introduced. At this point, the tree has sprouted just a couple of leaves and its root system is in early development.

The truffle spore is introduced to the roots of the sapling and the sapling returned to the enclosed nursery, where it will remain for the first year of its life. Once the tree has had this time to mature, an expert is brought in to verify the presence of the fungi around the roots of the tree. Only when the fungus has been identified will Terry plant the tree on his property.

Pierre Jean Pebeyre, France's largest truffle wholesaler, has visited Terry's property. The French visitor remarked on Australians' impatience. 'Pebeyre told me that the French don't even look for truffles until the trees have been growing for ten years,' recalls Terry, 'but in Australia we found the first truffle after only four years of growing'.

Terry lives for the day when he can pull a truffle from beneath every tree. But for this to happen he must give it time. Some of Terry's oldest trees stopped fruiting when they were interfered with during research, and are only just returning to fruit now. 'I've had experts from France and other countries visit this farm and there's nothing that says we can't do this. 'Nobody has told me I'm barking up the wrong tree here,' so I am continuing to grow this business and hopefully a wonderful export industry for Tasmania.'

POACHED *truffles*

500 ml (18 fl oz) Mushroom and Madeira Consommé (page 257)

salt and freshly ground pepper

Madeira to taste

6 medium-sized fresh black winter truffles, brushed free of dirt

Choose truffles that are firm, unblemished and extremely pungent.

Poaching them in a delicate mushroom and Madeira-flavoured stock preserves them and prolongs their lifespan. They are incredibly versatile and at Bécasse we have myriad uses for them: they can be finely chopped and added to sauces and vinaigrettes or used in stuffings and terrines.

Gently heat the consommé to just below a simmer. Taste and adjust seasoning then add the Madeira.

Add the truffles and poach gently for around 20 minutes, or until they are tender and the consommé is very aromatic. Remove the truffles from the consommé and place them in a sterilised jar with an airtight rubber seal. Pour in enough consommé to cover the truffles – they must be completely submerged. Transfer to the refrigerator to cool, leaving the lid open. Once cold, seal and store in the refrigerator for up to 6 months.

Makes 6 poached truffles

TRUFFLE *linguine*

with Sautéed White Asparagus and Truffle Hollandaise

TRUFFLE LINGUINE

250 g (9 oz) strong flour

½ teaspoon salt

180 ml (6 fl oz) egg yolks (around 12 yolks)

1 teaspoon extra-virgin olive oil

1 fresh black winter truffle, chopped very finely

SAUTÉED WHITE ASPARAGUS

12 spears white asparagus, trimmed and peeled

30 g (1 oz) unsalted butter

salt and freshly ground pepper

few drops lemon juice

TO SERVE

300 ml Truffle Hollandaise Sauce (page 264), kept warm

½ Poached Truffle (page 50), finely shaved

¼ cup flat-leaf parsley leaves, finely sliced to a chiffonnade

TO MAKE THE LINGUINE, mix the flour and salt and sift twice. Tip onto your work surface and make a well in the centre. In a separate bowl, whisk together the egg yolks, oil and truffle. Pour into the flour and use your hands to gradually work the liquid into the flour to form a solid mass.

Knead for about 10 minutes until the dough is smooth and slightly springy. Divide into 3 even portions, wrap each in cling film and refrigerate for at least 30 minutes to allow the gluten to relax. This will prevent shrinkage later.

Roll each piece of dough through your pasta machine, working down from the thickest setting to the third-finest setting. Dust each sheet lightly with flour and roll through the linguine attachment. Hang in a cool dry place for about 30 minutes.

TO SAUTÉ THE ASPARAGUS, drop them into a pan of boiling salted water and cook for 1 minute. Heat the butter in a pan until lightly foaming. Add the asparagus and sauté for a few minutes. Season and add the lemon juice.

WHEN READY TO SERVE, bring a large pan of salted water to the boil and add a splash of olive oil to help prevent the linguine sticking together. Cook the linguine for 90 seconds, stirring around in the water from time to time. Drain well.

Divide the linguine into 6 portions and use a carving fork to twirl each portion into neat little bobbins on each serving plate. Arrange 2 asparagus spears on top of each portion and spoon on the warm hollandaise. Garnish with shavings of truffle and the parsley and serve immediately.

Serves 6 as an entrée

CARPACCIO OF TRUFFLE AND *granny smith apple*

with Seared Foie Gras, Watercress and Roasted Hazelnuts

1 litre (2¼ pints) water

150 g (5 oz) sugar

1 vanilla pod, split and seeds scraped

2 Granny Smith apples

juice of 1 lemon

2 fresh black winter truffles

330 g (11 oz) foie gras*

1 tablespoon sherry vinegar

100 ml (3½ fl oz) hazelnut oil

80 g (2¾ oz) hazelnuts, roasted, skins removed and halved

2 cups watercress leaves

fleur de sel

freshly ground white pepper

Put the water, sugar, vanilla pod and seeds into a pan and bring to a gentle simmer over a medium heat. Meanwhile, peel and core the apples. Cut each in half lengthwise and use a very sharp knife or a mandolin to cut into thin half-moon slices. Drop the apple slices into the simmering liquid then immediately remove the pan from the heat. Leave the apples to cool and infuse.

When ready to serve, finely slice the black truffles and arrange the slices in a neat overlapping circle on each plate. Top with a circle of apple slices.

Heat a heavy-based frying pan over a high heat until almost smoking. Use a very sharp knife dipped in hot water to cut the foie gras into 6 slices and season lightly. Sear on each side in the dry pan for about 10 seconds, until golden brown. Add the sherry vinegar, then remove the pan from the heat. Drain the foie gras slices on kitchen paper. Add the hazelnut oil to the pan then add the hazelnuts and swirl around well. Put the watercress leaves in a small mixing bowl. Add a spoonful of the pan juices and toss gently.

Place a slice of foie gras on top of the apple slices and top with a few watercress leaves. Season with fleur de sel and a little pepper. Spoon over some of the pan juices and garnish each plate with roasted hazelnuts.

Serves 6 as an entrée

Note: Raw foie gras is not available in Australia, but you can purchase good quality poached (mi-cuit) foie gras from specialist food stores. Pâté de foie gras is quite different and should not be substituted in this recipe.

RAGOÛT OF YABBY TAILS AND *sweetbreads*

with Leeks, Peas, Macaroni and Truffle Velouté

MACARONI

30 pieces of Macaroni (page 270)

RAGOÛT

18 x 150 g (5 oz) yabbies, heads removed and de-veined

12 baby leeks, trimmed and cut into thirds

30 ml (1 fl oz) non-scented cooking oil

18 x 50 g (1¾ oz) Calves' Sweetbreads (page 270)

80 g (2¾ oz) unsalted butter

120 g (4 oz) shelled peas

few drops lemon juice

salt and freshly ground pepper

TRUFFLE VELOUTÉ

300 ml (10 fl oz) Albufera Sauce (page 263)

1 Poached Truffle (page 50)

splash of Madeira

few drops lemon juice

salt and freshly ground pepper

TO SERVE

300 ml (10 fl oz) Yabby Bisque (page 260), kept warm

1 fresh black winter truffle, finely shaved

MAKE 30 MACARONI, following the instructions on page 270.

TO MAKE THE RAGOÛT, bring a large pan of salted water to the boil and blanch the yabbies, a few at a time, for 10 seconds. Refresh in iced water and when cool enough to handle remove the shells. Refrigerate until ready to serve.

Bring another large pan of salted water to the boil and blanch the peas, leeks and macaroni pieces for 2 minutes, then drain and refresh in iced water.

Meanwhile, heat a large heavy-based frying pan over a medium-high heat. Add the oil followed by the sweetbreads and caramelise until golden brown. Add the butter and heat to a nut-brown foam. Add the yabby tails to the pan and sauté everything together for a few moments. Add the lemon juice and swirl around gently. Add the drained vegetables and macaroni and toss everything together well. Season with salt and pepper.

TO MAKE THE TRUFFLE VELOUTÉ, heat the Albufera sauce then pour into a blender. Add the whole truffle and blitz on high for 3 minutes until smooth. Add the Madeira and lemon juice and season with salt and pepper.

TO SERVE, divide the ragoût evenly between 6 plates. Spoon the truffle velouté and yabby bisque neatly around each plate and garnish each serving with truffle shavings. Serve immediately.

Serves 6 as an entrée

VELOUTÉ OF *celeriac*

with Salt Cod Mousse and Truffle

CELERIAC VELOUTÉ

1 medium celeriac, well scrubbed

3 sprigs thyme

1 bay leaf

1 litre (2¼ pints) White Chicken Stock (page 254)

100 g (3½ oz) butter

½ onion, finely sliced

3 cloves garlic, finely sliced

salt and freshly ground pepper

50 ml (1¾ fl oz) milk

SALT COD MOUSSE

400 g (14 oz) blue eye cod, skin, pin bones and bloodline removed

100 g (3½ oz) Wet Salt (page 9)

zest of 1 lemon

2 sprigs thyme

1 bay leaf

4 cloves garlic, roughly crushed

300 ml (10 fl oz) milk

freshly ground pepper

75 g (3 oz) Potato Purée (page 277), or 1 small baked potato

1 x 5 g (⅛ oz) gelatine leaf, softened in cold water

30 ml (1 fl oz) garlic oil

salt and freshly ground pepper

squeeze of lemon juice

50 ml (1¾ fl oz) pure cream, whipped to soft peaks

TO SERVE

½ cup finely sliced chives

1 fresh black winter truffle, finely cut into thin batons

This soup is velvety smooth and has an earthy flavour that perfectly complements the salty cod and pungent truffle.

Salting cod is a traditional Mediterranean technique for preserving fish. The cod is salted for several days before being air-dried, and usually much of the original flavour disappears. At Bécasse we have modified this method, salting the cod for a few hours, rather than days. After a brief rinse, the fish is gently poached in an aromatic stock until it is just cooked. This way it retains the maximum amount of freshness and flavour.

TO MAKE THE CELERIAC VELOUTÉ, peel the celeriac and put it in a pan of acidulated water to stop it discolouring. Place the peelings in a saucepan with the thyme and bay leaf. Add the chicken stock and bring to the boil. Lower the heat and simmer gently for 20 minutes. Strain through a chinois or fine sieve and set the stock base aside.

Heat the butter in a pan and when it is lightly foaming, add the onion and garlic and sweat over a low heat for 8 minutes, or until soft and transparent. Finely slice the celeriac and quickly add to the pan with the onion and garlic. Sweat gently for a further 8 minutes, without colouring, until the celeriac softens.

Add the stock base and bring to the boil. Lower the heat, season well then simmer gently for 20 minutes. Add the milk and cook for a further 2 minutes, then remove from the heat.

Pour the soup into a blender and blitz on high for around 5 minutes to a very smooth purée. Taste and adjust seasoning then strain through a chinois or fine sieve.

TO SALT THE COD, put the wet salt into a mortar with the lemon zest and half of the thyme, bay leaf and garlic and pound to a smooth paste. Rub evenly over the cod then transfer to the fridge for 2 hours to marinate.

Put the milk in a pan with the remaining thyme, bay leaf and garlic cloves. Season with pepper and bring to a gentle simmer over a low heat.

Wash the salt mixture off the cod under cold running water and pat dry. Add to the hot milk and poach gently until just cooked – it should still be firm and slightly translucent in the centre. Remove the cod from the milk, wrap in a damp cloth and refrigerate until cold. Reserve the poaching milk.

continued …

continued

TO MAKE THE SALT COD MOUSSE, set aside about 300 g (10 oz) of the cod to flake and use as garnish. Put the rest into a food processor with the potato and whiz to a smooth purée. Pass through a drum sieve to remove any remaining lumps.

Squeeze excess water out of the gelatine. Put in a small pan with 2 tablespoons of the reserved poaching milk, and heat gently to dissolve. Tip into a blender with the cod purée and blitz for a few moments. With the blender on low, slowly trickle in the garlic oil until the mixture emulsifies and thickens to a velvety smooth purée. Strain through a chinois or fine sieve then taste and adjust seasoning. Add the lemon juice and whipped cream and fold through gently. Tip into a small bowl and refrigerate until set – about 2 hours.

TO SERVE, gently warm the soup over a low heat then use a hand-blender to whisk it to a frothy foam. Divide the soup between warmed soup bowls and scatter on the reserved pieces of flaked cod. Use a dessertspoon to form small quenelles of salt cod mousse and place 3 in each bowl. Top each bowl with a sprinkling of chives and truffle and serve immediately.

Serves 6 as an entrée

Goat's cheese

WOODSIDE CHEESE *wrights*

Tucked away in the picturesque Adelaide Hills about an hour from Adelaide city is the small rural community of Woodside. The area is a tourism centre, featuring handmade and boutique fine food manufacturers. One such artisan is Kris Lloyd, who heads the Woodside Cheese Wrights.

Lloyd's family owns the Coriole range of wine, olive oil and olives, produced nearby, and since 1994 the company has been manufacturing cheeses, made mostly from local goat's milk. She is the general manager of a small staff and head cheese maker.

Lloyd's attitude differs significantly from other producers of specialised or boutique food items in Australia; instead of closely guarding her knowledge, she is keen to share information with others, to increase overall knowledge of cheese making in Australia. Lloyd has travelled extensively through Europe, particularly in Italy and France, to discover more about her craft. She has initiated a cheese co-operative with other local cheese makers, sharing information and techniques with each other. She is also working with education institutions, rewriting the cheese-making apprenticeship curriculum.

Most of the cheeses at Woodside are made from goat's milk. However, Jersey milk is also used to make Charleston Jersey Brie, a smooth, creamy brie made in large wheels with a buttery yellow interior. Milk production is seasonal (goats and cows produce more milk during the summer months) and the seasons also affect flavours in the cheese.

There's a lot that makes Woodside cheese a different product from other cheeses on the market. Lloyd insists that the milk for one batch be sourced from single-herd goat dairies. 'It follows that a better, and consistent raw product is going to create a fantastic end product,' she says.

One of her suppliers is Anders Oksbjerg who lives in nearby Mypolonga. Three times a week fresh goat's milk is delivered to Lloyd and made into cheese that is salted and aged within the temperature and humidity-controlled 'caves' on site. Oksbjerg is one of only five farmers licensed to sell unpasteurised goat's milk in Australia.

Oksbjerg must submit milk samples every month for analysis. Tests are carried out for pathogens as well as for antibiotics present in the milk, which must be kept below prescribed levels for human consumption. Despite these tight restrictions Oksbjerg is a keen campaigner for unpasteurised goat's milk as he believes the exposure to certain bacteria actually boosts the immune system and general health. Oksbjerg believes people should at least be given the choice. 'People aren't eating enough raw food,' he says. 'By only ingesting sterile food, we're developing more allergies and intolerances.'

A METICULOUS *process*

The Woodside Cheese Wrights use batch pasteurisation (carried out in small batches) by which the milk is heated to 63°C and maintained for 30 minutes, to eliminate any pathogens. 'Our way is slow, but it creates a better product,' claims Kris Lloyd. Higher pasteurisation temperatures speed up the process but can adversely affect the milk integrity.

Once pasteurised, the milk is cooled and a starter culture added, followed by rennet. The starter culture is allowed to ripen, putting back into the mix the good bacteria stripped by the pasteurisation. These bacteria multiply and acidify, which is a vital part of the cheese-making process. Rennet is an enzyme that coagulates the mixture.

Next the curds (solids) and whey (liquid) are separated. A large cutter called a cheese harp cuts the curd first one way, then the other. The whey is partially drained off and the curd is poured into cheese hoops. This is called 'moulding', and creates the cheese's shape.

Once in the cheese hoop, the whey keeps draining slowly. The following morning, the drained cheese shapes (which at this point have a mild, subtle flavour) are immersed in a bath of brine or hand salted, as is the case with a large cheese wheel that may be susceptible to breaking in the brine bath. This salting process enhances flavour in the developing cheeses.

After salting, the cheeses are drained again, before having white mould spores added to them. The mould works quickly to envelop the cheese and creates a colony of protective white mould on the outside, while on the inside the bacteria continues to modify the taste and texture of the cheese. The cheeses are placed in one of several controlled-environment 'caves'. The temperature and humidity of the caves are maintained (at 12°C and 96 per cent respectively) to ensure maximum proliferation of the mould on the outside of the cheese. Colder temperatures would stunt the growth of the white mould and less humidity would extract moisture from the cheese. Depending on the type, the cheeses remain in the cave anywhere from ten days to four weeks.

GOAT'S CURD

There is no way to disguise faults in a curd cheese the way you can, to some extent, with other cheeses that are salted, treated or ashed, so it requires precise, disciplined handling. To make the goat's curd, the same procedure as for all Woodside Cheeses is followed: the milk is pasteurised and treated with starter culture and rennet. After the whey is drained off in cheesecloth bags overnight it is lightly salted and packaged for sale immediately.

Its flavour is light and tangy, with an almost fluffy finish. The versatility of goat's curd means it is suitable for both sweet and savoury recipes. This is a fresh, young cheese, smelling of grass and milk.

EDITH'S ASH

This traditional French-style goat's cheese is named after its creator, a woman named Edith from a small town near Burgundy in France. After two weeks' culturing, it is rolled in fern ash, which alters the acid balance of the cheese. This modification introduces a distinct savoury flavour to the cheese as it continues to mature in the weeks following. After eight weeks, the bacteria will have almost entirely softened the interior of the cheese. That is why soft-rinded cheeses are best consumed within one week of their expiry date, and kept at room temperature, because the flavour and bacteria have developed fully. A fully mature Edith's Ash will have a ball of thick cheese in the middle, surrounded by a cheese of finer, runnier consistency closer to the rind. Edith is recognised for its strong yet refined flavour and texture.

CABECOU

Cabecou was developed in the Quercy, Rouergue and Perigord regions of France. Its origins are believed to date back to the Arab invasions that brought goats to these areas. The name 'Cabecou' means 'little goat' in French and refers to the size of the cheese rather than its source. Cabecou attracts strict specifications: 4–5 centimetres in diameter, 15 millimetres in height and not exceeding 40 grams in weight. Its fat content is 45 per cent. Woodside makes Cabecou in 20-gram discs. Due to its small size the cheese matures very quickly and its shelf life is only about two weeks. The flavour is tender and delicate, and the cheese is versatile in cooking.

CAPRICORN

Capricorn is Woodside's version of a camembert, made with goat's milk. The cheese is made in the same style as a camembert: salted and matured in a cave. A special bacteria is added to enhance flavour, which can turn patches of the rind a reddish colour. Lloyd carefully pares back the mould so as to avoid a thick rind around what is a delicate, velvety cheese.

The French insist that it is best eaten *moitié affiné* – half and half – mould having penetrated the interior somewhat, but with the heart still white and not yet creamy. Ripening from the outside in, this cheese can be eaten from two weeks after the make date (the date the milk it is made from is pasteurised), however at this early stage the full flavour and texture potential will not be reached. Four weeks after being made, Capricorn is fully ripe and oozing a subtly flavoured cheese: tangy and salty, the middle (less ripened) section with a definite bite.

DEEP-FRIED *zucchini flowers*
with Chive and Shallot-Whipped Goat's Curd and a Herb Salad

CHIVE AND SHALLOT-WHIPPED GOAT'S CURD

3 shallots, finely diced

250 ml (8¾ fl oz) dry white wine

200 g (7 oz) fresh goats' curd

100 ml (3½ fl oz) pure cream

1 cup snipped chives

salt and freshly ground pepper

few drops lemon juice

DEEP-FRIED ZUCCHINI FLOWERS

300 ml (10 fl oz) non-scented cooking oil

6 female zucchini flowers

100 g (3½ oz) seasoned plain flour

salt and freshly ground pepper

HERB SALAD

2 cups fresh herbs and salad leaves
(a selection of baby frisée, French tarragon,
chervil, lamb's lettuce (mâche), baby red
chard, baby watercress sprigs)

fleur de sel

drizzle of extra-virgin olive oil

few drops lemon juice

TO PREPARE THE WHIPPED GOAT'S CURD, put the shallots and white wine in a small pan and bring to the boil. Reduce over a high heat until the wine has nearly all evaporated and the shallots are soft. Remove from the heat and cool.

Put the goat's curd and cream in a mixing bowl and whip to soft peaks. Fold in the shallots and snipped chives, season with salt and pepper and stir in the lemon juice. Refrigerate until ready to serve.

TO DEEP-FRY THE ZUCCHINI FLOWERS, heat the oil in a deep pan to 190°C (375°F), or until a cube of bread colours and sizzles to the surface within 30 seconds. Split the flowers in half lengthwise and dredge lightly in the seasoned flour, patting off any excess. Deep-fry a few at a time until they are golden and crisp, turning gently in the oil to ensure they cook and colour evenly. Remove from the oil and drain on kitchen paper. Season well with salt and pepper.

TO SERVE, divide the hot zucchini flowers between 4 serving plates. Use a dessertspoon to form small quenelles of whipped goat's curd and place on each flower. In a mixing bowl, toss together the mixed herbs and salad leaves and arrange a small mound on the zucchini flowers. Season with fleur de sel and finish with a drizzle of oil and a few drops of lemon juice. Serve immediately.

Serves 4 as an entrée

TERRINE OF *beetroot*

with Edith's Ash and Baby Tarragon

GOLDEN BEETROOT

3 large golden beetroots, washed carefully to remove grit and sand

2 litres (4¼ pints) water

100 ml (3½ fl oz) verjuice

60 ml (2 fl oz) chardonnay vinegar

pinch of saffron threads

50 g (1¾ oz) sugar

1 teaspoon salt

freshly ground white pepper

RED BEETROOT

3 large red beetroots, washed carefully to remove grit and sand

2 litres (4¼ pints) water

100 ml (3½ fl oz) red wine

100 ml (3½ fl oz) ruby port

60 ml (2 fl oz) cabernet sauvignon vinegar

50 g (1¾ oz) sugar

1 teaspoon salt

freshly ground white pepper

TERRINE

6 x 5 g (⅛ oz) gelatine leaves, softened in cold water

400 ml (14 fl oz) golden beetroot poaching liquor

400 ml (14 fl oz) red beetroot poaching liquor

TO SERVE

2 x 400 g (14 oz) Edith's Ash goat's cheeses

¼ cup baby tarragon

200 ml (7 fl oz) golden beetroot poaching liquor, reduced by two-thirds to a syrup

Each beetroot is poached separately in a different flavoured liquor to maintain its colour and flavour. The beetroot should be completely submerged while poaching, so you may need to adjust quantities accordingly.

We use a small hors d'oeuvres terrine mould for this recipe, which is about 5 cm (2 in) high, 5.5 cm (2¼ in) wide and roughly 30 cm (12 in) long. Try to buy one with removable sides. The terrine needs a minimum of 6 hours' pressing time and is really best made the day before you intend to serve it.

TO POACH THE GOLDEN BEETROOTS, place them in a medium-sized pan and cover with the remaining ingredients. Taste and adjust the flavour balance to your liking. Heat to just below a simmer, then poach gently, uncovered, for about 2 hours, or until the beetroots are tender. Remove from the heat and allow to cool slightly in the poaching liquor. When cool enough to handle, peel the beetroots. Pour the liquor through a sieve lined with muslin and reserve.

TO POACH THE RED BEETROOTS, repeat the above process.

TO MAKE THE TERRINE, soften 3 gelatine leaves in a small bowl of cold water. Heat 60 ml (2 fl oz) of the 400 ml (14 fl oz) golden beetroot poaching liquor in a small pan. Squeeze any excess water out of the gelatine and add it to the pan, whisking to dissolve completely. Tip into the remaining golden beetroot poaching liquor and refrigerate until it starts to thicken and set.

Soften the remaining 3 gelatine leaves in another small bowl of cold water and repeat the above process with the same quantities of red beetroot poaching liquor.

Cut all the beetroots into 5 mm (¼ in) slices and trim to form rectangles the same width as the mould. Double-line the terrine mould with cling film, leaving a generous overhang. Pour in enough red beetroot jelly to create a 5 mm (¼ in) layer and allow to set. Add a layer of red beetroot then pour in enough golden beetroot jelly to create a 5 mm (¼ in) layer and allow to set. Add a layer of golden beetroot and then another layer of red beetroot jelly. Continue layering jelly and beetroot to the top of the mould. Fold the cling film over the top and refrigerate overnight or for a minimum of 6 hours.

HALF AN HOUR BEFORE SERVING, bring the cheese to room temperature. Slice each cheese into 4 wedges. Unmould the terrine and remove the cling film. Use a very sharp knife, dipped in hot water, to cut it into 8 slices. Place a slice of terrine on each plate with a wedge of cheese. Garnish with a few sprigs of baby tarragon and drizzle with the golden beetroot syrup.

Serves 8 as an entrée

Note: When building the terrine, allow each jelly layer to set soft, rather than firm. This helps the layers stick together and minimises the risk of the terrine splitting when you slice it.

DOUBLE-BAKED *cabecou soufflé*

with a Celery Leaf and Frisée Salad and Walnut Vinaigrette

150 g (5 oz) dried breadcrumbs

50 g (1¾ oz) walnuts, roasted, skins rubbed off and finely chopped

salt and freshly ground pepper

100 ml (3½ fl oz) Clarified Butter (page 264)

SOUFFLÉ BASE
60 g (2 oz) butter

60 g (2 oz) plain flour

300 ml (10 fl oz) warm milk

340 g (12 oz) Cabecou goat's cheese

1 teaspoon salt

freshly ground pepper

6 egg yolks

10 egg whites, at room temperature

pinch of salt

few drops lemon juice

SALAD
150 g (5 oz) walnuts

¼ bunch celery, leaves reserved, stalks peeled and finely sliced

large handful frisée, golden leaves from the centre

salt and freshly ground pepper

200 ml (7 fl oz) Walnut Vinaigrette (page 266)

1 cup Deep-Fried Parsley Leaves (page 283)

This is a chunky, rustic fail-proof soufflé, with a crusty shell, fluffy interior and melting pieces of soft tasty Cabecou cheese.

Mix the breadcrumbs with the chopped walnuts and season well. Brush 8 x 150 ml (5 fl oz) soufflé moulds with the clarified butter and line with the breadcrumb mixture. Refrigerate until required.

TO MAKE THE SOUFFLÉ BASE, melt the butter in a heavy-based pan over a medium heat until it begins to foam but not colour. Stir in the flour with a wooden spoon and cook over a medium heat for a couple of minutes without colouring. Slowly add the warm milk, stirring all the while. Bring to the boil, then reduce the heat and simmer for 5 minutes.

Remove from the heat and allow to cool slightly. While still warm, tip into a food processor and begin to process. Crumble 140 g (5 oz) of the goats' cheese add it to the mixture with the motor running. Process until smooth. Season with salt and pepper. With the motor still running, add the egg yolks, one at a time, to form a smooth, glossy mixture. Tip into a large mixing bowl, cover with cling film and leave until required. You can prepare the soufflés to this stage up to 1 day ahead.

TO COOK THE SOUFFLÉS, preheat the oven to 190°C (375°F). Put the egg whites into a spotlessly clean mixing bowl and whisk to soft peaks. Add the salt and lemon juice and continue whisking to stiff peaks. Dice the remaining goats' cheese and stir it into the soufflé base. Stir in half the egg whites to slacken the mixture. Quickly and gently fold in the remaining egg whites, being careful not to over mix. Divide between the 8 moulds and level the surfaces with a spatula.

Bake the soufflés in the centre of the oven for 15 minutes, until risen and golden. Remove from the oven and leave to cool. They will deflate and shrink. Turn them out of the moulds and set aside until ready to reheat. They will keep quite happily for a couple of hours.

TO MAKE THE SALAD, roast the walnuts until golden brown then remove from the oven and put them in a large mixing bowl. Blanch the celery slices for 30 seconds then refresh in iced water. Add them to the mixing bowl with the celery leaves and frisée. Season and toss gently with the walnut vinaigrette.

WHEN READY TO SERVE, preheat the oven to 190°C (375°F). Arrange the soufflés on a baking tray and reheat for 10 minutes. They will rise again and look golden and puffy.

Divide the salad between 8 serving plates and scatter on the deep-fried parsley. Arrange a hot soufflé on top and drizzle over a little more vinaigrette. Serve immediately.

Serves 8 as an entrée or light main course

SALAD OF *raw cèpes*

with Capricorn Goat's Cheese, Shallots and Thyme

1 x 400 g (14 oz) Capricorn goat's cheese, chilled

12 large fresh cèpe (porcini) mushrooms

2 shallots

8 sprigs thyme, leaves picked

drizzle of extra-virgin olive oil

freshly ground white pepper

fleur de sel

Make sure you choose a very ripe Capricorn goat's cheese for this recipe.

About 20 minutes before you are ready to serve, remove the cheese from the refrigerator and slice crosswise into 4 even discs. Leave to sit at room temperature to soften and for the flavour to develop while you prepare the salad.

Finely slice the cèpes and arrange the slices in a neat overlapping circle on each plate. Shave the shallots on a mandolin (or use a very sharp knife to slice them as thinly as you can) and scatter them over the cèpes.

Carefully place a disc of cheese on top of the salad. Sprinkle with thyme leaves and drizzle on a little oil. Finally, season with pepper and fleur de sel.

Serves 4 as an entrée

Shellfish

SALTY SEAS

A PERSONAL *approach*

In 1998 a Tasmanian-based not-for-profit youth training and employment scheme – the Beacon Foundation – turned its benevolent hand to the Tasmanian coastal town of St Helens. Georges Bay, on which St Helens is situated, had become so infested with Pacific oysters they were clogging the waterways, creating a hazard for tourists in the area. The Beacon Foundation established a short-term project to rid Georges Bay of the shellfish while training some of its unemployed local youth in the basics of oyster handling.

One of the employees was Anita Paulsen, who grew up in nearby Devonport and had dreamed of becoming a marine biologist as a child. When the Beacon Foundation project was over, Anita and business partner Lex Weekes decided to continue, broadening the produce traded to incorporate sea urchins, vongole clams, angasi oysters, scallops, crayfish and live fish. They put a great deal of energy into research and development, including sourcing new products and consistently marketing to top-end restaurants on the Australian mainland. Paulsen and Weekes have become ambassadors for the Tasmanian seafood industry.

OPPOSITE: From left to right: Lex Weekes, Dale Ridges, Anita Paulsen

The Salty Seas factory has a series of saltwater holding tanks that are used to purge the shellfish of impurities, sand and grit from the sea floor. Salty Seas washes its produce in saltwater direct from Binalong Bay, enhancing both flavour and appearance of the shellfish. The water is filtered using ultra-violet filters, as well as bio-filtration, fractionators and sand filters.

Their days begin early, sometimes as early as 1 a.m. if there is a big shipment to go out that day. Local divers and fishermen are contracted or sell to Salty Seas on a day-to-day basis depending on what is required. Dealing directly with restaurants, Paulsen and Weekes are able to keep a finger on the pulse of their business, and the immediacy with which they can act is unique – with the factory on the edge of the bay, Salty Seas can fill orders at short notice and with astonishing reach. Perhaps it is this personal and flexible approach that earned the company the prestigious *Gourmet Traveller*/Jaguar Award of Excellence for a Primary Producer in 2002.

Tasmanian waters are subject to quota restrictions to ensure the ongoing proliferation of all species of commercially coveted seafood. And at 23 metres in depth at its deepest point, Georges Bay is teeming with sea life.

Dale Ridgers, a contract diver, is usually in the water by 9 a.m. and completes two dives in his working day, finishing his last dive and delivering to the Salty Seas factory not long after 1 p.m. Ridgers and the other divers who supply Salty Seas unload their dinghies at the front door of the factory, which sits on the edge of Media Cove, on the Golden Fleece Rivulet that feeds into the heart of Georges Bay.

Between dives, Dale Ridgers stashes his haul in the open water at what is known as a 'depuration site', a series of suspended nets to cleanse the shellfish of impurities, sand and grit while allowing them to remain in robust health, enjoying the the pristine tidal waters of Georges Bay. As required and when each species has gone through its prescribed depuration period, Dale removes them from the water and transports them to the Salty Seas factory.

The only problem with this system is the poacher. 'Yes, I've had the odd catch go missing,' he chuckles, 'but on the whole it hasn't been too much of a problem'. He points out that poachers really only operate on a small, domestic scale and only ever when the water and outside temperature make being in the sea an attractive option. 'It gets pretty cold down here, you know.'

A truck arrives daily at 5 p.m., and all produce must be ready for this transport to make the flights out of Launceston (several hours' drive on the winding roads from St Helens). Following the collection, a couple of hours are spent returning the factory to its sterilised conditions before Paulsen, Weekes and their staff review upcoming orders for the following day and clock off at about 7 p.m. 'You have to like it,' Weekes reflects on his labour-intensive occupation.

SCALLOP (*Pecten fumatus*)

Harvest areas for scallops are rotated annually to ensure adequate restocking of the Tasmanian seas' produce. The season runs from June to November, slowing into October as the molluscs begin to spawn. Rich, salty and sweet, I prefer Tasmanian scallops because of their generous size and the clean waters they come from. Because Salty Seas' scallops are washed in salt water, the quality of the product is enhanced; when cleaned in fresh water a scallop will act as a sponge and absorb the water, making it more difficult to caramelise and prone to spitting in the frying pan. It will also affect its flavour, colour and texture.

ANGASI OYSTER

(*Ostrea angasi*)

Also commonly known as the 'flat oyster', the angasi oyster is native to Tasmania as well as the New South Wales coastline, extending to Queensland. This mollusc is unique for its strong, sweet and slightly earthy flavour when compared with other oysters. Angasi oysters grow on the bottom of Georges Bay, at depths of between 1 and 20 metres. The season runs from March to November. Georges Bay is currently Tasmania's only authorised harvesting area for this particular type of oyster.

VONGOLE CLAM
(Katalysia scalrina)

Available year-round and also called 'Katalysia clams', these molluscs are known for harbouring small pearls in their shells (which can be a nasty surprise if you bite on one). The clam is harvested from sand beds at nearby Ansons Bay and depurated for seven days to rid shells of the little pearls, impurities and other grainy matter that may reside within. Vongole clams have enjoyed a surge in popularity in recent years due to their plump, tender meat.

SEA URCHIN
(Echinus esculentus)

Sea urchins belong to the marine species family *Phylum echinodermata* (spiny-skinned animals) – the same family as starfish, sea cucumbers and sea lilies. Harvested in the waters and mouth of Georges Bay, sea urchins are a delicacy in Japan that sell for a high price in their market. They are collected by hand from the sea floor – in shallow waters and to a depth of 70 metres. The edible part is the roe, or ovaries. There are five of these 'tongues' of roe in each sea urchin and it has an extraordinarily fresh, salty flavour with a distinctive floral aroma.

PAN-FRIED *red mullet*

with Cuttlefish Confit and Sea Urchin Jus

3 x 400 g (14 oz) red mullet (rouget)

100 ml (3½ fl oz) extra-virgin olive oil

¼ teaspoon orange zest

1 clove garlic, finely chopped

4 coriander seeds, finely ground

pinch of saffron threads

2 sprigs thyme, leaves picked

6 basil leaves, torn into small pieces

CUTTLEFISH CONFIT

½ medium onion, cut into
5 mm (¼ in) dice

1 clove garlic, roughly crushed

2 sprigs thyme

200 ml (7 fl oz) olive oil

salt and freshly ground pepper

4 slices white bread, cut into
5 mm (¼ in) dice

salt and freshly ground pepper

2 small cuttlefish, cleaned and
finely sliced

30 sun-dried cherry tomatoes

1 tablespoon grated parmesan

¼ cup flat-leaf parsley leaves, very finely
shredded to a chiffonade

few drops lemon juice

SEA URCHIN JUS

300 ml (10 fl oz) Rouget Jus (page 262)

1 tablespoon extra-virgin olive oil

few drops orange juice

18 sea urchin tongues

80 ml (2¾ fl oz) sea urchin juice*

salt and freshly ground pepper

Red mullet or rouget is also called barbonia and is known in France as rouget-barbet. It is highly prized in the Mediterranean region. The best rouget are those with a bright reddish-pink skin streaked with gold and with a black striped dorsal fin, two scales under its eyes and a pair of barbels beneath the chin.

With the soft red mullet and cuttlefish, crunchy croutons, sweet tomatoes and tangy parmesan, this is a truly lively dish.

TO PREPARE THE RED MULLET, use a very sharp knife to scrape off the scales from the tail to the head – they are delicate and come away easily. Slice away the fillets and remove any pin bones. Arrange the fillets skin side up on a shallow tray. Drizzle over the olive oil and sprinkle the remaining ingredients evenly over the fish pieces. Cover and refrigerate for 2 hours.

FOR THE CUTTLEFISH CONFIT, put the diced onion in a small heavy-based pan with the garlic and thyme. Pour on the oil and season well with salt and pepper. Cook at a very low even temperature, between 70–80°C (160–175°F) for around 45 minutes. Don't allow the oil to simmer – you should just see the odd bubble rising to the surface. Use a slotted spoon to transfer the onions to a small colander and drain. Reserve the flavoured oil but discard the aromatics.

Heat a few tablespoons of the flavoured oil in a frying pan and fry the diced bread until golden brown, turning to brown evenly. Drain well on kitchen paper and season with salt and pepper.

Put the cooked onions and sliced cuttlefish into a heavy-based pan with 2 tablespoons of the flavoured oil. Cook over a very low heat, stirring gently. You just want to warm the cuttlefish through – be careful not to overcook it. As it warms, it softens and turns opaque. At this point, remove the pan from the heat. Add the croutons, tomatoes, grated cheese and parsley and stir gently to combine. Season with salt and pepper and add a drop of lemon juice. Keep warm.

TO PREPARE THE SEA URCHIN JUS, put the rouget jus in a small pan and bring to a gentle simmer. Add the oil, orange juice, sea urchin tongues and juice and season to taste.

WHEN READY TO SERVE, preheat the oven to 140°C (275°F), remove the fish fillets from the refrigerator and bring to room temperature. Cook, still in the marinade, for about 6 minutes, until medium-rare and aromatic.

Divide the cuttlefish confit between 6 warm serving plates. Arrange the red mullet fillets on top and spoon over the sea urchin jus. Serve immediately.

Serves 6 as an entrée

Note: Each spine-covered urchin shell (known as the test) yields a small amount of juice.

CIVET OF JOHN DORY, CLAMS AND *angasi oysters*

1 x 1.8 kg (4 lb) John Dory, filleted and skinned

12 live angasi oysters, rinsed well to remove dirt and grit

500 g (18 oz) large clams (vongole), soaked in several changes of cold water to remove any sand

1 litre (2¼ pints) Clam Stock (page 257)

salt and freshly ground pepper

30 medium pasta bows, blanched for 6 minutes in boiling, salted water and refreshed in iced water

60 g (2 oz) dried wakame seaweed, reconstituted in cold water

40 g (1⅓ oz) dried hijiki seaweed, reconstituted in cold water

½ cup finely sliced chives

few drops lemon juice

The direct translation of 'civet' is simply 'stew', however in a more culinary sense civet generally refers to a wild game stew made from rabbit, hare, venison or boar, thickened with the animal's own blood and traditionally served with small onions. The name is derived from the French word 'cive' – spring onion – a traditional garnish.

This is my version of a seafood civet, full of the strong salty taste of the ocean.

Remove any sinews from the John Dory and trim the edges. Cut each fillet into three even portions, then cut each portion in half to yield 12 pieces in total. Set aside.

Open the oysters, and remove them from their shells, taking care to retain all the juices. Rinse the clams.

Put 500 ml (18 fl oz) of the clam stock into a pan and warm gently to just below a simmer. Keep warm while you poach the seafood.

Put the rest of the clam stock into a large, heavy-based pan, bring to a simmer and add the clams. Cover with a tight-fitting lid and simmer gently for 2 minutes until the shells begin to open. Remove the lid from the pan and lower the heat.

Season the John Dory fillets lightly with salt and pepper and place them in the pan on top of the clams. Poach gently, uncovered, for 2 minutes, then turn the fillets over. Add the pasta bows and swirl the pan gently to mix them in. Cook for a further minute to warm through. Add the seaweed and oysters to the pan and poach for 30 seconds. Turn the oysters and poach for a further 30 seconds.

Add the reserved oyster juices and chives and season to taste with salt and freshly ground pepper. Finish with a squeeze of lemon juice.

Use a hand-blender to whisk the reserved clam stock for 10–15 seconds to a frothy foam. To serve, divide the civet evenly between 6 warm serving bowls, making sure that each person has 2 fillets of John Dory. Spoon on the foaming sauce and serve immediately.

Serves 6 as a main course

CARAMELISED *scallops*
with a Fricassée of Clams and Salsify

FRICASSÉE OF CLAMS AND SALSIFY

500 g (18 oz) large clams (vongole), soaked in several changes of cold water to remove any sand

½ medium carrot, finely sliced

1 stick celery, finely sliced

¼ small leek, finely sliced

½ bulb fennel, core removed and finely sliced

3 cloves garlic, roughly crushed

4 sprigs thyme

200 ml (7 fl oz) dry white wine

30 g (1 oz) unsalted butter

300 g (10½ oz) Glazed Salsify (page 280)

100 ml (3½ fl oz) Red Wine Sauce (page 262)

GARNISH

300 g (10½ oz) Potato Purée (page 277)

65 ml (2⅓ fl oz) milk

65 ml (2⅓ fl oz) pure cream

65 g (2⅓ oz) unsalted butter

2 tablespoons Chlorophyll (page 268)

2 tablespoons Garlic Purée (page 282)

salt and freshly ground pepper

150 g (5 oz) Garlic and Herb Butter (page 265), melted

CARAMELISED SCALLOPS

6 large fresh scallops

salt and freshly ground pepper

2 teaspoons non-scented cooking oil

60 g (2 oz) unsalted butter

few drops lemon juice

TO PREPARE THE FRICASSÉE, put the rinsed clams in a large mixing bowl with the carrot, celery, leek and fennel, garlic, thyme and wine. Heat a large heavy-based pan until very hot. Tip everything in and cover the pan with a tight-fitting lid. Cook on a high heat for a few moments, shaking the pan from time to time to ensure even cooking. As the clams begin to open, transfer them from the pan to a colander to drain. Keep warm until ready to serve. Discard the vegetables and herbs and freeze the liquor for use in another recipe.

To prepare the salsify, heat a frying pan over a medium heat. Add the butter and fry to a nut-brown foam. Add the salsify and toss in the foam until golden and caramelised. Add the Red Wine Sauce and swirl the pan over the heat to form a glossy emulsified sauce. Remove from heat and keep warm until ready to serve.

TO PREPARE THE GARNISH, warm the potato purée over a moderate heat. Meanwhile, put the milk, cream and butter into a separate small pan and bring to the boil. When the butter has melted use a hand-blender to blitz it briefly to an emulsion, then tip into the purée. Add the chlorophyl and garlic purée and whisk everything together well. Season with salt and pepper and keep warm until ready to serve.

TO CARAMELISE THE SCALLOPS, heat a large frying pan until nearly smoking. Season the scallops lightly with salt and freshly ground pepper. Add the oil to the pan and add the scallops, flat side down. Sear for a few seconds then add the butter and heat to a nut-brown foam. Remove the pan from the heat and carefully turn the scallops over. Season again and add the lemon juice and baste for a few more seconds. The whole process should take no more than a minute – you are aiming for scallops that are cooked medium-rare: caramelised and golden on the outside, but still translucent in the centre.

TO SERVE, place a spoonful of the warm potato purée in the centre of each serving plate and top with a scallop. Arrange the clams and salsify around the plate and drizzle with the warm pan juices and a little garlic and herb butter. Serve immediately.

Serves 6 as an entrée

NAGE OF *angasi oysters*
with Scallop and Ginger Tortellini

SCALLOP AND GINGER TORTELLINI

500 g (18 oz) Scallop Mousse (page 269)

1 small bulb fennel with the fronds attached

80 g (2³/4 oz) fresh ginger

1 lime

splash of Noilly Prat

splash of Pernod

salt and freshly ground pepper

250 g (9 oz) Pasta Dough (page 269), at room temperature

1 egg, lightly beaten with a little water to form an egg wash

ANGASI OYSTER NAGE

1 small carrot, peeled

1 stick celery, trimmed and peeled

1 small desirée potato, peeled

1 litre (2¹/4 pints) Oyster and Ginger Nage (page 259)

18 live angasi oysters, rinsed well to remove dirt and grit

¹/2 cup finely snipped chives

few sprigs fresh chervil

¹/2 cup baby basil

A nage is a delicately flavoured, aromatic broth in which shellfish and crustaceans are lightly poached and served. It is often finished with a dash of cream and fresh herbs.

The juice from angasi oysters is strong and salty – almost elemental. It's a bit like swallowing a mouthful of sea when you're playing in the waves at the beach.

TO MAKE THE TORTELLINI FILLING, put the scallop mousse in a mixing bowl set on ice. Core and finely dice the fennel, reserving the fronds. Blanch the fennel in boiling salted water and refresh in iced water. Drain and pat dry.

Peel the ginger and dice it finely. Blanch in boiling water seasoned with a little salt, sugar and lemon. Refresh in iced water. Repeat 2–3 times, depending on the strength of the ginger. You want it to be aromatic with a hint of heat, but not overpowering. Drain and pat dry.

Finely chop the fennel fronds and add to the mousse with the blanched fennel and ginger. Fold through gently. Zest the lime over the bowl of mousse to capture the aromatic oils with the zest. Add a squeeze of lime juice then add the Noilly Prat and Pernod and season with salt and pepper.

Place a teaspoon of mousse on a small square of cling film and twist to seal tightly. Poach in a pan of gently simmering water for 2 minutes. Taste and adjust the balance of seasonings if necessary. Cover the bowl with cling film and refrigerate until required.

TO MAKE THE TORTELLINI, dust your work surface lightly with flour. Roll the pasta dough through a pasta machine, working down from the thickest setting to the finest setting to form a smooth, thin sheet. Lay the pasta sheet on your work surface and cut out 18 rounds using a 9 cm (3¹/2 in) cutter.

Place a spoonful of chilled scallop mousse, about 25–30 g (1 oz), on each pasta round. Brush the edge lightly with the egg wash then fold over to form a half-moon. Use your fingers to pinch the dough together and seal, then trim the edge neatly with the pastry cutter. Twist the 2 corners in until they meet and pinch them together using a little more egg wash. Repeat to make a total of 18 tortellini.

continued …

continued

TO PREPARE THE ANGASI OYSTER NAGE, dice the vegetables very finely to form a brunoise. Blanch them in boiling salted water for a few seconds then refresh in iced water. Drain and pat dry. Put the oyster and ginger nage in a large pan and bring to a gentle simmer. Shuck the oysters and strain the liquor through a fine sieve. Add both to the pan with the blanched vegetables and snipped chives.

TO SERVE, bring a large pan of salted water to the boil. Cook the tortellini, a few at a time, for 4 minutes then transfer to a large bowl and season lightly with salt and pepper.

When all the tortellini are cooked, divide them between 6 hot serving bowls. Ladle on the nage, distributing the oysters and vegetables evenly. Garnish each bowl with a few leaves of chervil and baby basil and serve immediately.

Serves 6 as an entrée

Crustacea

MULATAGA

AN ECOLOGICAL *responsibility*

Mulataga founder Dennis Gaunt grew up in Geraldton, a few hundred kilometres north of Perth, Western Australia. 'From an early age I was inducted into the fishing industry,' he says. As the years passed, Gaunt noticed the numbers of shellfish in the sea dropping and in the early 1980s decided to investigate the dwindling viability of aquaculture in the state. To an (at the time) unenthusiastic audience, Gaunt pitched his ideas about assisted regeneration in our oceans. With a balance between ecological responsibility and business sense ('We're green but we're also pragmatic: we've got to live and eat'), Gaunt approaches fishing with what he calls an 'environmental underlay'.

The company's name was selected from an Aboriginal dictionary. 'Moolataga' roughly translates as 'ancient or Dreamtime river fish'. The name was eventually adapted to 'Mulataga', with origins from the Noongyar tribe from the south-west of Western Australia.

When he first established the business, Gaunt decided to farm yabbies rather than saltwater crustacea, as the privately owned dams made easier work than government-controlled public waterways. The business was one of the first to tap into the yabby market – now a huge source of revenue for Australia. 'That was the beginning of [Mulataga's] drive into aquaculture,' he says. The company now collaborates with the Fisheries Department on research and development projects, in particular learning more about the growth cycles of the crystal crab.

Today Mulataga operates fishing vessels from Broome and Lake Argyle to the Rainbow Coast (stretching across the south-west corner of Western Australia from Cape Leeuwin to Esperance) spanning a distance of more than 800 kilometres by road. The hostile West Australian coastline is home to many species that over the years have become Mulataga's specialties.

Mulataga's headquarters and packing factory are situated at the end of the runway at Perth International Airport. Live shellfish are purged in holding tanks (at the same temperature as the water they were found in) to cleanse them of dirt, excrement or sand, and are then packaged for live shipment to restaurants around the globe. In holding rooms live marron and yabbies are held at a chilled temperature to slow their heartbeat and minimise distress.

The *Roy Larsson*, one of Mulataga's fishing craft, is based in Albany, on the coast of southern Western Australia. Starting out its life as a Tasmanian fisher and ferry, the boat now ventures out on trips ranging from two to ten days, depending on weather and haul. Designed for heavy weather, it has a steel frame and upper wheelhouse where the skipper sits. Storms can be violent in this region and with these features the *Roy Larsson* is better equipped than most boats. 'For this kind of work and in this area,' Dennis Gaunt explains of the Rainbow Coast, 'you need a vessel and people with character'. It is hard and dangerous work.

The crew of *Roy Larsson* take her up to 50 kilometres offshore to retrieve the crayfish pots planted around the sea floor. The catch can vary between 20 and 200 shellfish per trip, and is stored in a saltwater-filled hold beneath the lower deck of the boat. Before the crew shift the catch to the storage area, they clamp the crustacea's claws; a king crab is capable of lopping off a human finger in a second.

Every catch is logged, including the depth at which each species of shellfish was found, and latitude and longitude bearings. Each species has a restriction on minimum weight or length, set by the Department of Fisheries, and must be returned to the ocean should they not meet these standards, keeping the ocean's stores at healthy levels.

The *Roy Larsson* in Albany, Western Australia

THE MARRON *farm*

Ken Court lives at 'Yarrabah', a 200-hectare property about 45 minutes south-east of Perth. The name 'Yarrabah' is from the Aboriginal language, derived from 'the running water' (yarra) and the 'red gums' (bah) of the area. Court's farm features 34 dams, each devoted to the cultivation of marron. These resilient creatures are well suited to the area with its healthy rainfall.

Marron moult and are at their most vulnerable during the summer months. The plated armour that protects the marron's vital organs is shed, revealing a soft skin that is slowly replaced with hard armour that grows again over a few months. For this reason marron are harvested during the winter, when they are more hardy.

They are kept at Yarrabah until they are about two-and-a-half years old, and at a weight of roughly 250 grams. Marron can, however, grow up to 500 grams. The farm harvests about 30,000 marron annually. They are fed on a diet of pilchards and blue mackerel, and a low-protein grain that supplements the natural food source in the dam – the grasses growing at its edge that make up three-quarters of the marron's feed. With a fully developed hard shell, marron are tough creatures and can survive out of water for some time. 'They're bulletproof,' Court claims. 'They'll walk across a paddock.'

Harvesting is literally a case of pulling the plug on the dams and allowing gravity to do its work. Over the course of a week, as the water level gradually goes down, the marron gather in the deeper end of the dam. Then the water is drained more briskly and each crustacean is automatically guided into a piece of plastic pipe, through which they rocket downhill into a grading facility. After being graded the marron are purged for five or six days, ready for the Mulataga pick-up.

Ken Court's Marron Dams at Yarrabah near Perth, Western Australia

THE YABBY *farm*

Husband and wife team Cocky and Judy Roberts have been farming yabbies for fifteen years. They were among the original suppliers of Mulataga yabbies and have a depot on their property, collecting and purging yabbies from surrounding local yabby farms.

The yabby season runs year-round. Traps are set using a piece of oily fish (often a sardine or mackerel) as bait, and the yabbies fall into a rectangular trap. To maximise numbers, the traps usually sit for at least 24 hours before they are pulled in by a length of string and the yabbies collected.

A rather crude device acts as a grading system. A shallow plastic box with slats as a base is filled with the yabbies collected in the traps. Those that fall through the spaces between the slats are returned to the dam; those that remain are deemed large enough for harvest. The company has devised cooling and transportation systems to keep the crustacea as calm as possible during transport.

KING MARRON
(*Cherax tenuimanus*)

Reaching a maximum body length of around 18 centimetres (closer to 40 centimetres when including the claws), marron thrive on the sandy bottom of deep rivers. Although native to Western Australia, there are species found in New South Wales and South Australia. When cooked, the flesh is moist and firm.

YABBY
(*Cherax albidus*)

Yabbies are resilient creatures that can survive out of water for days. Yabbies are smaller than marron and the flesh is sweet and held in high regard by chefs. In its natural environment, the yabby is found in slow-flowing water to a depth of five metres. More are farmed in Western Australia than in any other Australian state or territory.

GOLDEN OR CRYSTAL CRAB
(*Chaceon bicolor*)

Also known as the 'golden lucky crab' and the 'Australian deep-sea crystal crab', the golden crab is found in deep oceans (up to 1000 metres in depth) and is abundant just off the continental shelf of Western Australia. This crab can vary from a weight of about 600 grams to three kilograms, and is popular for its sweet flavour. The shell is thin, making it easy to prepare, and it has a high meat yield of about 36 per cent.

GIANT 'KING' CRAB
(*Pseudocarcinus gigas*)

A deepwater species, the giant crab (known as the 'giant Tasmanian crab' or 'giant deepwater crab') is prized for its delicate, sweet flavour and tender texture. This species is the largest found in Australian waters and is the world's heaviest. It can reach 45 centimetres across its carapace (body diameter minus the claws) and a weight of more than 17 kilograms. It is slow growing and long-living, and numbers have dwindled as a result of waters being overfished.

CHAMPAGNE CRAB
(*Hypothalassia armata*)

This species is found all around the eastern and southern coastlines of Australia: spanning southward from Mackay in Queensland and up to Port Hedland in Western Australia, in waters 30 to 540 metres in depth. At 15 centimetres across the carapace, the champagne crab is not big, but is in constant demand for its delicate flavour.

RED PEARL CRAB
(*Maia squinado*)

Commonly known as the 'spider crab', the red pearl crab is easily identifiable by the brilliant-red textured bubbles on its carapace and legs. The spider crab family have eight legs on their body, in addition to the pincers. The sweet, smoothly textured meat makes this a favourite.

CARPACCIO OF *golden beetroot*

with Champagne Crab and Baby Sorrel

CARPACCIO

16 medium golden beetroot, washed
carefully to remove grit and sand

3 litres (6½ pints) water

200 ml (7 fl oz) verjuice

100 ml (3½ fl oz) chardonnay vinegar

pinch of saffron threads

80 g (2¾ oz) sugar

1 teaspoon salt

freshly ground white pepper

1 x 1 kg (2 lb 2 oz) champagne crab

½ cup finely snipped chives

100 ml (3½ fl oz) Lemon Vinaigrette
(page 266)

fleur de sel

freshly ground white pepper

1 cup baby sorrel

The carapace of the champagne crab has protective spikes covering it. Once the crab is dead these spikes should be removed with a cook's blowtorch to prevent any mishaps while you are removing the meat.

TO POACH THE GOLDEN BEETROOTS, place them in a medium-sized pan and cover with the remaining ingredients. Taste and adjust the flavour balance to your liking. Heat to just below a simmer and poach gently, uncovered, for about 2 hours, or until the beetroots are tender. Remove from the heat and allow to cool slightly in the poaching liquor. When cool enough to handle, peel the beetroots.

Pour the liquor through a sieve double-lined with muslin. Bring 200 ml (7 fl oz) of the strained liquor to the boil, then lower the heat and simmer for 15 minutes until reduced by two-thirds to a syrup. Remove from the heat and leave to cool.

TO COOK THE CRAB, bring a large pan of salted water to the boil, then lower the heat to a simmer. Place the crab in the pan and simmer gently for 10 minutes. Remove the crab from the water and leave until cool enough to handle.

Remove the legs and claws from the crab, crack them and remove the meat. Crack the body shell and remove all the meat from the carapace. Carefully pick through all the crab meat removing any specks of shell or cartilage. Transfer to a clean mixing bowl and add the snipped chives, vinaigrette, fleur de sel and pepper. Toss gently to combine.

TO SERVE, use a mandolin or very sharp knife to slice the beetroot as finely as possible. Arrange the slices in a neat overlapping circle on each plate.

Spoon a neat layer of crab meat on top of the beetroot, garnish with a few leaves of baby sorrel and drizzle with the golden beetroot syrup.

Serves 6 as an entrée

SALAD OF CRISP SPICED *pork belly*

with Snow Crab and Vietnamese Dressing

1 x 1.2 kg (2 lb 10 oz) snow crab

300 ml (10 fl oz) non-scented cooking oil

½ cup Vietnamese mint leaves

½ cup Thai basil leaves

6 large shallots, finely sliced

½ small green mango, very finely julienned

½ bunch spring onions, very finely shredded

250 ml (8¾ fl oz) Vietnamese Dressing (page 267)

salt and freshly ground pepper

few drops fresh lime juice

400 g (14 oz) Spiced Confit Pork Belly (page 276), chilled

At Bécasse we marinate the pork belly in a spiced dry salt for 24 hours, then gently confit it in a spiced braising liquor. If time is not on your side, a piece of barbecued pork from Chinatown will work as a good alternative.

To cook the crab, bring a large pan of salted water to the boil then lower the heat to a simmer. Place the crab in the pan and simmer gently for 12 minutes. Remove the crab from the water and leave until cool enough to handle.

Remove the legs and claws from the crab, crack them and remove the meat. Crack the body shell and remove all the meat from the carapace. Carefully pick through all the crab meat removing any specks of shell or cartilage. Transfer to a clean mixing bowl and set aside.

Heat the oil in a small deep pan to 180°C (350°F), or until a cube of bread colours and sizzles to the surface within 30 seconds. Deep-fry half the Vietnamese mint leaves until golden brown and crisp, about 10–15 seconds. Repeat with half the Thai basil. Deep-fry the sliced shallots for 45–60 seconds. Drain the fried herbs and shallots on kitchen paper and keep warm until required.

Put the green mango and spring onions in the mixing bowl with the crab meat. Roughly tear the reserved fresh Thai basil leaves and add them to the bowl. Add a few tablespoons of dressing, season with salt and freshly ground pepper and add a few drops of lime juice. Toss gently then taste and adjust seasoning if necessary.

Slice the chilled pork lengthwise into 12 long, thin slices. Fry over a high heat until golden and brown. Remove from the pan and drain briefly on kitchen paper.

To serve, place a ring mould on the centre of a serving plate. Line the inside of the mould with 2 slightly overlapping pieces of pork. Spoon in a generous amount of the crab mixture and press it down firmly into the mould. Carefully lift up the mould and repeat for the other 5 serves. Top each stack with the deep-fried herbs and shallots. Shred the remaining fresh Vietnamese mint leaves very finely and sprinkle them around the plate. Drizzle on a little dressing and serve while the pork is still warm.

Serves 6 as an entrée or light main course

24 x 150 g (5 oz) live yabbies

1 large carrot, peeled and cut into long batons

2 sticks celery, peeled and cut into long batons

1 large zucchini, cut into long batons

1 large yellow zucchini, cut into long batons

2 tablespoons olive oil

1 large red capsicum, cut into long batons

1 large eggplant, cut into long batons

salt and freshly ground pepper

splash of sherry vinegar

SPICY MARINADE

8 whole coriander seeds, crushed to a powder

3 cardamom seeds, crushed to a powder

1 pinch saffron threads

100 ml (3½ fl oz) fresh orange juice

50 ml (1¾ fl oz) fresh lime juice

100 ml (3½ fl oz) verjuice

400 ml (14 fl oz) extra-virgin olive oil

¼ small red chilli, very finely chopped

salt and freshly ground pepper

TO SERVE

100 g (3½ oz) unsalted butter

400 ml (14 fl oz) Yabby Bisque (page 260), kept warm

200 ml (7 fl oz) Herb Oil (page 268)

½ cup baby basil leaves

8 basil leaves, very finely shredded to a chiffonade

Escabèche is a traditional Spanish marinade, particularly used for fish or small game birds. The fish or birds are fried then covered with a hot spicy marinade. They are left to cool in the marinade for 24 hours or so and then served at room temperature.

This spicy vegetable escabèche makes a delicious tangy accompaniment that cuts through the richness of the yabbies.

TO PREPARE THE YABBIES, put them in the freezer for an hour or so before cooking. Bring a large pan of salted water to the boil and blanch the yabbies, a few at a time, for 10 seconds. Refresh in iced water and when cool enough to handle remove the heads, shells and intestinal tract. Refrigerate until ready to serve.

TO PREPARE THE VEGETABLES, blanch the carrot, celery and zucchini batons until just tender, then refresh in iced water. Drain, pat dry and set to one side.

Heat the oil in a large frying pan and sauté the capsicum and eggplant batons for a few minutes until lightly browned. Season with salt and pepper then deglaze the pan with a splash of vinegar. Combine all vegetables and set aside until required.

TO MAKE THE SPICY MARINADE, heat a heavy-based frying pan and lightly toast the crushed coriander and cardamom seeds with the saffron threads until they smell aromatic. Add the orange and lime juice and the verjuice, bring to the boil and simmer for a few minutes until reduced by a third. Remove the pan from the heat and whisk in the olive oil and chilli. Season to taste. Pour over the vegetables while still hot and leave to marinate for 2 hours.

TO SERVE, melt the butter in a saucepan until lightly foaming. Add the yabby tails and sauté until golden and lightly caramelised. Season well and drain on kitchen paper.

Gently warm the marinated vegetables. Divide them between 8 warm serving plates and arrange the yabby tails on top, allowing 3 per serve. Spoon on some of the pan juices then drizzle the yabby bisque and herb oil around the plate. Garnish with the baby basil leaves and the basil chiffonade.

Serves 8 as an entrée

MARRON TAILS ROASTED WITH *aromatics*

with Sautéed King Crab, Pea Shoots and Ginger

ROASTED MARRONS

4 x 350 g (12 oz) live marrons

80 g (2¾ oz) Aromatic Confit Salt
(page 10)

4 cloves garlic, roughly crushed

6 sprigs thyme

20 ml (⅔ fl oz) non-scented
cooking oil

SAUTÉED KING CRAB,
PEA SHOOTS AND GINGER

1 x 1.8 kg (4 lb) live king crab

50 g (1¾ oz) unsalted butter

2 cloves garlic, finely chopped

200 g (7 oz) pea shoots, leaves picked

200 g (7 oz) bean sprouts,
roots removed

salt and freshly ground pepper

few drops fresh lemon juice

TO SERVE

200 ml (7 fl oz) Marron Bisque (see Yabby
Bisque, page 260), kept warm

200 ml (7 fl oz) Ginger Beurre Blanc
(page 264), kept warm

Deep-Fried Ginger (page 284)

Use the heads and claws from the marrons to make the yabby bisque. When you prepare the Aromatic Confit Salt (page 10), roughly crush the spices instead of pounding them to a powder.

TO PREPARE THE MARRONS, put them in the freezer for an hour or so before cooking. Preheat the oven to 180°C (350°F). Bring a large pan of salted water to the boil and blanch the marrons, one at a time, for 10 seconds. Refresh in iced water and when cool enough to handle remove the heads and claws. Stretch the marron tails out flat on your work surface. To keep them straight while roasting, insert a dessert spoon underneath each marron, just inside the cartilage, and tie with string.

Put the aromatic salt into a mortar and pestle with the garlic and thyme and pound to a paste. Heat a large ovenproof frying pan and add the oil. Add the marron tails to the pan and sauté for 2 minutes, turning them around in the pan until the flesh begins to caramelise and the shell turns bright orange. Add the spice paste to the pan and toss gently to coat the marron tails. Put in oven and roast for 6 minutes, turning them every few minutes. Remove from the oven and rest in a warm plate for another 6 minutes.

TO PREPARE THE CRAB, put it in the freezer for an hour or so before cooking. Bring a large pan of salted water to the boil, then lower the heat to a simmer. Place the crab in the pan and simmer gently for 18 minutes. Remove the crab from the water and leave until cool enough to handle.

Remove the legs and claws from the crab, crack them and remove the meat. Crack the body shell and remove all the meat from the carapace. Carefully pick through all the crab meat removing any specks of shell or cartilage. Transfer to a clean mixing bowl and set aside.

TO SAUTÉ THE CRAB AND VEGETABLES, melt the butter in a saucepan with the garlic, until lightly foaming. Add the crab with the pea shoots and bean sprouts and toss for 1–2 minutes until the crab is just warmed through and the leaves begin to wilt. Season with salt and freshly ground pepper and stir in a drop of lemon juice.

TO SERVE, carefully remove the shell from the marron and carve into neat medallions.

Divide the sautéed crab and vegetables between 4 warm serving plates and arrange the sliced marron tails on top. Drizzle on the marron bisque and the ginger beurre blanc and garnish with the deep-fried ginger.

Serves 4 as a main course

Tuna, mulloway and kingfish

THE STEHR GROUP

THE STEHR *Group*

Port Lincoln is the gateway to the Great Australian Bight and a fishing hub servicing markets such as Asia and the USA. It is home to the most diverse commercial fishing operations in Australia, with established tuna, prawn, lobster, sardine, crab, abalone, oyster, mussel and scallop businesses. Generous fishing quotas are in place to encourage industry, but are also regulated to discourage overfishing. Aquaculture employs between 15 and 20 per cent of Port Lincoln's population, with another 15 to 20 per cent working in related industries.

The Stehr Group founder Hagen Stehr emigrated to Australia from Germany as a boy. He started out with an abalone boat, which he traded for a prawn trawler after a while. Hagen Stehr started his business with long-line fishing and 'poling' (hauling the fish from the water by hand while standing on a platform) and his tuna fishing methods developed. He founded the Stehr Group of companies in 1969. 'Initially we were just wild-catch fishermen,' Marcus Stehr, Hagen's son, explains. There are still only five tuna fishing enterprises in the Port Lincoln area and Stehr is keen for the industry to grow.

Over the years, Hagen Stehr has forged a strong identity in the fishing industry. He is chairman of the Australian Fishing Association and is a well-known member of the fishing community in the Port Lincoln area and beyond. In 1997 he was awarded the Order of Australia medal; Stehr has been credited with elevating fishing to an artisan level.

The aquaculture arm of the Stehr Group has expanded from focusing on yellowtail kingfish initially to mulloway (also known as suzuki or jewfish) and southern bluefin tuna. Much research and development has gone into the propagation of southern bluefin tuna, and the Stehr Group is in the process of building an onshore facility to continue this project. Closing the breeding cycle (being able to grow tuna from initial spawn through to harvested adult, all in captivity) could eliminate much of the cost of searching for and catching young tuna in the Great Australian Bight.

SOUTHERN BLUEFIN TUNA *ranching*

Flying into Port Lincoln across the Spencer Gulf, round fish pens can be seen from the air, flowing in threads from the harbour to open water. The Stehr Group operates over a dozen pens during the winter season and more in the summer. Each tuna pen spans 40 or 50 metres in diameter and can be as deep as 15 metres. Insuring the fish in these pens alone costs around A$250,000 annually, which is perhaps an indication of the value of the tuna fishing industry in Australia.

Rearing tuna is a far more complicated process than raising any other fish from a hatchery. Because tuna are very sensitive to their environment, and spawn only in deep water, the conditions under which they might spawn in captivity have not yet been perfected in Australia. Hagen Stehr actively promotes research in this area through spawning programs, with assistance from the government.

Spotter planes fly over the expanse of the Bight between December and March on the lookout for the discolouration in the water, which marks the presence of a large school of young tuna. It is while these tuna are migrating that they are captured, using a method called 'purse seining'. The planes direct boats, loaded with hauls of live pilchards in their holds, towards the tuna. The pilchard bait is released and a large net encircles the school and traps as many fish as possible – in the thousands.

Beneath the water, the tuna are transferred to a pen which is then towed at a speed of one knot all the way back to the outer reaches of Port Lincoln, where the tuna are positioned to grow in water rich in oxygen thanks to strong currents circulating. Here the fish are fed Australian pilchards and imported fatty fish until they've grown sufficiently to sell on the open market. The process of fattening tuna for market takes about four months.

Preparing the tuna for market is a unique practice. Early in the morning, a diving team of four enters the pen and encircles the fish with a net that lies below them. As the sun rises, the net is tightened and raised toward the surface, making the area of water shallow enough for divers to chase each fish individually. They slide a hand into its gills (which appears to pacify the giant fish) and lead it to the edge of the boat.

The Japanese method of killing tuna is used in Australia. It is known as iki jime. A corer is pushed into the brain of the fish and a slim wire rod is slid in and along the fish's spinal column, disconnecting the nerves from the spinal cord and preventing rigor mortis, which can adversely affect the flavour of the fish. The gills are removed, the fish is weighed and within a couple of minutes, the tuna is bathed in salted ice for its journey to the factory. This keeps the flesh fresh without freezing it, so it will taste its best hours or days later.

There is at least one tuna expert on board the fishing vessels at all time, judging the quality of the fish for prospective buyers. This person is in constant contact with the markets, informing them on the quality of the fish coming out of the southern seas.

Being a member of a tuna dive team is not without its dangers; great white sharks, breeding at the nearby and aptly named Dangerous Reef, are frequent visitors to the pens, to try and feed on the fattening tuna. They have been known to tear through the netting and eat the trapped fish, before becoming trapped in the net themselves. Divers are faced with the unenviable reality of not knowing what else is in the pen with them when they enter the cold water before sunrise. The work is physically taxing; there have even been cases of tuna having broken human arms with a flick of their tail.

Once back on dry land, the tuna are taken to a processing plant not far from the water's edge. Here they are gutted, thoroughly cleaned, weighed, measured, and evaluated. A sliver of meat is cut from the base of each fish's tail and closely inspected. The Japanese market (which is where a large portion of the Stehr Group's tuna ends up) favours a fatty meat of a deep red hue. From the cut at the base of the tail, the fat beneath the skin, as well as the intramuscular fat, can be clearly evaluated. Australian-reared tuna is more fatty than the fish grown and harvested in Japan, making the product a desirable one for the Japanese sashimi market.

The most expensive part of the tuna flesh is the belly (*toro* in Japanese), which has the most concentrated marbling of fat. On the current market this part of the fish will earn A$250 a kilogram.

Tuna must never be frozen if it is to retain its premium asking price, so the fish have capsules of an innocuous gel ice placed in their bellies and around their bodies. It is in this form that the fish are shipped around the country and overseas. Pallets of tuna leave Port Lincoln by road to Adelaide (some 700-plus kilometres away) or by air straight from the local airport, a few minutes out of town.

As each fish has been weighed and examined, it can be 'identified' and traced from this point all the way to its final destination in the markets or individual kitchens.

CLEAN SEAS *hatchery*

The Stehr Group's hatchery operates at Arno Bay, a sparsely populated town 115 kilometres north of Port Lincoln. In warehouses also containing state-of-the-art laboratories, mulloway and yellowtail kingfish are reared from larvae to young fish, and continue their development in pens of filtered ocean water similar to the ones that will house them later in the open water.

Morten Deichmann completed his biology degree in his native Denmark before embarking on a career path that has taken him around the world. Deichmann worked on Cyprus, in Italy, Bangkok and regional Thailand before arriving in Australia in 2003. He now engineers the management of all the fish at the hatchery – from spawning right through to their departure for the sea pens.

Through artifical light and controlled water temperatures the fish are encouraged to think it's the spawning season, and they spawn for longer. Fertilised eggs are then collected from the spawning tanks and placed in incubation tanks, where they hatch into larvae four or five millimetres in length. These larvae are fed rotifers – tiny zooplankton which themselves feed on cultivated algae grown at the hatchery by a marine biologist. Plastic vats at the hatchery hold thousands of litres of the algae, which bubble a brilliant green.

The larvae progress to artemia – commonly known as brine shrimp or sea monkeys. These shrimp grow to between 10 and 15 millimetres in length and are also cultivated at the hatchery. After a month of feeding, the larvae are weaned onto a more solid diet of fish meal pellets, which speed their growth, for a further month. At this stage, the fish weigh about five grams, are about 10 centimetres long, and are ready to be transferred to sea pens to reach maturity. This is a process of at least two years as the fish grow in their ocean homes. The water locations are selected for their rich oxygen content and clear currents.

SASHIMI OF *bluefin tuna*
with Pickled White Radish, Cucumber and Baby Coriander

PICKLED WHITE RADISH

200 g (7 oz) white radish (daikon)

100 ml (3½ fl oz) sake

50 ml (1¾ fl oz) mirin

½ teaspoon salt

1 teaspoon sugar

500 ml (18 fl oz) water

freshly ground white pepper to taste

1 small cucumber

4 small red radishes

1 cup baby coriander leaves

1 x 400 g (14 oz) bluefin tuna belly (toro)

½ lemon

drizzle extra-virgin olive oil

fleur de sel

freshly ground pepper

The first time I tasted bluefin tuna belly – toro – it was prepared by Australia's premier master sushi chef Ryuichi Yoshii, at his eponymous Sydney restaurant, Yoshii. I was amazed by the flavour and texture and have been addicted to it ever since. To me, toro is the ocean's equivalent of the highest quality Wagyu beef: dense, marbled, and full of flavour.

This salad uses the three different parts of the belly, each with a varying degree of marbled fat and a unique flavour.

TO PICKLE THE WHITE RADISH, peel and cut it into neat ribbons, about 2 mm (⅛ in) thick. Place the remaining pickling ingredients in a medium saucepan and bring to a gentle simmer over a medium heat. Taste and adjust the balance of sweetness and acidity according to your palate.

Add the white radish and bring back to a simmer. Remove the pan from the heat and allow to rest and infuse for 20 minutes. Chill radish in the pickling solution until required.

TO PREPARE THE VEGETABLE GARNISH, peel the cucumber and cut into ribbons of a similar size to the white radish. Use a mandolin or very sharp knife to slice the red radish.

WHEN NEARLY READY TO SERVE, trim any fat and sinew from the tuna belly. Slice into 3 sections, the oh toro, chu toro and akami (page 000). Slice each of these into 4 neat slivers. This should be done immediately before serving.

TO SERVE, toss the cucumber, red and white radish with a little of the pickling solution. Season with salt and pepper, a squeeze of lemon juice and a drizzle of extra-virgin olive oil.

Arrange a slice of the oh toro, chu toro and akami on each serving plate. Season with salt and pepper, a squeeze of lemon juice and a drizzle of extra-virgin olive oil. Carefully add the vegetables and garnish with a few coriander leaves. Serve immediately.

Serves 4 as an entrée

Bluefin tuna belly

Bluefin tuna loin and belly

TARTARE OF MULLOWAY WITH
Iranian osietra caviar
and Chive Crème Fraîche

CHIVE CRÈME FRAÎCHE

300 ml (10 fl oz) crème fraîche

100 ml (3½ fl oz) thickened cream

½ cup finely snipped chives

fleur de sel

freshly ground white pepper

few drops lemon juice

1 x 500 g (18 oz) mulloway fillet

50 g (1¾ oz) Iranian osietra caviar

extra-virgin olive oil

fresh chervil

While I consider Iranian caviar to be superior to others, the choice of sevruga or osietra comes down to personal preference. I would use osietra for this dish as it has a cleaner, more refined flavour; a hint of acid with a fresh briny flavour and a slight bitter aftertaste.

This dish is really all about the pleasure of contrasting different textures and flavours. The mulloway has a smooth, creamy richness that is superbly offset by little salty bursts of caviar – it is truly sublime.

TO PREPARE THE CHIVE CRÈME FRAÎCHE, put the crème fraîche and cream in a chilled mixing bowl and whisk to soft peaks. Fold through the chives and season with the fleur de sel, a little pepper and lemon juice. Cover with cling film and refrigerate.

TO PREPARE THE TARTARE OF MULLOWAY, use a very sharp knife to skin the fillet then remove the bloodline and trim away any sinews. Cut into neat 5 mm (¼ in) dice and place in a mixing bowl.

Gently fold through half the caviar and a splash of oil. Divide the tartare evenly between 8 serving plates, using a ring mould to create neat little discs. Spread a thin layer of caviar on the top of each disc before carefully lifting away the ring mould.

Use a dessertspoon to form small quenelles of the chive crème fraîche and arrange them around the tartare. Drizzle with a little extra-virgin olive oil and garnish with a few sprigs of chervil. Serve straightaway.

Serves 8 as an entrée

BLUEFIN TUNA *belly*

with Eggplant Caviar and a Warm Verbena Tea Vinaigrette

EGGPLANT CAVIAR

2 large eggplants

80 g (2¾ oz) salt

60 ml (2 fl oz) non-scented cooking oil

8 sprigs thyme

4 sprigs rosemary

4 cloves garlic, crushed

freshly ground white pepper

olive oil

1 x 600 g (20 oz) bluefin tuna belly (toro), trimmed of bloodline and any sinews

Eggplant Crisps (page 284)

Verbena Tea Vinaigrette (page 266)

lemon verbena leaves, finely shredded

TO PREPARE THE EGGPLANTS, cut them in half lengthwise then use a sharp pointed knife to score the flesh deeply in a criss-cross fashion. Rub a generous amount of salt into the flesh and place the eggplants, flesh side down, on a wire rack set in the sink to drain for about 2 hours. Carefully brush away all the salt and pat the eggplants dry with kitchen paper.

Preheat your oven to 180°C (350°F). Heat a medium-sized baking tray over a moderate heat then add the oil. Fry the eggplants, flesh side down, for a few minutes, until golden brown. Remove the tray from the heat and turn the eggplants over. Stud the flesh with the herbs and garlic, season with salt and freshly ground pepper and drizzle with oil.

Cover the baking tray with foil and roast for 30 minutes until the flesh is soft and tender. Scoop the flesh out of the skins and chop it roughly. To remove any excess moisture, spoon the eggplant flesh into a square of muslin and hang in a cool place to drain for a couple of hours.

TO SERVE, cut the tuna into 20 even slices and divide between the serving plates, allowing 5 slices per serve. Use a dessertspoon to form small quenelles of eggplant caviar and place them between the tuna slices. Place an eggplant crisp on top of each quenelle and spoon over the warm vinaigrette. Garnish with the shredded lemon verbena leaves and serve immediately.

Serves 6 as an entrée or 4 as a main course

MARINATED *yellowtail kingfish*
with Prawn, Gazpacho Vinaigrette and Sorbet

MARINATED YELLOWTAIL KINGFISH

1 x 500 g (18 oz) yellowtail kingfish (hiramasa) fillet

60 g (2 oz) salt

30 g (1 oz) sugar

1 lime

½ small red chilli, de-seeded

2 star anise

6 coriander stalks

8 coriander seeds

GAZPACHO VINAIGRETTE

1 small purple onion

½ small cucumber

4 very ripe roma tomatoes

1 small red capsicum

1 small yellow capsicum

200 ml (7 fl oz) extra-virgin olive oil

salt

few drops Tabasco

lemon juice

GAZPACHO SORBET

6 very ripe vine-ripened tomatoes

2 tablespoons tomato paste

200 ml (7 fl oz) gazpacho purée (see method)

2 tablespoons liquid glucose

20 ml (²/₃ fl oz) vodka

lemon juice

salt

few drops Tabasco

GARNISH

16 extra-large king prawns

salt and freshly ground pepper

½ cup baby basil leaves

Yellowtail kingfish, also known as hiramasa or Australian yellowtail, is native to southern Australian waters. The intensely fat-marbled belly makes excellent sashimi and the robust texture of the loin stands up very well to cooking.

TO PREPARE THE YELLOWTAIL KINGFISH, use a very sharp knife to skin the fillet then remove the bloodline and pin bones and trim away any sinews.

Put the remaining marinade ingredients into a blender and blitz to a fine paste. Smear the paste all over the fish, wrap it tightly in cling film and leave to marinate in the refrigerator for 8 hours.

TO MAKE THE GAZPACHO VINAIGRETTE, cut the vegetables square (reserving the trim and 2 of the tomatoes) and dice to a neat brunoise. Put in a mixing bowl and set aside.

Roughly chop the trim, place in a blender with the 2 tomatoes and blitz to a smooth purée. Strain through a fine sieve. Reserve 200 ml (7 fl oz) of the purée for the sorbet and mix the rest through the diced vegetables. Add the olive oil and season with salt, Tabasco and lemon juice. Stir well and set aside until ready to serve.

TO MAKE THE GAZPACHO SORBET, cut the tomatoes into quarters and discard the seeds. Put them into a blender with the remaining ingredients and blitz to a smooth purée. Taste and adjust the seasonings if necessary. Push the purée through a chinois or very fine sieve, then refrigerate until cold. Pour into an ice cream machine and churn according to the manufacturer's instructions.

PREPARE THE PRAWNS by removing their heads and intestines. Blanch the tails for 1 minute in a saucepan of boiling salted water. Place the prawns in a bowl with a couple of cubes of ice to cool. When cool enough to handle, peel the prawns and slice them in half, lengthwise. Season with salt and pepper.

TO SERVE, gently wash the marinade off the yellowtail kingfish and pat dry. Use a sharp knife to cut into 24 neat slices. Divide the slices between 8 serving plates, allowing 3 slices per person. Place a spoonful of gazpacho vinaigrette between the slices and top each mound with 2 prawn halves and a neat quenelle of sorbet. Garnish with a few leaves of baby basil and serve immediately.

Serves 8 as an entrée

BROCHETTE OF *yellowtail kingfish*
with Artichokes Barigoule

1 x 600 g (20 oz) yellowtail kingfish (hiramasa) fillet

salt and freshly ground pepper

30 ml (1 fl oz) non-scented cooking oil

80 g (2¾ oz) unsalted butter

juice of 1 lemon

12 Artichokes Barigoule (page 283)

¼ cup flat-leaf parsley leaves, finely shredded to a chiffonade

Prepare the artichokes according to the method on page 283, substituting a bunch of baby carrots for the 1 in the recipe.

TO PREPARE THE YELLOWTAIL KINGFISH, remove the pin bones and use a very sharp knife slice the fillet into 6 x 100 g (3½ oz) neat rectangular portions. Score each portion crosswise through the skin, about two-thirds of the way through the flesh, so that it resembles brochette. Season with salt and pepper.

Preheat your oven to 180°C (350°F). Heat a large ovenproof frying pan over a high heat, until almost smoking. Add the oil, then the fish pieces, skin side down. Fry for about 3 minutes, or until the skin is crisp and golden. Transfer the pan to the oven and cook for 2 minutes.

Return the pan to the stove, add the butter to the pan and heat to a nut-brown foam. Add the lemon juice and turn the fish pieces over for a few seconds so that the pan juices are absorbed into the scored flesh – the fish should be cooked medium-rare. Remove from the pan and leave to rest in a warm place for a minute.

TO SERVE, cut the artichokes in half lengthwise and warm through gently in the barigoule liquor. Add the parsley and toss together well. Place 4 artichoke halves in each warm serving bowl, top with a fish brochette and serve immediately.

Serves 6 as an entrée or 4 as a main course

Ocean trout and saltwater char

PETUNA SEAFOOD

SMALL STEPS TO A *big business*

The word 'Petuna' is a combination of the names of Peter and Una Rockliff, whose fishing empire was born almost half a century ago. Peter, who had always loved fishing and spent childhood holidays at the coast with fishermen, had worked hard on the land to buy his first boat, *Alva*, a 25-foot long seasonal vessel with an open hull.

During the spring of 1949 Peter travelled to Bridport on Tasmania's north-east coast in search of fishing opportunities. There he met Una and they married soon afterwards. The couple's next boat was *Rowana*, a 32-foot vessel with a tiny cabin and by 1954 Peter was fishing full-time for cray. He would be at sea for up to ten days at a time and, in the days before radio contact, this was difficult for Una and their three children.

Peter took his first crewman during the 1960s, fishing for scallop and shark around Tasmanian waters, and in 1971 finished building the *Petuna*. She was large, sturdy and had the capacity to venture further from the shore than previous vessels, enabling the Rockliffs to discover unfished cray grounds.

Later the Rockliffs built the *Petuna Enveavour*, Tasmania's first trawler. At this time trawling as a fishing method was still largely unknown. The number of trawlers operating in the area leapt from one to sixty in a short time as fishermen discovered it allowed them to bring in huge numbers of fish, and to travel farther from shore than before. Trawling attracted its fair share of criticism, however, and was blamed for the overfishing of certain waters and damage to the sea floor.

The couple began to investigate aquaculture as an alternative, and in 1991 Petuna bought a 50 per cent share in Sevrup Fisheries in Cressy, south of Launceston.

Over the years the company has cultivated salmon, golden trout and saltwater char, as well as developing a superior strain of ocean trout, a species now synonymous with the name Petuna.

Petuna's produce is processed at the Devonport factory. In pristine conditions ensured by strict decontamination procedures, fish are cleaned, filleted and packaged for distribution throughout Australia and international export. There is also an onsite smokehouse. With the airport only minutes from the factory, it is possible for Petuna fish to be served in New York restaurants a mere 48 hours after leaving Tasmanian shores.

Although their son-in-law, Tim Hess, now oversees the daily running of the business, Peter and Una Rockliff remain hands-on at Petuna, and in 2004 were awarded the Order of Australia medal for their contribution to the fishing industry.

OPPOSITE: Una and Peter Rockliff at Petuna headquarters

A HATCHERY ON *the hillside*

Kevin Chilman and his wife Josie work at the Sevrup Fisheries hatchery, breeding and grading salmon and ocean trout, readying them to be transported to sea pens in Macquarie Harbour, near Strahan, where they grow to full size.

At Sevrup, Chilman's chief responsibility is maintaining brood-stock quality in order to produce fingerlings (tiny fish of only a few centimetres) of consistent number and quality. They are capable of producing 650,000 fingerlings annually for transfer to sea cages. To meet this demand, five million eggs must be incubated in the hatchery every year.

Ocean trout spend five weeks in incubation before hatching, and Chilman ensures direct contact with UV light is avoided in the incubation pens, as the light can penetrate the eggs and kill the fish. Once hatched, the fish sink to the bottom of the tanks, feeding from the egg's yolk, which remains attached to the body for around eight weeks after hatching. When the yolk is consumed, the hatchling rises to the water's surface in search of food.

The first solid the fish consumes is a formula containing vitamins, proteins and fats. The formula is made locally at Cambridge, which has established itself as a centre for development in marine biology. Isolated strains of algae are also cultivated in Cambridge for use in the hatcheries.

The fish are theoretically ready for transportation once they reach a weight of 120 grams, but are kept at the hatchery for up to a year for rigorous grading. At the time of our visit, 80,000 ocean trout were being held in an outdoor pen, awaiting grading and their final journey to the sea pens, where they spend another year to eighteen months.

Grading is a time-consuming procedure: each fish is inspected individually for any defects. Size and colour are also checked, and any fish that don't make the grade are sold to farm dams to be sold locally. This is a costly but necessary elimination process. According to Chilman the market is becoming more and more particular and the grading ensures that only the finest quality fish make their way to the grow-out pens and eventually to market.

The process of moving fish from a freshwater environment to salt is known as 'smultifying'; a young salmon going through this transition is referred to as a 'smult'. World Heritage-protected Macquarie Harbour, where the fish are grown in sea pens, is a mixture of freshwater on the surface and saltwater beneath, a result of the Franklin and Gordon rivers flowing through the harbour out to sea.

As the salmon, trout and char mature, each fish moves instinctively to an area where the salinity is optimal for its own needs. The darker freshwater towards the surface also serves to protect the fish from direct sunlight that causes discolouration. These conditions are ideal for maturing fish in the salmonid family – water that is too saline can cause disease in immature fish gills.

In Australian aquaculture, in order to produce fish all year round, the conditions of the spawning period are synthesised, tricking fish into spawning during the Australian winter as well as in summer.

Macquarie Harbour is known for its penal settlement, Sarah Island, which was used by the government between 1821 and 1832 to house its most dangerous criminals. The now deserted 11-acre island can be seen from the sea pens just off Liberty Island, nine miles out from Smiths Cove where a Sevrup office and net restoration workshop are situated. The sea pens are each weighted with anchors around the circumference of the pens to prevent tidal flow dragging the enclosures and reducing their volume. In twenty metres of water, the seven-metre pens house thousands of fish each. Divers work in the pens twice a week, clearing out any dead fish and monitoring the state of the nets. The lease agreement with the government also dictates that Petuna is responsible for cleaning the sea floor beneath the pens.

Fish are harvested onsite: they are removed and bathed in carbon dioxide which stuns them. By the time the fish regain consciousness, they have been cut open and die rapidly in water aboard the harvesting vessel, before being placed in an ice slurry which keeps the flesh at a temperature of 2°C. Allowing the fish to regain consciousness is a deliberate tactic as their final movements hasten the expulsion of blood from the body. Once in ice, the fish are moved back to land and shipped to Devonport for further processing and then transport around Australia and abroad.

Petuna has recently established a new breed of saltwater char. Also known as Arctic char, this fish is indigenous to northern waters towards the Arctic Circle, and was first commercially fished during the 19th century off Labrador. It is caught in freshwater streams or farmed in saltwater for differing flavour. This versatility also affects flavour; char raised in saltwater yields a deeper coloured and sweeter tasting flesh than its freshwater cousins.

Herbed and marinated ocean trout with lemon sour cream and verbena

Tartare of smoked and raw ocean trout with purple shiso sorbet

Mille-feuille of ocean trout brandade with a salad of shaved white Alba truffle

ASSIETTE OF OCEAN TROUT *hors d'oeuvres*

Here are three little dishes that can be served individually or together,
as small entrées or hors d'oeuvres. They demonstrate the versatility of this wonderful fish,
by highlighting a range of textures and possible flavour marriages.

Herbed and Marinated Ocean Trout with Lemon-Sour Cream and Verbena

HERBED AND MARINATED OCEAN TROUT

1 x 300 g (10½ oz) ocean trout fillet, skinned, bloodline and pin bones removed

50 g (1¾ oz) Citrus Salt (page 12)

1 tablespoon Dijon mustard mixed to a paste with 2 tablespoons cold water

4 tablespoons mixed herbs (a selection of flat-leaf parsley, chives, chervil and coriander), finely chopped

LEMON-SOUR CREAM

150 ml (5 fl oz) sour cream

50 ml (1¾ fl oz) thickened cream

1 lemon

fleur de sel

freshly ground white pepper

TO SERVE

18 Deep-Fried Lemon Verbena Leaves (page 283)

1 tablespoon extra-virgin olive oil

TO PREPARE THE OCEAN TROUT, rub all over with wet citrus salt, wrap tightly in cling film and leave to marinate in the refrigerator for 6 hours.

Remove the cling film and thoroughly rinse the fish under running water. Pat dry. Brush the skinned, flat side of the fish with a little mustard paste and sprinkle with chopped herbs. Wrap the fish tightly in cling film again and put in a shallow dish. Put a plate on top of the fish and weight down with a 1 kg (2 lb 2 oz) weight. Refrigerate for 4 hours.

TO PREPARE THE LEMON-SOUR CREAM, put the sour cream and thickened cream in a mixing bowl and whip together to form soft peaks. Zest the lemon over the bowl to capture the aromatic oils with the zest. Add a squeeze of juice and season with salt and freshly ground pepper. Refrigerate until required.

TO SERVE, carefully unwrap the ocean trout taking care not to lose the herbs. Use a very sharp knife to cut it crosswise into fine slivers and arrange neatly on serving plates. Use a dessertspoon to form small quenelles of lemon-sour cream and place on top of the fish. Garnish with a few deep-fried lemon verbena leaves and a drizzle of extra-virgin olive oil.

Serves 6 as part of an hors d'oeuvres selection, or 2 as an entrée

ASSIETTE OF OCEAN TROUT *hors d'oeuvres*

Tartare of Smoked and Raw Ocean Trout

with Purple Shiso Sorbet

TARTARE OF SMOKED AND RAW OCEAN TROUT

1 x 150 g (5 oz) ocean trout fillet, skinned, bloodline and pin bones removed

1 x 150 g (5 oz) cold-smoked ocean trout fillet, skinned, bloodline and pin bones removed

½ cup finely sliced chives

½ tablespoon extra-virgin olive oil

fleur de sel

freshly ground white pepper

PURPLE SHISO SORBET

3 cups purple shiso

2 tablespoons liquid glucose

100 ml (3½ fl oz) water

small pinch of salt

TO PREPARE THE TARTARE, cut both pieces of trout into neat 5 mm (¼ in) dice. Put in a mixing bowl and refrigerate until ready to serve.

TO MAKE THE SORBET, snip the shiso leaves off their stalks, reserving a small handful for garnish. Put them into a blender with the glucose, water and a tiny pinch of salt. Blitz on high for 3 minutes to form a smooth, fine purée. Pass the purée through a chinois or very fine sieve. Tip into an ice cream machine and churn according to the manufacturer's instructions. Freeze until required.

TO SERVE, add the chives, oil and seasoning to the trout tartare and mix through gently. Taste and adjust seasonings if necessary.

Divide the tartare evenly between 6 serving plates, using a ring mould to create neat little discs. Carefully lift away the ring mould. Use a dessertspoon to form small quenelles of sorbet and place on top. Garnish with a few leaves of purple shiso and serve straightaway.

Serves 6 as part of an hors d'oeuvres selection, or 2 as an entrée

ASSIETTE OF OCEAN TROUT *hors d'oeuvres*

Mille Feuille of Ocean Trout Brandade with
a Salad of Shaved White Alba Truffle

OCEAN TROUT BRANDADE

2 tablespoons salt

1 medium desirée potato, skin on

400 ml (14 fl oz) milk

2 cloves garlic

3 sprigs thyme

salt and freshly ground pepper

1 x 300 g (10 oz) ocean trout fillet, skinned, bloodline and pin bones removed

1 teaspoon garlic oil

80 ml (2³/₄ fl oz) thickened cream

TUILES

2 sheets Tunisian brik pastry (or substitute filo pastry)

60 ml (2 fl oz) Clarified Butter (page 264)

salt and freshly ground pepper

TO SERVE

few handfuls baby cress

60 ml (2 fl oz) Lemon Vinaigrette (page 266)

1 small fresh white Alba truffle

TO MAKE THE BRANDADE, preheat your oven to 220°C (425°F). Make a little mound of salt on a small baking tray and sit the potato on top. Bake for 25 minutes then turn the potato over in the salt and bake for a further 25 minutes. Use a skewer to test whether the potato is cooked – it must be soft right through to the centre, but take care not to overcook it. Cut the potato in half and scoop out the flesh.

Meanwhile heat the milk in a small saucepan with the garlic, thyme, salt and pepper. Simmer gently for 2 minutes to infuse. Remove the pan from the heat and add the ocean trout. Return the pan to the heat and poach fish very gently for around 6 minutes until just cooked. Remove the fish from the milk, cover it with a damp cloth and refrigerate until cool. Reserve the milk.

When the fish is cold, break into rough flakes and put in a food processor with the potato, garlic oil, and a little of the milk. Process until velvety smooth. Push the purée through a drum sieve into a chilled mixing bowl.

Whip the cream to soft peaks and fold through the purée. Taste and adjust seasoning if necessary then refrigerate until ready to serve.

TO MAKE THE TUILES, preheat the oven to 180°C (350°F). Cut the brik pastry into 18 neat rectangles, brush each with clarified butter and season lightly. Bake the pastry rectangles between 2 flat baking trays (to keep them flat) for 8–10 minutes, or until crisp and golden. Drain on kitchen paper and leave to cool.

To assemble the mille feuilles, place a tuile on each serving plate. Use a dessertspoon to form small quenelles of brandade and place one on each tuile. Top with another tuile and another quenelle, and finish with a tuile.

Put the baby cress in a mixing bowl and gently toss with the vinaigrette. Arrange a small mound next to each mille feuille and garnish with shavings of truffle.

Serves 6 as part of an hors d'oeuvres selection, or 2 as an entrée

SEARED *saltwater char*

with Wilted Spinach, Champagne and Sorrel Sabayon, Iranian Osietra Caviar

CHAMPAGNE AND SORREL SABAYON

150 ml (5 fl oz) champagne

4 egg yolks

2 cups sorrel leaves

few drops lemon juice

salt and freshly ground pepper

SEARED SALTWATER CHAR

30 ml (1 fl oz) non-scented cooking oil

6 x 180 g (6 oz) saltwater char fillets, skin and pin bones removed

salt and freshly ground pepper

80 g (2¾ oz) unsalted butter

squeeze lemon juice

WILTED SPINACH

30 g (1 oz) unsalted butter

300 g (10 oz) baby spinach leaves

2 cloves garlic

salt and freshly ground pepper

few drops lemon juice

TO SERVE

50 g (1¾ oz) fresh Iranian osietra caviar

TO MAKE THE SABAYON, put the champagne and egg yolks in a bowl over a saucepan of gently simmering water. Whisk briskly for about 10 minutes until the mixture bulks up and thickens to a pale, foamy sabayon. Remove from the heat.

Slice the sorrel leaves to a fine chiffonnade and fold them through the sabayon with the lemon juice and seasoning.

TO SEAR THE SALTWATER CHAR, heat a large ovenproof frying pan over a medium-high heat and add the oil. Season the char fillets and add them to the pan, flat side down. Fry for a few minutes until golden and caramelised. Add the butter and heat to a nut-brown foam. Add the lemon juice and turn the fish pieces over for a few seconds in the pan – the fish should be cooked medium-rare. Remove from the pan and drain briefly on kitchen paper. Leave to rest in a warm place for a minute.

TO SERVE, heat the butter in a large heavy-based saucepan until lightly foaming. Add the spinach and garlic cloves and turn in the butter until the spinach begins to wilt. Season with salt and pepper and add the lemon juice. Remove from the heat, discard the garlic cloves and drain well.

Place a mound of spinach in the centre of each of each serving plate and spoon over a generous amount of sabayon. Arrange the fish on the spinach. Use a teaspoon to make small quenelles of caviar and use to garnish the fish. Serve immediately.

Serves 6 as a main course

CRISP SKIN *saltwater char*
with Spiced Pork Crackling, Slow-Braised Abalone and Dashi Vinaigrette

SLOW-BRAISED ABALONE
500 g (18 oz) black-lip abalone

100 g (3½ oz) salt

50 g (1¾ oz) dried konbu seaweed

50 g (1¾ oz) dried bonito flakes

1.5 litres (3 pints) water

300 ml (10 fl oz) sake

100 ml (3½ fl oz) light soy sauce

60 ml (2 fl oz) mirin

30 g (1 oz) fresh ginger, finely sliced

SPICED PORK CRACKLING
80 g (2¾ oz) Aromatic Confit Salt (page 10)

4 tablespoons five-spice powder

300 g (10 oz) fatty pork skin

2 tablespoons non-scented cooking oil

50 g (2 oz) unsalted butter

2 tablespoons salt

2 tablespoons sugar

SALAD
1 bunch spring onions

1 cup Thai basil leaves

1 cup Vietnamese mint leaves

¾ cup samphire (sea asparagus)

continued …

Make sure you choose a piece of pork skin with plenty of fat for the spiced crackling. Fat absorbs the marinade better than the skin, and during the cooking it puffs up in the pan to make crackling that is delectably tasty, crisp and light.

The abalone is braised very slowly in a fragrant dashi stock, and ends up buttery-soft and full of flavour. The aromatic stock is then used for the vinaigrette.

TO BRAISE THE ABALONE, remove the meat from its shell and discard all the innards. Rub the flesh thoroughly with salt to clean it then immediately rinse well under cold running water and pat dry.

TO MAKE THE DASHI STOCK, put the konbu, bonito and water in a large saucepan and heat to 80°C (175°F). Infuse for 30 minutes then strain through a chinois or fine sieve. Discard the solids and place the stock back in the saucepan.

Add the sake, soy sauce, mirin and ginger to the pan and place it back on the heat. Add the abalone, and cook at a steady 80°C (175°F) for 6 hours.

Remove the abalone from the pan, reserving the poaching stock, and refrigerate until cold and set – this will make it easier to slice.

Use a very sharp knife to slice the abalone into very fine slivers and put in a shallow dish. Strain the dashi stock, and set aside 300 ml (10 fl oz) to make the vinaigrette. Pour the rest over the abalone and leave to marinate until ready to serve.

TO MAKE THE SPICED PORK CRACKLING, mix the aromatic salt with 2 tablespoons of the five-spice powder and massage it well into the pork skin and fat. Leave for at least 2 hours for the flavours to infuse.

Thoroughly brush the salt off and slice into 5 mm (¼ in) slivers. Heat a frying pan over a moderate heat and add the oil. Sprinkle in the slivers of pork skin and move around in the pan for a few minutes until they start to crisp. Add the butter and heat to a nut-brown foam. Continue to cook the crackling slivers until they turn golden brown, crisp and puffy. Drain on kitchen paper.

Mix together the salt, sugar and remaining five-spice powder. Sprinkle over the crackling while still warm.

PREPARE THE SALAD by finely slicing the spring onions and putting them into a mixing bowl with the herbs.

Blanch the samphire in rapidly boiling water for 45 seconds and refresh in iced water. Drain well and add to the salad.

continued …

CRISP SKIN *saltwater char*

continued

DASHI VINAIGRETTE

300 ml (10 fl oz) dashi stock (see method)

2 teaspoons sesame oil

100 ml (3½ fl oz) olive oil

100 ml (3½ fl oz) peanut oil

CRISP SKIN SALTWATER CHAR

salt and freshly ground pepper

8 x 150 g (5 oz) saltwater char fillets, skin and pin bones removed

30 ml (1 fl oz) non-scented cooking oil

60 g (2 oz) unsalted butter

few drops lemon juice

TO MAKE THE DASHI VINAIGRETTE mix all the ingredients together well.

WHEN READY TO SERVE, heat a large ovenproof frying pan over a medium-high heat and add the oil. Season the char fillets and add them to the pan, flat side down. Fry for a few minutes until golden and caramelised. Add the butter and heat to a nut-brown foam. Add the lemon juice and turn the fish pieces over for a few seconds in the pan – the fish should be cooked medium-rare. Remove from the pan and drain briefly on kitchen paper. Leave to rest in a warm place for a minute.

Lightly dress the salad with the dashi vinaigrette, divide it evenly between 8 serving plates and top with slivers of the marinated abalone. Arrange a fillet of char on top of the salad and drizzle over a little extra vinaigrette. Garnish with the spiced pork crackling and serve straightaway.

Serves 8 as a main course

CONFIT OF SMOKED *ocean trout belly*

with Cauliflower and Horseradish Beignets

CONFIT OF SMOKED OCEAN TROUT BELLY

1 x 600 g (20 oz) smoked ocean trout belly, skin, bloodline and pin bones removed

300 ml (10 fl oz) Rendered Duck Fat (page 274)

300 ml (10 fl oz) olive oil

400 ml (14 fl oz) non-scented cooking oil

zest of 1 lemon

3 sprigs thyme

4 cloves garlic, roughly crushed

CAULIFLOWER AND HORSERADISH PURÉE

¼ small cauliflower

60 g unsalted butter

½ small onion, finely sliced

2 cloves garlic, finely sliced

100 ml (3½ fl oz) White Chicken Stock (page 254)

2 sprigs thyme

salt and freshly ground pepper

50 ml (1¾ fl oz) pure cream

1 fresh horseradish, grated and divided into thirds (or substitute around 3 tablespoons good quality purchased horseradish purée)

CAULIFLOWER AND HORSERADISH BEIGNETS

12 cauliflower florettes (see above)

150 ml (5 fl oz) Parsley Oil (page 268)

200 ml (7 fl oz) lager

salt and freshly ground pepper

150 g (5 oz) plain flour

TO SERVE

500 ml (18 fl oz) non-scented cooking oil

80 g (2¾ oz) sifted, seasoned plain flour

salt and freshly ground pepper

few drops lemon juice

6 Deep-Fried Parsley Leaves (page 283)

250 ml (9 fl oz) Parsley Coulis (page 268)

TO CONFIT THE OCEAN TROUT preheat the oven to 80°C (175°F). Bring the fish to room temperature and cut into 6 x 100 g (3½ oz) portions. Put the rendered duck fat into a shallow ovenproof dish with the oils, lemon zest, thyme and garlic. Warm very gently on the stovetop until just warm to the touch, around 45°C (115°F). Slip the fish pieces into the oil and cover with a piece of greaseproof paper cut to fit the dish. Transfer to the oven and cook for 45 minutes. Remove from the oven and leave to cool in the oil.

TO MAKE THE CAULIFLOWER AND HORSERADISH PURÉE, start by cutting 12 even-sized florettes from the cauliflower and set them aside to make the beignets. Weigh 200 g (17 oz) of the cauliflower trimmings and slice them thinly.

Heat a heavy-based saucepan over a medium-high heat and add the butter. When it foams, add the onion and garlic and sweat for 6 minutes until they soften without colouring. Add the sliced cauliflower and sweat for a further 5 minutes until it is soft. Add the chicken stock to the pan with the thyme, salt and pepper. Bring to the boil, then lower the heat and simmer for 10 minutes, or until thick. Add the cream and a third of the grated horseradish. Return to the boil, then remove the pan from the heat. Tip into a blender and blitz to a very smooth purée. Pass through a chinois or fine sieve and keep warm until ready to serve.

TO MAKE THE CAULIFLOWER AND HORSERADISH BEIGNETS, put the 12 cauliflower florettes into a bowl with the parsley oil and another third of the grated horseradish. Toss well and leave to marinate for 30 minutes.

Prepare the batter by putting the lager in a mixing bowl with the remaining horseradish and season with salt and pepper. Gradually whisk in the flour until you have a smooth thin batter. Set aside until ready to serve; it will keep well for up to 2 hours.

WHEN READY TO SERVE, heat the oil in a heavy-based saucepan to 190°C (375°F) or until a cube of bread colours and sizzles to the surface within 30 seconds or so. Toss the marinated cauliflower florettes in the seasoned flour, shaking off any excess. Dip each florette in the batter then deep-fry until crisp and golden. Remove from the oil and drain on kitchen paper. Season with salt and pepper and a drop of lemon juice while hot.

Remove the trout pieces from the oil, drain on kitchen paper and season with salt and pepper and a drop of lemon juice. Arrange them on 6 warm serving plates. Top with 2 hot beignets and a leaf of deep-fried parsley. Decorate the plate with the parsley coulis and the cauliflower and horseradish purée.

Serves 6 as an entrée

Squab pigeon

GLENLOTH GAME

A BIRD WITH A *background*

A popular dish as far back as the Middle Ages, pigeon has also enjoyed stints as a domestic animal, a racing bird and a courier. In the empires of Egypt and Ancient Rome, it was contrary to laws of the period for a common man to own pigeons, so elevated was their status as 'carriers', delivering messages to and from the military in dangerous and remote situations.

Squab, juvenile pigeon processed before the formation of their flight feathers, is a delicacy increasing in popularity in restaurants the world over. Squab is prized for its rich and tender breast meat – at its most plump and flavoursome only before the birds can fly; once flight is possible the meat becomes tough and body fat is lost through exercise. Other indicators of quality in squab are an unblemished skin, a deep, gamey aroma and burgundy-coloured breast meat.

The town of Wycheproof in north-west Victoria is home to Glenloth Game, owned and operated by Ian and Rhonda Milburn. The couple farm squab and free-range chicken, and process them on-site. Their processing centre also caters for guinea fowl, pheasant and rabbit from other farms in the vicinity.

While the Mediterranean conditions in Wycheproof – the long, hot summers and short winters – are ideal for minimising disease in the birds, the accompanying lack of water makes it a tough environment. Milburn's father was a water diviner and it appears that he has inherited his father's skill, having found a bore 50 metres below the surface of the land that supplements the farm's water requirements.

Pigeons cannot be battery-farmed; newly hatched squab must be reared by their parents. Mating pairs stay together for life and produce up to ten chicks annually, from the age of about one to roughly eight or nine years of age. For the first days of their lives, the hatchlings are fed by both parents with a substance known as 'pigeon milk'. It is high in protein and carbohydrate, and pre-digested in the parents' stomachs (it cannot be emulated synthetically). After these critical first days, they progress to regurgitated grain from their parents' beaks.

The most desirable attribute in a squab, aside from its tender breast meat, is weight. Squab don't grow much heavier than 600 grams (dressed weight – the weight of the bird with feathers and innards removed) and most are around the 350 to 450 gram mark. The heavier the dressed weight of the squab pigeon, the more it will sell for.

Glenloth employ parent stock of White King and Swiss Mondaine pigeon breeds, finding them the most consistent in quality and size. Strict quarantine laws now prevent the importation of squab strains into Australia, so the strains already here are all breeders are able to work with.

THE GLENLOTH *business*

There are now about fifteen squab breeders supplying Glenloth, down from twenty-nine a few years ago. 'It is difficult to make farming squab economically viable,' Ian explains. 'The fluctuating prices and increasingly costly food make things difficult, and particularly the severe drought Australia has suffered in recent years.'

Pigeons eat whole grains of wheat, peas and corn, which are divided in sections in their feed bin. Depending on the time of year their consumption of the individual grains varies. Overall they would consume more peas, however their consumption of corn goes up over winter as it gives them more energy.

After being gutted and cleaned, each squab is chilled to a temperature between 1 and 3°C as protection; pathogens *E. coli* and salmonella cannot survive in temperatures below 8°C.

Glenloth Game is appreciated within the food industry for its consistency of quality, which has been attributed to the mixing of its own feeds.

CARPACCIO OF *squab*

with a Herb Salad and Pea Vinaigrette

CARPACCIO OF SQUAB

50 ml (1³/₄ fl oz) Madeira

salt and freshly ground pepper

¹/₂ x 5 g (¹/₈ oz) gelatine leaf, softened in cold water

skinless breast fillets from 2 x 500 g (18 oz) squab

2 teaspoons non-scented cooking oil

PEA VINAIGRETTE

200 g (7 oz) podded fresh peas

120 ml (4 fl oz) Herb Oil (page 268)

3 tablespoons finely chopped chervil and tarragon

salt and freshly ground pepper

HERB SALAD

handful frisée, golden leaves from the centre

1 cup chervil sprigs

¹/₄ cup baby tarragon sprigs

splash extra-virgin olive oil

few drops lemon juice

fleur de sel

freshly ground white pepper

This is a version of the old classic, pigeon 'n' peas, Bécasse-style. It's a dish of many textures: I love the contrast of the buttery-soft squab with the firm juicy peas and crisp salad leaves. And although it is a light salad, the flavours are vibrant and intense.

TO PREPARE THE SQUAB CARPACCIO, put the Madeira in a small saucepan over a high heat and bring to the boil. Season with salt and pepper. Squeeze out the excess moisture from the softened gelatine and stir into the Madeira until completely dissolved. Strain through a chinois or a fine sieve and leave to cool to room temperature.

Lay the squab breasts on your work surface in pairs, skin side down. Brush each breast lightly with the Madeira and put one on top of another, aligning the thick end of one with the thin end of the other. Wrap each pair of squab breasts tightly in cling film, rolling gently to form 2 firm cylinders. Refrigerate for at least an hour to set.

Remove the squab from the refrigerator, remove the cling film and season. Heat a small frying pan until almost smoking. Add the oil then sear the squab portions all over until lightly coloured. Remove from the pan and wrap each pair tightly in cling film again. Roll once more to form 2 firm cylinders. Put into the freezer for 1–2 hours until just set – you don't want them to freeze.

TO MAKE THE PEA VINAIGRETTE, blanch the podded peas in simmering water for 3 minutes until tender. Refresh immediately in iced water then drain and pat dry. Pop the peas out of their skins and put the bright green little halves into a small mixing bowl. Add the oil, herbs and seasoning and stir well. Set aside until ready to serve.

TO MAKE THE SALAD, toss the frisée and herbs with the extra-virgin olive oil and lemon juice and season lightly.

TO SERVE, remove the squab from the freezer and slice each cylinder into 10 even slices. Remove the cling film from each piece and place 5 slices on each plate. Arrange a small mound of salad next to the squab and drizzle with the pea vinaigrette. Season the squab discs with fleur de sel and pepper and serve immediately.

Serves 4 as an entrée

TERRINE OF SQUAB, *foie gras and artichoke*

MARINATED SQUAB BREASTS

8 x 500 g (18 oz) squab

salt and freshly ground pepper

50 ml (1¾ fl oz) non-scented cooking oil

100 g (3½ oz) unsalted butter

¼ cup thyme

300 ml (10 fl oz) Game Bird Marinade
(page 265), kept warm

MARINATED FOIE GRAS

1 x 500 g (18 oz) cooked foie gras*

430 ml (15 fl oz) Foie Gras Marinade
(page 265)

CONFIT SQUAB LEGS

100 g (3½ oz) Aromatic Confit Salt
(page 10)

1 litre (2¼ pints) duck fat

4 cloves garlic, roughly crushed

3 sprigs thyme

1 bay leaf

TERRINE

24 Confit Globe Artichokes (page 276),
cut into 1 cm (½ in) slices

500 ml (18 fl oz) Game Jelly (page 258)

fleur de sel

freshly ground white pepper

This is a fairly complex recipe to prepare but is worth it for the striking end result. It is visually very pretty and full of rich, buttery flavours that are beautifully cut by the tangy pickled artichokes. The breasts and the legs of the squab are prepared separately and you can use the carcasses to prepare the game jelly (page 258).

TO PREPARE THE SQUAB, bring them to room temperature and preheat your oven to 180°C (350°F). Remove the legs, wings and undercarriage from the squab, leaving the breasts attached to the remaining carcass: this is what's known as the crown. Remove the heads, necks, throat sacks and wishbones. Chop the wings and undercarriage into small pieces and set to one side for the game stock. Reserve the legs for the confit.

Season the squab crowns well all over. Select a large baking tray that will comfortably accommodate all of them. Heat over a medium-high heat then add the oil. Place the squab in the tray then add the butter and heat to a nut-brown foam. Turn the squab around in the pan until golden and caramelised, which will take 6–8 minutes.

Sit the birds upright in the pan and transfer to the oven. Roast for 2 minutes then remove from the oven and place the birds on their backs on a cooling rack. Tuck the thyme into the cavities then pour in all the pan juices. Leave in a warm place to rest for 6 minutes.

Use a very sharp knife to slice the breasts away from the carcasses, remove the skin and trim away any sinews. Slice all the breasts horizontally so you have a total of 32 flat halves. Place them in a large dish and pour on the warm game bird marinade. Use your hands to work this thoroughly into the meat. Cover with cling film and refrigerate for 6 hours to marinate.

TO PREPARE THE FOIE GRAS, use a very sharp knife dipped in hot water to slice the foie gras lengthwise into long thin slices – about the same thickness as the pigeon breast pieces.

Place them in a large dish and pour over the warm foie gras marinade. Cover with cling film and leave to steam for about 20 minutes. Transfer to the refrigerator and marinate for 6 hours.

TO CONFIT THE SQUAB LEGS, sprinkle half the aromatic salt onto a large shallow dish and place the squab legs on top. Sprinkle over the rest of the salt then cover tightly with cling film and refrigerate for an hour.

Preheat your oven to 110°C (225°F). Wash away the salt and pat the legs thoroughly dry. Melt the rendered duck fat in a large ovenproof dish. Add the garlic, thyme and bay leaf then add the squab legs, making sure they are completely submerged in the fat. Cover with a piece of greaseproof paper cut to the size of the dish. Cook in the oven for 2 hours until the meat is very tender and comes away from the bone. Drain the legs in a colander and when cool enough to handle remove the meat and shred into small pieces. Set aside until required.

continued …

TERRINE OF SQUAB, *foie gras and artichoke*

continued

TO ASSEMBLE THE TERRINE, lightly grease a standard loaf or brioche tin and double-line it with cling film, leaving a generous overhang. Bring all the terrine ingredients to room temperature and arrange as follows: divide the marinated squab breast pieces into 2 piles of 16; divide the marinated foie gras slices into 2 piles; divide the confit leg meat into 3 even piles and divide the artichoke slices into 2 piles.

Build the terrine in layers, starting with the confit leg meat, followed by a layer of pickled artichokes, a layer of foie gras and a layer of squab breast pieces. Season each layer with salt and pepper and drizzle with the game jelly as you go. Repeat the sequence of layers, ending with a layer of confit leg meat. Fold the cling film over the top and weight down with a 2 kg (4 lb 4 oz) weight. Refrigerate overnight.

TO SERVE, remove the terrine from the refrigerator, unwrap it and cut into 12 slices while still cold and firm. Bring to room temperature before serving.

Serves 12 as an entrée

Note: Raw foie gras is not available in Australia, but you can purchase good quality poached (mi-cuit) foie gras from specialist food stores. Try to buy it in lobes if you can. Pâté de foie gras is quite different and should not be substituted in this recipe.

SQUAB *pot au feu*

with Foie Gras and Thyme Dumplings, Stuffed Neck and Confit Wings

2 x 500 g (18 oz) squab

8 extra squab wings

100 g (3½ oz) Aromatic Confit Salt
(page 10)

CONFIT WINGS AND LEGS

1 litre (2¼ pints) Rendered Duck Fat
(page 274)

3 cloves garlic

4 sprigs thyme

½ bay leaf

STUFFED NECKS

100 g (3½ oz) shiitake mushrooms,
cut into quarters

1 clove garlic

2 sprigs thyme

salt and freshly ground pepper

SQUAB CROWNS

2 squab crowns (see method)

salt and freshly ground pepper

few tablespoons Rendered Duck Fat
(page 274)

2 litres (4¼ pints) Squab or Game
Consommé (page 258)

12 x Foie Gras and Thyme Dumplings
(page 269)

12 baby leeks, blanched in simmering
salted water until tender then refreshed
in iced water

This recipe is inspired by pot au feu – a French classic with many regional variations. In the traditional version, the base is an aromatic flavoursome broth in which all the meat and garnish are braised with herbs. Our version is a little different as the component parts are prepared separately, and then served in a light consommé. It makes for a rather more complex and layered dish full of wonderful flavours and textures.

For this recipe you need whole squabs with the necks and heads intact. You will also need to buy a few extra squab wings, or use any left over from another dish.

The consommé, dumplings and aromatic salt will need to be made ahead of time so remember this in your planning.

TO PREPARE THE SQUAB, remove the legs, wings, undercarriages, necks and heads from the squab leaving the breasts attached to the remaining carcass: this is what's known as the crown. Remove the wishbones and throat sacks.

Set aside all the wings (12 in total) and the legs with the 2 squab necks. Trim the wing tips from the wings and remove the thick bones. Pull the skin back to reveal the second, fine bone with a nugget of meat attached. Remove the bones from the necks and turn them inside out. Sprinkle some of the salt onto a flat tray and arrange the wings, legs and necks on top. Cover with the rest of the salt and leave to marinate for an hour.

TO CONFIT THE WINGS AND LEGS, preheat your oven to 110°C (225°F). Rinse away the salt from the wings and legs and pat them dry. Heat the duck fat in a casserole dish with the garlic and herbs. Add the wings and legs so they are completely submerged. Cover with a piece of greaseproof paper cut to the size of the dish. Place in the oven and cook for 2 hours, until the meat is tender and easily comes away from the bone. Remove the wings and legs from the pan (reserving the fat for later) and drain them in a colander until cool enough to handle. Set the wings to one side. Remove the meat from the legs and shred into small pieces.

TO STUFF THE NECKS, rinse away the salt and pat them dry. Turn the necks back the correct way and tie them tightly at the narrow end.

Heat a tablespoon of the rendered duck fat in a heavy-based frying pan and sauté the mushrooms for a few minutes. Add the garlic and thyme and sauté until golden brown. Season with salt and pepper then drain and leave to cool.

Roughly chop the mushrooms and mix them with the shredded leg meat. Stuff the squab necks with this mixture, packing it in firmly so each neck is plump and round. Secure the open end firmly with string.

Put the stuffed necks into the casserole dish with the flavoured duck fat and cook in the oven for 20 minutes at 110°C (225°F). Remove from the oven, drain briefly then set aside with the wings.

continued …

SQUAB *pot au feu*

continued

TO POACH THE SQUAB CROWNS, bring them to room temperature and season with salt and pepper. Heat the consommé in a heavy-based saucepan to 80°C (175°F).

Heat a heavy-based frying pan until hot. Add a tablespoon of the rendered duck fat followed by the seasoned squabs. Fry for 3 minutes until the skin is golden brown and caramelised. Remove from the pan and pat dry on kitchen paper to thoroughly remove any fat.

Put the squab in the consommé with the dumplings and poach gently for about 8 minutes. Remove the squab from the consommé, but leave the dumplings sitting in the consommé. Leave the squab to rest in a warm place for about 4 minutes.

WHEN READY TO SERVE, heat a heavy-based frying pan until hot. Add a little rendered duck fat and fry the squab wings and stuffed necks until golden brown and caramelised.

Heat the blanched leeks in the consommé with the dumplings.

Slice the 4 breasts off the carcasses, remove the skin and carve each breast off the bone into 3 pieces. Season well and divide between 4 warm serving bowls. Carve each of the necks into 6 slices and divide between the 4 bowls with the wings, dumplings and leeks. Ladle on the hot consommé and serve at once.

Serves 4 as a main course

CONFIT DODINE OF *squab*

with a Salad of Walnuts, Salsify and Muscatels

STUFFING

2 teaspoons non-scented cooking oil

6 small Calves' Sweetbreads (page 270)

salt and freshly ground pepper

30 g (1 oz) unsalted butter

drop lemon juice

3–4 fresh or reconstituted dried trompette mushrooms, finely shredded (available from good food stores)

200 g (7 oz) Chicken Mousse (page 269)

8 Confit Duck Gizzards (page 275), cut into large dice

60 g (2 oz) pistachio nuts, blanched and peeled

1 tablespoon finely chopped parsley

splash of Armagnac

continued …

A dodine is a wonderful 'special occasion' dish, which is a little tricky to prepare but quite spectacular. Poultry or game birds (often duck) are boned and stuffed with a mixture of the breast meat, confit leg meat and offal. The birds are then sewn back to their original shape in order to confit, then caramelised.

You will need good knife skills to bone the birds. But it's well worth taking the time to learn the techniques as, once learned, they can be used time and time again for all manner of poultry and game dishes.

TO PREPARE THE STUFFING, heat a frying pan over a high heat then add the oil. Season the sweetbreads lightly with salt and pepper and add them to the pan. Add the butter and heat to a nut-brown foam. Fry the sweetbreads, turning them in the foam until they are golden and caramelised. Add the lemon juice and stir briefly then remove from the pan and drain on kitchen paper until cool.

Add the mushrooms to the same pan, add a little more butter and sauté the mushrooms. Season well with salt and pepper then drain and leave to cool.

Put the chicken mousse in a small bowl and gently fold in all the remaining ingredients, including the sweetbreads and mushrooms. The stuffing will be quite lumpy, but this adds to the visual appeal when the squabs are carved.

To test the flavour balance of the stuffing, wrap a teaspoonful in cling film, secure tightly and poach for 2 minutes. Taste and adjust the seasonings if required.

TO PREPARE THE SQUAB, place breast side down on a secure chopping board and, using your sharpest boning knife, make a neat incision lengthwise down the undercarriage of the bird. Carefully bone down the left side, disconnecting the wing and leg from the ball and socket joints where they are attached to the main carcass. Keep your knife flush against the carcass in order to remove all the meat. Continue working your knife under and along the breast until you reach the centre of the breastbone. Repeat this procedure down the right side of the bird until you meet the centre breastbone. Then remove carcass – it should come away as one whole piece leaving the bird behind. Chop the carcass into small pieces and reserve for the jus gras.

Remove the wing tips and clean the wing bones that are still attached to the bird. Bone out and remove the thigh bones from the birds. The wing tips and the thigh bones can be used to make the jus gras.

Repeat the boning-out process with the other squab then lay the 2 birds out on the board, breast side down, and open them up as wide as you can. Remove the throat sacks from the necks and scrape away any excess fat.

Divide the stuffing mixture in two and place in the cavities. Try to make sure the sweetbreads and mushrooms are evenly distributed down the centres of the birds. Bring the sides up around the stuffing to reform the birds and sew neatly along the join with string. Spear through the legs with toothpicks to secure them.

CONFIT DODINE OF *squab*

continued

CONFIT SQUAB DODINE

2 x 500 g (18 oz) squab, heads and claws attached

1.5 litres (3 pints) Rendered Duck Fat (page 274)

4 cloves garlic, roughly crushed

6 sprigs thyme

1 bay leaf

salt and freshly ground pepper

30 ml (1 fl oz) non-scented cooking oil

100 g (3½ oz) unsalted butter

SALAD OF WALNUTS, SALSIFY AND MUSCATELS

200 ml (7 fl oz) Squab Jus Gras (page 262)

200 g (7 oz) Glazed Salsify (page 280)

100 g (3½ oz) roasted walnuts

100 g (3½ oz) dried muscatels, seeded

1 teaspoon finely chopped parsley

TO CONFIT THE SQUAB, preheat your oven to 120°C (245°F). Pour the duck fat into a deep ovenproof dish that is just large enough to fit the 2 squab and add the garlic, thyme and bay leaf to the pan. Heat gently then add the squab to the dish – they should be completely submerged. Cover with a piece of greaseproof paper, cut to the size of the dish, and cook for 15 minutes.

Lift the squab out of the fat, drain briefly and season with salt and pepper. Heat a frying pan over a medium-high heat then add the oil. Add the squab to the pan, followed by the butter and heat to a nut-brown foam. Turn the squab around in the pan until deep golden-brown and caramelised. Remove from the heat and leave to rest in a warm place for a few minutes.

TO PREPARE THE SALAD, heat the jus gras in a large frying pan. Add the salsify, walnuts and muscatels and stir until warmed through. Add the parsley and mix thoroughly.

TO SERVE, remove the string from each bird and carve in half lengthwise. Arrange on warm serving plates and spoon around the warm salad and plenty of jus gras.

Serves 4 as an entrée

Pork

BANGALOW SWEET PORK

THE SWEET PORK *company*

Byron Bay is just north-west of Australia's most easterly point in New South Wales. A lighthouse marks the promontory where many a holidaymaker has stayed up all night to watch the sun reach its first point in Australia on a new day. And in the hills behind the bustling holiday town is where you'll find the cutting edge in pork farming, at Bangalow Sweet Pork.

Joe Byrne, a wiry, straight-talking man in his sixties, has invested a significant number of years and 'just as many wheelbarrow-loads of money' in creating pork that is tender, rich in flavour and low in saturated fats. He's passionate about the quality of his product and has worked with agricultural scientist Jim Berting for more than thirty years to create the premium brand.

When Byrne is presenting his product to butchers, 'The first thing I tell them is that we're expensive and we're fat,' he chuckles. It has taken him years to open people's minds to the idea that pork is a meat that must carry fat; that there are different kinds of fats in meat – both good and bad for health; and that the fat in pork is where all the flavour is found. 'Pigs don't have fur or feathers to keep them warm,' he says, 'so they're bound to have more naturally occurring fat to compensate'.

So far, almost fifty butchers Australia-wide sell pork from Bangalow Sweet Pork and as the word spreads, so does customers' desire for a tastier product. 'We don't go out of our way to make our pigs fat,' Byrne says, 'but we don't restrict them, either'. It is this monumentally different attitude to the production of pork that distinguishes Sweet Pork from the rest of the pork on the market.

TURNING BACK THE *clock*

The Sweet Pork Company is rewriting the rules of pork farming and consumption in Australia. In the past, consumers have been led to believe that the leanest cut of pork is preferable, under the misconception that fat is always bad. This pressure pushed farmers to produce pork that was extremely lean. 'The problem with that,' Joe explains, 'is that it tastes like cardboard. All the flavour of meat is gleaned from the fat. If you put chicken fat into beef sausages, they taste like chicken.' Pork reared to be low in fat is often tough, dry and lacking in flavour. It was this realisation that paved the way for Byrne and Berting to develop their unique pork product.

The Sweet Pork Company pays great attention to the feeding and management of farm livestock, in the belief that this close proximity will lead to a better product. Berting has lived in the Bangalow area since 1980 and has spent the majority of this time refining pig feed. The three farmers currently producing pigs for the Bangalow Sweet Pork are well versed in Berting's secret feed recipe but have signed non-disclosure agreements. Although Byrne and Berting won't reveal what goes into the feed for their pigs, they're only too happy to discuss what doesn't.

You won't find growth promoters, antibiotics or chemical metabolism modifiers in the animals at the Sweet Pork Company. These are used elsewhere to prohibit the development of fat in the animals, to speed up the growth process and therefore the meat yield. Similarly, fish meal is commonly used elsewhere in feed. While extremely high in protein and helpful in producing a very lean carcass, which has been in fashion in recent years, fish meal tends to make pork meat taste fishy. 'It's simply not what pork is supposed to taste like,' Berting says.

With the policy of avoiding all chemicals in the meat and allowing the pigs a more natural diet and a longer, gradual weight gain, Sweet Pork has a high fat content and is a more expensive cut of meat. But for the exemplary taste and delicate texture, it is very much worth it.

'Pork used to taste wonderful when I was a kid, but this paranoia about fat nowadays has spoiled how pork is meant to taste,' Byrne says. He is keen to educate his customers to change their priorities. Along with Australia's obsession with fat, the problem is, according to Byrne, a lack of understanding and experience in pig farming. Old methods have been lost to mechanised farming techniques and the philosophies that underpin those long-trusted techniques have disappeared.

'Few of the newcomers to the industry in the past twenty years would have had the benefit of any experience in pig production that wasn't in a "factory farming" situation,' Berting says. 'All research in feeding, breeding, housing and health is governed by the pressure – mostly from supermarkets – to produce a cheaper article, heedless of the quality. Worse still, the term "quality" has been misrepresented to mean "absence of fat".'

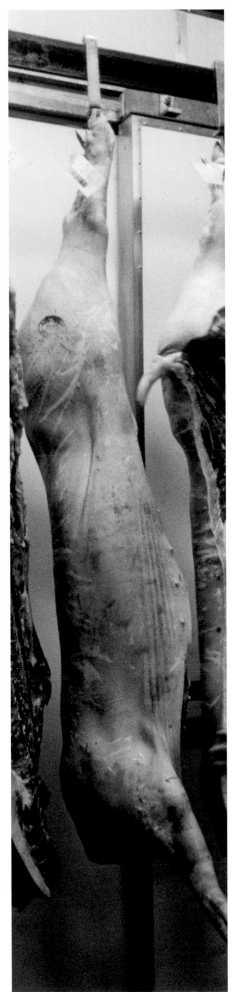

THE SCIENCE OF *taste*

Jim Berting studied agriculture with a postgraduate year in animal nutrition and genetics. After he completed his postgraduate studies he developed an interest in pig farming and it was fortunate that his studies were well suited to work in this area. Jim's contribution to the Sweet Pork Company has been to address the connection between genetics and the quality of feed for pigs, the principal secret of the company's success. Because of the relatively short generational interval in pigs (sows can produce two litters of eight piglets annually), it is possible to make changes to a pig's genetic makeup rapidly. Breeds that have been experimented with include Hampshire, Wessex and Saddleback.

Berting explains that pigs take on the flavour of the food they're fed in the last eight weeks of their lives. In Europe, pigs are sometimes kept in an orchard to graze on the fruit for the last few weeks of their lives, as it is said to bring a sweetness to their meat.

The breakdown of fats in Bangalow Sweet Pork's meat is interesting in comparison to other brands. Mono-unsaturated fat constitutes 53.3 per cent; saturated fat 36.6 per cent; with poly-unsaturated fats making up the rest of the total fat content. Other farmed pork might have a lower total fat content, but of that content a far greater portion is made up of saturated fat, which is more likely to increase blood cholesterol in humans. People need some fat in their diet in order to process the vitamins A, D, E and K, as well as for other vital functions, but an unsaturated fat is better for this purpose as it carries less risk of forming cholesterol deposits in the arteries.

Bangalow Sweet Pork pigs are fed a diet that also enhances omega 3 and omega 6 production – a good thing for the human diet as we need these fats and our bodies don't produce them.

The intramuscular fat in Bangalow Sweet Pork is marbled throughout the flesh, and it's this that gives the meat its succulent texture and sweet taste. Cooks should bear in mind that while using this product it's a good idea to cook the pork meat with all the fat left on it (including the 'depot' fat that lies between the skin and muscle) and remove it after cooking. 'Just because there's more fat on Sweet Pork doesn't mean you're obligated to eat it all,' Byrne says.

Through nurturing a natural approach, the Sweet Pork Company is farming a product that defies the trend towards non-fat meat products while embracing flavour and healthy fats at the same time.

CARAMELISED BOUDIN NOIR, SCALLOPS AND
butternut pumpkin
with Herb Foam and Sherry Jus

1 butternut pumpkin

non-scented cooking oil

80 g (2¾ oz) unsalted butter

4 sprigs thyme

1 sprig rosemary

2 cloves garlic, roughly crushed

salt and freshly ground pepper

200 ml (7 fl oz) Pork Jus (page 260)

1 tablespoon dry sherry

1 kg (2 lb 2 oz) Butternut Pumpkin Purée (page 278)

1 litre (2¼ pints) Herb Foam (page 267)*

2 x Boudin Noir (page 273), each cut into 3 thick slices

few drops lemon juice

6 extra-large fresh scallops

fleur de sel

Use the Boudin Noir recipe on page 273 or a good quality purchased one. Our boudin recipe is one that was developed with Raymond Blanc and is quite exceptional. The traditional savoury sausage base has been enhanced with the careful addition of spices, apples and braised meat from the pig's head.

TO PREPARE THE PUMPKIN, begin by cutting it crosswise. For this dish you only need the thinner seedless end – use the bulbous end for another recipe. Peel the pumpkin and cut crosswise into 2 x 4 cm (1½ in) slices. Use a 4 cm (1½ in) pastry cutter to cut 3 smaller discs from each slice, so you have 6 in total.

Heat a frying pan over a medium-high heat. Add a splash of oil followed by the discs of pumpkin and cook gently on one side only, for about 5 minutes until lightly coloured. Now add the butter and cook over a medium heat until it foams – you want it to foam up over the pumpkin. Add the thyme, rosemary and garlic and season well. Lower the heat and cook the pumpkin for around 20 minutes, until tender and caramelised a deep golden-brown all over. Turn it around in the pan from time to time to ensure it colours evenly. Remove the pan from the heat and keep warm.

WARM THROUGH THE PORK JUS with the sherry in a small saucepan and keep hot until required. Similarly, warm through the pumpkin purée and keep hot until ready to serve.

HEAT THE HERB FOAM and when hot, transfer to an espuma cream gun. Shake the can well and rest upside down for 15 minutes before use.

TO CARAMELISE THE BOUDIN NOIR, heat a heavy-based frying pan over a medium heat, add a little butter and cook until it foams. Add the slices of boudin noir and season well. Gently caramelise on both sides and finish with a drop of fresh lemon juice.

TO CARAMELISE THE SCALLOPS, heat another large frying pan until nearly smoking. Season the scallops lightly with salt and freshly ground pepper. Add a splash of oil to the pan and add the scallops, flat side down. Sear for a few seconds then add a generous tablespoon of butter and heat to a nut-brown foam. Remove the pan from the heat and carefully turn the scallops over. Season again and add a few drops of lemon juice. Baste the scallops for a few more seconds. The whole process should take around 1 minute – you are aiming for scallops that are cooked medium-rare: caramelised and golden on the outside, but still translucent in the centre.

WHEN ALMOST READY TO SERVE, place a disc of pumpkin, a slice of boudin noir and a scallop on each plate. Decorate the plate with the pumpkin purée, the herb foam and the pork jus. Sprinkle with a little fleur de sel and serve immediately.

Serves 6 as an entrée

Note: You will need to buy an espuma cream gun and gas canisters from a specialist cookery shop.

SLOW-POACHED *fillet of pork*

with Gribiche Vinaigrette and Crisp Pig's Tail

SLOW-POACHED FILLET OF PORK

400 g (14 oz) pork fillet, trimmed of all sinews

400 ml (14 fl oz) Pork Jus (page 260)

100 ml (3½ fl oz) sparkling cider

½ tablespoon non-scented cooking oil

salt and freshly ground pepper

CRISP PIG'S TAIL

1 Braised Pig's Tail (page 272)

300 ml (10 fl oz) non-scented cooking oil, for deep-frying

1 teaspoon Dijon mustard

100 g (3½ oz) plain flour

salt and freshly ground pepper

TO SERVE

sea salt

small handful frisée, golden leaves from the centre

250 ml (8¾ fl oz) Gribiche Vinaigrette (page 267)

TO SLOW-POACH THE PORK, cut the fillet into 4 even-sized portions and wrap each tightly in cling film. Refrigerate and rest overnight – this helps to shape the pork into neat round discs.

When ready to poach, take the pork fillets from the fridge, remove the cling film and bring to room temperature. Gently warm the pork jus in a medium saucepan. Bring to a gentle boil and add the cider. Return to a gentle boil, season with salt and pepper and immediately remove from the heat.

Allow to cool to the point where it is just hot to the touch, then return to the heat and keep at a very low constant temperature, around 70°C (160°F).

Heat a heavy-based frying pan on a high heat until almost smoking. Add a teaspoon of oil and season the pork fillets generously. Sear them quickly in the hot pan, turning to ensure an even colour. This should only take a few seconds. Transfer the pork fillets to the saucepan with the pork jus. Cover with a piece of greaseproof paper cut to size and poach very gently at 70°C (160°F) for 25 minutes. Remove pork from the poaching liquor and leave to rest in a warm place for 8 minutes.

TO PREPARE THE CRISPY PIG'S TAIL, remove all the cartilage from the pork tail leaving the skin in one neat piece. Cut the tail into thin, even long strips.

Put the oil in a small deep saucepan and heat to 180°C (350°F) or until a cube of bread colours and sizzles to the surface within 30 seconds.

Whisk the mustard with a few tablespoons of water in a small mixing bowl. Put the flour in another mixing bowl and season well. Toss the strips of pig's tail in the mustard then toss in the seasoned flour. Shake off the excess and drop in the hot oil one by one. Deep-fry for a few minutes until golden and crisp, moving the strips around in the oil to prevent them from sticking together and to ensure they colour evenly. Drain on kitchen paper and season.

TO SERVE, carve the pork fillets finely into even slivers. Arrange on serving plates and season with a little sea salt. Toss the frisée in a little vinaigrette, and divide between the plates. Garnish with the strips of crispy pig's tails, drizzle on more of the vinaigrette and serve at once.

Serves 4 as a main course

ROAST RACK OF *pork*

with Choucroute and Charcutière Sauce

1 x 1.6 kg (3 lb 7 oz) pork rack, with 4 bones

50 g (1¾ oz) salt

100 ml (3½ fl oz) non-scented cooking oil

2 litres (4¼ pints) Choucroute (page 282)

400 ml (14 fl oz) Charcutière Sauce (page 263)

This dish is the perfect way to showcase Bangalow pork, with its sweet succulent meat, layer of tasty fat and crisp shell of crackling. To me this is what roast pork is all about.

Ask your butcher to 'French' the rack and remove the chine bone. Leave the skin and all the fat intact.

TO PREPARE THE PORK, clean each of the four bones by scraping away any remaining fat, meat and sinew so they are perfectly clean. Use a very sharp knife to score the skin from top to bottom at 5 mm (¼ in intervals), cutting right through the skin to the fat underneath. The scoring is important as it allows the salt to penetrate the skin and help draw out moisture and it also allows much of the fat to melt away in the cooking. This will result in a airy, crisp crackling.

Massage the salt into the pork skin, making sure you get it into all the incisions. Put the pork upside down on a wire rack set over a tray and refrigerate for at least 4 hours.

Preheat your oven to 220°C (425°F). Use a dry cloth to rub away any moisture from the pork. Heat a baking tray over a medium heat and add the oil. When hot, add the pork, skin side down, and cook for around 6 minutes until the skin has begun to colour. Put in the oven and roast for 20 minutes. Turn the rack over and roast for another 20 minutes. Remove from the oven and leave to rest in a warm place for 20 minutes.

While the pork is resting, warm through the choucroute and the charcutière sauce.

TO SERVE, carve the pork into 4 thick cutlets. Divide the choucroute between each serving plate and arrange a cutlet on top. Spoon the sauce around and serve straightaway.

Serves 4 as a main course

ASSIETTE OF *pig's head*

1 Braised Pig's Ear (page 272)

300 ml (10 fl oz) non-scented cooking oil for deep-frying

50 g (1¾ oz) seasoned flour

1 egg, lightly beaten with a splash of milk

100 g (3½ oz) seasoned dry breadcrumbs

fleur de sel

freshly ground white pepper

few drops lemon juice

100 g (3½ oz) unsalted butter

1 Braised Pig's Tongue (page 271), cut lengthwise into 4 even pieces

Braised Ballottine of Pig's Head (page 272), chilled and cut into 4 x 2 cm (¾ in) medallions

1 Braised Pig's Cheek (page 271), cut into 4 even pieces

GARNISH

1 Red Sensation pear

50 g (1¾ oz) sugar

20 ml (⅔ fl oz) Poire William

50 g (1¾ oz) unsalted butter

200 ml (7 fl oz) Savoy Cabbage Purée (page 278)

120 ml (4 fl oz) Pork Jus (page 260)

fleur de sel

freshly ground white pepper

200 ml (7 fl oz) Horseradish Chantilly (page 282)

As the title suggests, this is a plate of tasty little morsels, each showcasing a different part of the pig's head. I love dishes like this that use different parts of the same animal and prepare each using a different method. It's a brilliant way of showing how versatile the secondary cuts of meat can be if you're prepared to be a little adventurous. Although it is a bit of a 'restaurant' dish, it would be wonderful to present as part of a buffet table for a special occasion.

TO PREPARE THE PIG'S EAR, cut it into 8 long strips. Heat the oil in a small deep saucepan to 180°C (350°F) or until a cube of bread colours and sizzles to the surface within 30 seconds.

Prepare 3 mixing bowls of flour, beaten egg and breadcrumbs. Dredge the ear strips one by one in the flour, shaking off any excess flour. Dip in the egg and then the breadcrumbs, gently patting off any excess. You are aiming for a neat even coating. Drop the ear strips into the oil, one by one. Deep-fry for a few minutes until golden and crisp, moving the strips around in the oil to prevent them from sticking together and to ensure they colour evenly. Drain on kitchen paper and season with a little fleur de sel, white pepper and a few drops of lemon juice.

TO COOK THE PIG'S TONGUE AND BALLOTTINE OF PIG'S HEAD, heat a large heavy-based frying pan over a medium heat. Add the butter and heat to a nut-brown foam. Add the pieces of tongue and the ballottine medallions and fry gently on both sides until caramelised a deep golden-brown. Make sure you keep the temperature constant to prevent the butter burning – you want a nice even caramelisation.

TO PREPARE THE GARNISH, heat a small heavy-based frying pan over a very high heat until smoking. Cut the pear in half and remove the core. Cut each half into quarters and toss in the sugar. Place the pieces in the smoking pan and caramelise evenly on both sides. Add the Poire William to the pan; be careful as the heat may cause the alcohol to ignite. Add the butter to the pan, lower the heat and toss the pear around until the pieces are nicely glazed. The whole process should take no more than 2 minutes, so the fruit remains firm and does not overcook and become mushy. The pear pieces should end up glazed a dark shiny brown. Keep to one side until ready to serve.

Warm through the Savoy cabbage purée. In a separate pan, warm the pieces of pig's cheek in the pork jus.

TO SERVE, place a spoonful of the cabbage purée and a piece of glazed pear on each warm serving plate. Arrange a seasoned ballottine medallion, a piece of pig's tongue, the braised cheek and fried ear on the plate. Garnish with a quenelle of horseradish chantilly and drizzle over the pork jus. Serve immediately.

Serves 4 as a main course

PIG'S *trotters*

stuffed with Confit Pork Neck, with Truffle Potato Purée and Madeira Jus

PIG'S TROTTERS

4 fresh pig's trotters (hind legs), tunnel boned

20 ml (²/₃ fl oz) non-scented cooking oil

1 large carrot, peeled and roughly chopped

1 medium onion, roughly chopped

2 sticks celery, roughly chopped

½ small leek, roughly chopped

½ head garlic, crushed

80 g (2³/₄ oz) unsalted butter

6 sprigs thyme

1 bay leaf

1 litre (2¼ pints) Pork Jus (page 260)

1 litre (2¼ pints) Brown Veal Stock (page 256)

STUFFING

20 ml (²/₃ fl oz) non-scented cooking oil

2 medium onions, cut into neat dice

80 g (2³/₄ oz) unsalted butter

salt and freshly ground pepper

100 ml (3½ fl oz) Madeira

1 tablespoon thyme leaves

1 tablespoon finely chopped fresh black winter truffle

400 g (14 oz) Confit Pork Neck (page 275)

200 g (7 oz) Chicken Mousse (page 269)

GARNISH

400 g (14 oz) Potato Purée (page 277)

20 ml (²/₃ fl oz) milk

50 g (1³/₄ oz) unsalted butter

2 tablespoons finely chopped fresh black winter truffle

20 ml (²/₃ fl oz) Madeira

1 Poached Truffle, finely shaved (page 50)

A classic dish inspired by the master, Pierre Koffman.

For this dish it is vital to select perfect unblemished trotters from the hind legs. They can be tricky to bone, so you might prefer to ask your butcher to do it for you. Otherwise, use a very sharp knife to carefully ease the skin away from the bone and peel it down – a bit like taking off a glove. At the end you'll come to the small toe bones. Cut through these, being careful to keep the skin well out of the way. Leave the toe bones in place and straighten the skin, with the meat attached, back to its original position (see overleaf).

TO PREPARE THE PIG'S TROTTERS, preheat your oven to 110°C (225°F). Singe away any hairs from the trotters with a cook's blowtorch.

Heat a large ovenproof dish over a medium heat. Add the oil followed by the chopped vegetables and garlic. Cook for a few minutes until lightly browned. Add the butter and heat to a nut-brown foam. Lower the heat and cook gently until the vegetables have caramelised a deep even brown. Drain off the excess butter.

Add the herbs, pork jus and veal stock to the pan and bring to a gentle simmer. Add the pig's trotters and cover with a piece of greaseproof paper, cut to the size of the pan. Cover with a tight-fitting lid, transfer to oven and cook for 3 hours. Check every 30 minutes or so, to ensure they are cooking evenly.

Remove from the oven and check the trotters – they should be soft and gelatinous. Remove and discard the herbs and vegetables and put the dish on a medium heat. Bring to a gentle boil, then lower the heat and braise the trotters, uncovered, for around 30 minutes. Baste every 5–10 minutes until the braising liquid has reduced to a sauce and there is a thick, sticky glaze coating the trotters. Remove the trotters from the pan and allow to cool to room temperature. Reserve the braising liquor left in the pan for serving.

TO MAKE THE STUFFING, heat the oil in a large heavy-based frying pan. Add the onions and cook over a high heat until they start to brown. Add the butter to the pan and heat to a nut-brown foam. Lower the heat and cook the onions for about 25 minutes, until they soften and caramelise a deep golden-brown.

Skim off some of the pan juices and season the onions well. Add the Madeira and simmer until reduced to a thick syrup. Remove the pan from the heat and stir in the thyme and chopped truffle. Tip into a mixing bowl and leave to infuse and cool.

When the mixture is cool, flake the confit pork neck into the mixing bowl. Add the chicken mousse, season and fold together gently. To test the flavour balance of the stuffing, wrap a teaspoonful in cling film, secure tightly and poach for 2 minutes. Taste and adjust the seasonings if required.

continued …

continued

TO STUFF THE PIG'S TROTTERS, lay each one on a large square of cling film, open side down. Divide the stuffing evenly between the trotters, pushing it firmly up into the hoof cavity and gently reshaping. Wrap each trotter tightly in cling film and then a piece of aluminium foil. Steam for 20 minutes.

TO PREPARE THE GARNISH, gently warm the potato purée and mix in the milk, butter and chopped truffle.

In a separate pan, warm the reserved braising liquor with the Madeira to make a thin sauce.

TO SERVE, remove the trotters from the steamer, carefully snip open the foil and cling film, and gently ease the trotters out onto each serving plate. Use a curved pastry spatula or a large oval spoon to form quenelles of potato purée and top with shavings of truffle. Drizzle over the warm sauce and serve straightaway.

Serves 4

Lamb

THE CASTRICUM BROTHERS

KEEPING IT ALL IN THE *family*

Jacobus Castricum migrated from Holland to Australia in 1952, with a family history in the meat business dating back a century. In 1954 he bought a butcher's shop in the Melbourne suburb of Dandenong, and a year later a small domestic abattoir. This abattoir is the basis of the Castricum Brothers' business as it still operates today. Jacobus's sons – Peter, Jack, Con, Martin and Theo – still own the Castricum Brothers business today. Theo and Martin are actively involved in the day-to-day running of the processing plant; the others sit on the board of the company. Martin's son Matthew is one of three full-time livestock buyers, travelling throughout the south-east of Australia grading and selecting lambs for the Castricum label. Peter's son Gary is the company's managing director. It's a 100-per-cent family-owned business.

Lambing seasons vary from north to south of the country, and Matthew travels as far north as Dubbo in New South Wales and west to Mount Gambier in South Australia to secure the best lambs for distribution. This is also the way they secure a consistent supply of lamb all year round. The responsibility for the superior quality of Castricum lamb starts with the livestock buyers, then, according to Theo and Martin, the secret is in a good pasture. 'You can always get a scrawny lamb from good genes,' Martin explains. As the end result is priced according to weight, a good 'dressed weight' (the term used for a processed animal's weight), coupled with impressive muscle-to-fat ratio, is imperative.

The Castricum Brothers label guarantees consistently superior cuts of lamb, facilitated by thorough grading techniques and quality standards. Breeds that make the best eating, according to the Castricums, include Poll Dorset Cross, Corriedale, White Suffolk, Hampshire Down and Border Leicester Cross.

BELOW LEFT (from left to right): Martin Castricum with his son Mathew and brother Theo; RIGHT: Alan Fox.

QUALITY IN *quantities*

In order to maintain their high standards the Castricum brothers have developed a farmer supply alliance called 'Casmark', which over 1800 contributing farms in Victoria, South Australia and New South Wales are part of.

To meet the heavy demand for Castricum Brothers lamb in the worldwide market, the business employs a system of offering farmers forward pricing – this helps to guarantee particular weights and standards of meat. This system encourages farmers to spend their money up front on a better quality animal, as they know what price they will get for the lamb carcass when it is ready for slaughter. The price paid for these lambs in Australia is not influenced by market fluctuation abroad but purely by conditions at home. The drought that has crippled Australian farmers in recent years has forced lamb prices up, as the constant demand has become more challenging to meet.

The forward commitment to farmers made by the Castricum brothers is essentially gambling on the market, and it is not without risk. The company offers a price for lambs up to six months in advance. International export trade adds a further variable with fluctuating exchange rates, and is beyond the Castricum brothers' control. In offering forward contracts with farmers Castricum can manage its exchange rate risks by forward-covering the exchange rates. Ninety per cent of Castricum Brothers' lamb products are exported overseas – the main markets are the United States and Canada.

Australia is traditionally more renowned overseas for Merino wool than for its lamb, but this is changing. As well as North America, Castricum Brothers export to Asia, Europe and the Middle East, particularly Saudi Arabia. China is predicted to be a growing market in the future.

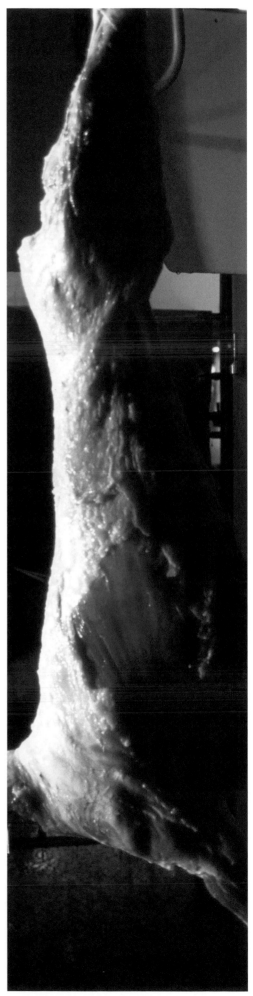

INSIDE THE *processing plant*

The Castricum brothers' abattoir is one of the most professional, efficient and technically advanced in Australia, and employs over 300 people. Lambs are processed swiftly, with minimum stress placed on the animals before their slaughter. A Halal butcher, denoted by his yellow trousers in among otherwise white-uniformed staff, kills lambs while facing Mecca. This is a requirement of Muslim customers and opens up the sale of Castricum Lamb within Muslim communities in Australia and internationally.

The abattoir processes 3000–4000 animals a day. It takes about 25 minutes to process each animal from live weight to dressed weight (from the holding pen to the chilling room).

The lambs are strung up by their feet and carried along a conveyor belt. Their skins are removed in a swift motion and their innards discarded. All lambs that go through the plant are screened, photographed and weighed by a sophisticated digital scanning device that is able to measure each animal's meat-to-fat ratio. This allows the Castricums to reward farmers for the amount of meat on the carcasses, rather than for the carcass weight alone. Leaner animals achieve a higher meat yield and are more prized as a result. This is one of the secrets of the success of Castricum lamb: the consistency of the product is guaranteed via such high-tech methods of processing.

Each carcass is colour-tagged according to its weight, and animals intended for international markets receive a separate label offering further information on the lamb's origin and destination. These tags also enable the Castricum brothers to trace the animals right back to their original farm. The carcasses are moved – thousands every day – to a chilling room, where they spend the night being refrigerated into rigid (therefore workable) form. It is just prior to refrigeration that any lamb requiring 'tender stretching' is singled out. Tender stretching is the process of hanging the carcass close to its natural standing position, with an even distribution of weight throughout the carcass. This creates exceptionally succulent meat. Not all carcasses are treated like this due to the space it takes up, but tender stretching of a lamb carcass will be carried out on request.

The last stop prior to transportation is the boning room. One hundred highly skilled butchers work on the production chain, slicing the carcasses into various cuts and joints. They work with breathtaking precision – finishing with a product that is vacuum-sealed and boxed, ready for consumption.

300 ml (10 fl oz) non-scented cooking oil

8 zucchini flowers

100 g (3½ oz) seasoned plain flour

salt and freshly ground pepper

12 x 40 g (1⅓ oz) Lamb's Sweetbreads (page 270)

1 tablespoon non-scented cooking oil

60 g (2 oz) unsalted butter

few drops lemon juice

12 parsley roots (optional), washed, blanched and refreshed

2 spears asparagus, peeled, blanched, refreshed and sliced

3 small red radishes, very finely sliced to neat rounds

8 vine-ripened cherry tomatoes, blanched, refreshed and peeled

small handful baby red chard

small handful baby frisée, golden leaves from the centre

small handful baby lamb's lettuce (mâche)

200 ml (7 fl oz) Black Olive Vinaigrette (page 266)

Heat the oil in a deep pan to 180°C (350°F), or until a cube of bread colours and sizzles to the surface within around 30 seconds. Remove the stigmas from the zucchini flowers and keep to use later. Dredge the flowers lightly in the seasoned flour, patting off any excess. Deep-fry a few at a time until they are golden and crisp, turning gently in the oil to ensure they cook and colour evenly. Remove from the oil and drain on kitchen paper. Season well with salt and pepper and keep warm.

Season the sweetbreads well. Heat a heavy-based frying pan over a high heat then add the oil. Carefully place the sweetbreads in the pan, smooth side down. Lower the heat a little and fry the sweetbreads without turning for 2 minutes until golden brown and caramelised. Add the butter and heat to a nut-brown foam. Lower the heat a little more and cook the sweetbreads for another minute in the foam, still without turning.

Add a few drops of lemon juice to the pan, turn the sweetbreads over and baste briefly in the foam. The flat side should be caramelised a lovely deep golden brown and they should still be creamy and soft in the centre.

Transfer the sweetbreads to a mixing bowl. Add the remaining salad ingredients, including the reserved flower stigmas, and toss everything together gently. Divide the salad between 4 serving plates and eat while still warm.

Serves 4 as an entrée

PETIT SALÉ OF *lamb breast*

with Swede and Carrot Dauphinoise and Jerusalem Artichoke Purée

CURED LAMB

4 sprigs thyme

2 sprigs rosemary

½ bay leaf

6 peppercorns

4 cloves

4 cloves garlic

1 kg (2 lb 2 oz) salt

100 g (3½ oz) sugar

1 x 2 kg (4 lb 4 oz) lamb breast (bone-in weight)

BRAISE

1 large carrot, chopped into large dice

1 medium onion, chopped into large dice

2 sticks celery, chopped into large dice

½ medium leek, chopped into large dice

½ head garlic

4 sprigs thyme

1 sprig rosemary

¼ bay leaf

TO SERVE

80 ml (2¾ fl oz) non-scented cooking oil

8 portions Swede and Carrot Dauphinoise (page 279)

40 g (1⅓ oz) unsalted butter

500 g (18 oz) Jerusalem Artichoke Purée (page 277)

1 tablespoon thyme leaves

This recipe is derived from the classic petit salé of dry salted young pork belly found throughout charcuterie preparations in early Roman times. You may retain the braising liquor once finished, as it makes a fantastic base for a hearty broth the following day. You should begin this recipe at least three days in advance.

TO CURE THE LAMB, put the herbs and spices into a large mortar and pound to a coarse powder. Add the garlic and pound to a paste. Tip the paste into a mixing bowl and add the salt and sugar. Use your fingers to rub everything together well, then massage a generous handful into the lamb.

Sprinkle more of the salt into a dish that is deep enough to hold the lamb. Put the lamb in the dish and pack the rest of the salt over and around it. Weight the lamb down then cover tightly with cling film and refrigerate. Leave for 3 days, during which time the dry salt will dissolve into a brine.

TO BRAISE THE LAMB, remove the lamb from the brine and rinse well under cold running water. Soak in several changes of cold water to remove all the salt.

Preheat the oven to 110°C (225°F). Put the lamb into a large deep casserole dish and cover with cold water. Heat gently to a simmer then skim away any surface fat and scum. Add the vegetables and herbs and cover with a piece of greaseproof paper cut to the size of the dish. Put in the oven and braise for 4 hours. Check every 30 minutes or so to turn the lamb and to make sure the liquid is not boiling. When cooked it should be meltingly tender – you should be able to pierce the meat easily with your finger.

Remove from the oven and carefully lift the lamb out of the braising liquor. Leave until just cool enough to handle then carefully remove the bone and any cartilage and sinews. Wrap the lamb loosely in cling film and put it on a flat tray. Cover with another flat tray and weight down. Refrigerate overnight.

continued …

continued

TO SERVE, remove the lamb from the refrigerator and cut into 8 even-sized rectangular pieces. Preheat your oven to 180°C (350°F). Heat a large heavy-based frying pan and when hot add half the oil. Add the lamb pieces, skin side down, and fry until golden brown and caramelised, about 4 minutes.

At the same time, heat another large heavy-based frying pan and when hot add the remaining oil. Cut the swede and carrot dauphinoise into 8 even-sized rectangular pieces and fry until golden brown and caramelised, about 4 minutes. Transfer both pans to the oven for 8 minutes.

Remove both pans from the oven and return to the stove top. Add a knob of butter to each pan and heat to a nut-brown foam. Cook for a few more minutes until the lamb and dauphinoise pieces are golden brown and caramelised.

Heat the Jerusalem artichoke purée and place a spoonful in the centre of each warm serving plate. Arrange a piece of lamb to one side. Carefully remove the golden top layer of the dauphinoise and arrange it on the other side. Place the remaining wedge of dauphinoise on top of the purée. Sprinkle with fresh thyme leaves and serve.

Serves 8 as a main course

NAVARIN OF LAMB *choux farci*

CHOUX FARCI

½ small onion, dice to a fine brunoise

250 ml (9 fl oz) white wine

500 g (18 oz) minced lamb neck or shoulder meat (about 25% fat)

1 teaspoon thyme leaves

1 tablespoon chopped sage leaves

salt and freshly ground white pepper

6 large green cabbage leaves, stems removed

2 x 250 g (9 oz) lamb back straps

2 x 8 point lamb racks

800 ml (1½ pints) Lamb Consommé (page 257)

salt and freshly ground pepper

30 ml (1 fl oz) non-scented cooking oil

16 baby carrots, peeled

2 Braised Lamb Tongues (page 271), sliced into quarters while cold

16 Braised Baby Onions (page 280)

24 Braised Turnips (page 280)

16 Turned Potatoes Cooked in Lamb Stock (page 279)

few sprigs chervil

few sprigs tarragon

Traditionally a navarin is a stew made with mutton. The name is derived from 'navet', the French word for turnip, which is the main vegetable accompaniment. The Bécasse version is more refined and modern: we replace the mutton with lamb and serve it in a delicate, herb-scented consommé accompanied by choux farci – little stuffed cabbage balls.

TO MAKE THE CHOUX FARCI, put the onion and wine in a saucepan and reduce to a syrup over a high heat. Mix with the lamb mince and herbs, season well and set aside.

Blanch the cabbage leaves for 3 minutes, then refresh in iced water. Pat dry. Place each leaf between 2 sheets of cling film and roll until flat and even. Remove the plastic wrap and use a 5 cm (2 in) pastry cutter to cut out 8 rounds from the leaves. Then use a 3 cm (1¼ in) pastry cutter to cut another 16 smaller rounds.

Divide the stuffing into 24 portions. Lay a large sheet of cling film across the work surface and place the 8 larger cabbage rounds on top, leaving plenty of space between them. Place a ball of stuffing on each, followed by a small cabbage round and flatten slightly. Repeat with another ball of stuffing and cabbage round, finishing with a ball of stuffing. Cut the cling film between each choux and wrap up tightly into neat balls. Prick each ball a few times with a toothpick. This will allow the choux farci to absorb the flavour of the consommé.

Preheat your oven to 190°C (375°F). Trim the sinews from the lamb back straps, leaving a fine layer of fat to protect the meat during the roasting. Trim the 2 lamb racks of sinews. Slice the loin away from one of the racks, reserving the bones to make the consommé.

Put the consommé in a medium saucepan, heat to just below a simmer and keep at this low heat. Season the lamb loin. Heat a heavy-based frying pan until almost smoking, then add the oil and sear the lamb loin until lightly browned all over. Place in the consommé and poach at 75°C (160°F) for 12 minutes, turning regularly to ensure even cooking. Remove from the pan and rest for 6 minutes.

Poach the choux farci in the consommé for 6 minutes. Add the baby carrots and simmer for a further 5 minutes, then add the pieces of tongue and remaining vegetables and cook for a further 2–3 minutes until everything has warmed through.

Meanwhile, put the lamb back straps and the lamb rack into the preheated oven and roast for 3 minutes. Turn the meat over in the pan and roast for a further 3 minutes. Remove from the oven and leave to rest for 3 minutes.

To serve, remove the plastic wrap from the choux farci and cut each in half. Carve the poached lamb loin and the 2 roasted lamb straps into 8 slices each. Carve the lamb rack into 8 cutlets. Divide the meat between 8 warm serving bowls. Divide the vegetables evenly between the bowls and ladle over the hot consommé. Garnish with sprigs of chervil and tarragon and serve straight away.

Serves 8 as a main course

CREPINETTE OF *lamb*
with Herb Crushed Potatoes and Ratatouille Jus

LAMB CREPINETTES

1 x 8 bone lamb rack

salt and freshly ground pepper

80 ml (2¾ fl oz) non-scented cooking oil

80 g (2¾ oz) lambs' liver, skinned, trimmed and diced

100 g (3½ oz) lambs' kidneys, skinned, trimmed and diced

160 g (5½ oz) Lambs' Sweetbreads (page 270), diced

30 g (1 oz) unsalted butter

few drops lemon juice

200 g (7 oz) Chicken Mousse (page 269)

1 tablespoon flat-leaf parsley, very finely chopped

200 g (7 oz) crepinette, cut into 4 squares

RATATOUILLE JUS

100 ml (3½ fl oz) extra-virgin olive oil

1 small red capsicum, diced finely to a brunoise

1 small yellow capsicum, diced finely to a brunoise

1 small green zucchini, diced finely to a brunoise

1 small yellow zucchini, diced finely to a brunoise

1 baby eggplant, diced finely to a brunoise

200 ml (7 fl oz) Lamb Jus (page 261)

2 firm ripe tomatoes, finely chopped

TO SERVE

50 ml (1¾ fl oz) non-scented cooking oil

60 g (2 oz) unsalted butter

400 g (14 oz) Herb Crushed Potatoes (page 279)

200 ml (7 fl oz) Raw Tomato Coulis (page 268)

TO PREPARE THE LAMB CREPINETTES, trim away all the sinew from the lamb rack then remove every second bone and cut the rack into 4 double cutlets. If you are unconfident about doing this yourself, ask your butcher to do it for you.

Heat a heavy-based frying pan until smoking. Season the lamb cutlets with salt and pepper and sear for a few seconds on each side until lightly browned. Remove from the pan and set aside.

Add the oil to the hot pan, followed by the diced liver and kidney. Toss in the pan for a few seconds and season with salt and pepper – be careful not to overcook, you want both the liver and kidneys to stay juicy and pink. Drain on kitchen paper and leave to cool.

Season the sweetbreads well. Add a little extra oil to the pan then add the sweetbreads, smooth side down. Lower the heat a little and fry the sweetbreads without turning for 3 minutes until golden brown and caramelised. Add the butter and heat to a nut-brown foam. Lower the heat a little more and cook the sweetbreads for another minute in the foam, still without turning.

Add a few drops of lemon juice to the pan, turn the sweetbreads over and baste briefly in the foam. The flat side should be caramelised a lovely deep golden brown and they should still be creamy and soft in the centre. Remove from the pan and leave to cool.

When cool, put the liver, kidney and sweetbreads into a large mixing bowl. Add the chicken mousse and parsley and season with salt and pepper. Mix thoroughly then divide the mixture into 4 even portions and mould firmly around the double cutlets. Wrap securely in the crepinette and season.

TO PREPARE THE RATATOUILLE JUS, heat the olive oil in a large heavy-based saucepan. Sweat all the diced vegetables except for the tomatoes, until soft and tender, around 2 minutes. Add the lamb jus to the pan and heat through. Keep warm until ready to serve. Add the tomatoes just before serving.

TO SERVE, preheat your oven to 180°C (350°F). Heat a heavy-based ovenproof frying pan until hot. Add the oil then fry the crepinettes for 4 minutes until golden brown and caramelised all over. Add the butter and heat to a nut-brown foam. Baste the crepinettes and roast in the oven for 8 minutes. Turn and baste them every few minutes. Remove from the oven and place on a rack to rest for 4 minutes.

Warm the herb crushed potatoes and place a spoonful in the centre of 4 warm serving plates. Arrange a lamb crepinette on top of the potato and spoon the ratatouille jus around the plate. Drizzle with tomato coulis and serve immediately.

Serves 4 as a main course

Wagyu beef

DAVID BLACKMORE

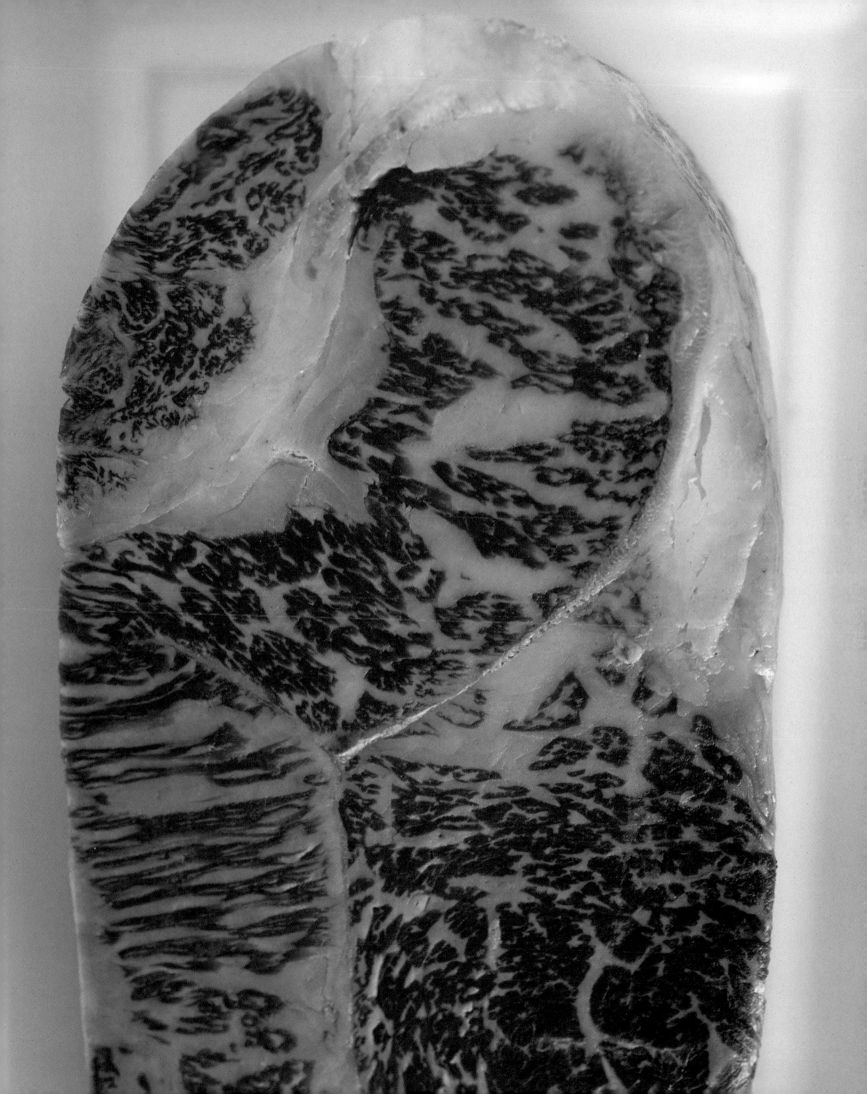

A CHEQUERED *heritage*

Wagyu (meaning 'Japanese cattle') cattle were introduced to rural Japan from the Asian mainland during the second century and used to pull ploughs in rural areas.

The Meiji Restoration (1868–1912) was a movement towards independent living characterised by a more powerful military, an educated public and a lifestyle relieved from the restrictions of feudal Japan. Prior to the Restoration consumption of milk and beef had been largely outlawed; the cow had been a valuable farm worker – certainly not a source of protein – for some 1200 years.

During the Meiji Restoration the Japanese government encouraged the import of foreign breeds of cattle in an attempt to broaden the local gene pool, but this was abandoned in 1910 as the cattle being produced didn't possess the qualities desired.

A strict line-breeding scheme commenced in 1959, using four Wagyu strains displaying superior traits. The result of the scheme was an increase in meat quality and an increase in milk production, as both milk and beef had crept into the Japanese diet at this time – largely a result of returning servicemen who had been fed meat on the battlefield to give them strength.

Only twice in the past century have live cattle and cattle genetics been exported from Japan. The first time was in 1976 when the University of Colorado received four Wagyu bulls for research purposes. These bulls were bred with American cattle, to make what is now known as American Purebred cattle. They are quite different from Japanese full-blood Wagyu cattle which can only be called so when both a Japanese heifer and bull are used in breeding.

One of Japan's premier breeders, Shogo Takeda, went to great lengths to export Wagyu cattle on another occasion, and in the 1990s 110 cattle were exported to the United States. This included the only live female Wagyu cow ever to be exported from Japan. For this indescretion Takeda was expelled from the Japanese Wagyu Association and has since been the target of much criticism from irate Japanese farmers keen to see their traditions remain in Japan.

Three strains of Wagyu are combined to create a breed hardy enough to withstand the harsh Australian conditions: Tajima, Shimane and Tottori. Tajima is the most famous, for providing the most dense marbling of all Wagyu beef. In Japan this beef is known as *matsuzaka* (female) or *kobe* (male) beef. The problem with farming Tajima in Australia is that they're small (bred for hilly terrains) and don't produce much milk (which makes a financial difference when you're feeding young). So the strain is mixed with the hardier Shimane cattle, which have larger stomachs and produce more milk.

WAGYU FARMING IN *Australia*

A charismatic businessman and fifth-generation farmer, David Blackmore was the first to import Wagyu cattle to Australia, in the 1990s. He imported the cattle through the United States as there was no established trade protocol between Australia and Japan at the time. Wagyu were a source of pride and there was intense pressure to retain the genes solely in Japan. 'It's their culture and heritage,' explains Blackmore. 'The Japanese still wish that the export had never happened.' Blackmore managed to obtain semen and embryos from the disputed export stock from Shogo Takeda and from those he introduced the first Wagyu genetics to Australia.

Blackmore now exports cattle to Japan, to meet the demand caused by increased beef consumption and a decrease in young Japanese entering the farming business. He also exports to the United States, Korea, Hong Kong and China.

Only Wagyu cattle that have a 100-per-cent pure bloodline from Japan are considered full-blooded Japanese cattle. And it is this beef that commands premium prices in Australia and around the world.

Blackmore is the pioneer of refining Wagyu genes in Australia. The Australian climate can be too harsh for the Wagyu's sensitive disposition, and Blackmore has undertaken extensive research in order to compensate for this. In addition to being kept in a covered and ventilated feedlot, Blackmore's cattle stand on sawdust, which is gentle on the hooves and thus reduces stress. 'Stress will give you bad beef,' claims Blackmore, 'so I want my herds to be as comfortable as possible'.

Blackmore won't be talked into divulging his secret recipe for the feed on which he rears his herds. He does, however, reveal one ingredient: beer. 'Stout is better as it contains more yeast,' he explains. 'It gets the bacteria in the stomach going.' While it might appear Blackmore tends the most spoilt herd of cattle in history, everything he does to ensure the animals' comfort is underpinned by a stern business objective, and Blackmore has made a profitable business providing what chefs, diners and farmers agree is the best eating beef on the market.

Some believe that Wagyu beef from southern parts of Australia is of a higher quality than that of beef from the north, mainly because the climate is gentler on the cattle with its cooler temperatures and lush pastures to nurture the delicate animals.

According to Blackmore, there are four pillars of quality Wagyu production: genetics, farm management, feed, and how the catttle are handled at the abattoir. Blackmore continues to benefit from ongoing support and advice from Mr Takeda, the Japanese farmer who first exported live Wagyu cattle to the United States.

' To compete in today's market, farmers have to let go of age-old traditions using antiquated ideas. They have to stop farming with their hearts and start farming with their heads. ' David Blackmore

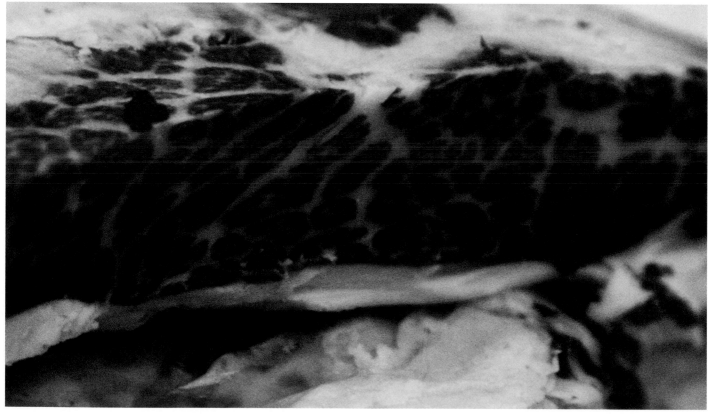

WAGYU *the product*

Wagyu beef is prized for its succulent texture and flavour, a result of the mono-unsaturated white fat throughout the muscle, which is commonly referred to as marbling. Marbling quality and density is what determines the grading of the beef, on an Australian scale that ranges from 1 to 9 (in Japan it is 1–12). In comparison, Angus beef generally marbles at a score of 2 or 3 on this scale.

Wagyu cattle are fed on special ration rather than grass, to ensure the milky white appearance of the intramuscular fat. The chlorophyll in grass can give beef fat a yellow tinge, and darken the colour of the meat. Given that sunlight also has a pigmenting effect on fat, Wagyu cattle spend most of their time sheltered from the sun. Wagyu cows feed on the by-products of beer brewing and popcorn production, as well as straw. The special diet promotes low levels of subcutaneous (outside) fat and higher intensity of intramuscular fat (marbling). Feeding the animals in such a way as to gain weight gradually – at a rate of about 800–900 grams per day rather than up to two kilos a day for some cattle breeds – increases their intramuscular fat levels. This bonus is twofold: the intramuscular fat is unsaturated, as opposed to the saturated fat found in subcutaneous fat; also, the fat is part of the final weight of the carcass, while subcutaneous fat is removed, so a higher price is paid.

The optimal age for processing an animal is thirty-four months. At this age it has matured sufficiently for the best qualities of the beef – the taste and the texture – to be enjoyed.

How this translates to your plate

Marbled fat starts to melt at 7°C, creating the tenderness that makes eating Wagyu beef such a pleasurable experience. The fat in Wagyu beef is a combination of two alpha lipoic acids (known as ALA): stearic acid and oleic acid. They are different from the cholesterol palmitic acid found in lean beef, and are recommended by the Heart Foundation as being good for heart health.

As the fat is marbled throughout the flesh, when it melts it does so back into the muscle itself. The flavour is flooded through the meat – fat being where any meat's flavour comes from. Wagyu experts place a piece of refrigerated meat on the back of their hand, to see how long it takes for the fat to start to leave a little melted slick on their skin. This tends to happen within ten seconds.

Marbling alone, however, is not an adequate way to judge the quality of a piece of meat. A farmer could cross an Angus cow with a full-blood Wagyu, slaughter the calf at twelve months and it could still be called Wagyu beef. What Blackmore's experience has shown is that maturing the animal slowly to more than thirty months develops the flavour in the beef. 'There's a real Japanese flavour,' says Blackmore. 'I've got them to Japanese standards.'

David Blackmore is certainly leading the way in the science of Australian Wagyu breeding, and even struggling to keep up with the demand.

CARPACCIO OF *girello*

with a Salad of White Asparagus Barigoule, Lemon and Parmesan

400 g (14 oz) Wagyu girello

fleur de sel

freshly ground white pepper

100 ml (3½ fl oz) Lemon Vinaigrette (page 266)

100 g (3½ oz) frisée, golden leaves from the centre

20 spears White Asparagus Barigoule (page 283)

2 tablespoons diced celeriac, blanched and refreshed

1 lemon, segments removed and sliced into small pieces

100 g (3½ oz) Parmigiano Reggiano shavings

few sprigs chervil

Girello is the Italian word for the eye-fillet of beef silverside.

Carve the girello into 4 even slices. Lay each piece between 2 layers of cling film and place on a heavy chopping board. Use a meat mallet or heavy rolling pin to bash the slices into large wafer-thin pieces. Trim to neat rounds and arrange on your serving plates. Season the girello with salt and pepper and drizzle with a little lemon vinaigrette.

Toss the frisée with more lemon vinaigrette and place a handful on top of each of the girello slices. Divide the asparagus spears evenly between each plate and scatter over the remaining ingredients. Serve straightaway.

Serves 4 as an entrée

CURED *tri tip*

with Parsnip, Truffle and Walnut Rémoulade

CURED TRI TIP

200 g (7 oz) Wagyu tri tip

300 g (10 oz) Curing Salt (page 11)

20 ml (²/₃ fl oz) non-scented cooking oil

PARSNIP, TRUFFLE AND WALNUT RÉMOULADE

2 small parsnips, peeled and sliced to a fine julienne

2 tablespoons flat-leaf parsley leaves, finely shredded to a chiffonade

1 tablespoon tarragon leaves, chopped

3 tablespoons mayonnaise

2 tablespoons truffle oil

½ fresh black winter truffle, finely diced to a brunoise

80 g (2³/₄ oz) shelled walnuts, lightly toasted

lemon juice

salt and freshly ground pepper

GARNISH

6 baby pears, halved and cored

50 g (1³/₄ oz) sugar

50 g (1³/₄ oz) unsalted butter

12 walnut halves, lightly toasted

1 small fresh black winter truffle, finely sliced

handful mixed salad leaves

100 ml (3¹/₂ fl oz) Truffle Vinaigrette (page 266)

The tri tip is a small area at the end of the rump. Together with the intercostal, rump cap and the short rib it is considered the most intensely marbled and prized cut of Wagyu beef.

TO CURE THE TRI TIP, cover it completely with curing salt, wrap it in cling film and weight it down with a 1 kg (2 lb 2 oz) weight. Refrigerate for 8 hours.

Thoroughly rinse off all the salt and pat dry. Heat a heavy-based frying pan until nearly smoking. Add the oil and quickly sear the tri tip until golden brown and caramelised all over. Remove from the pan and leave to cool. When cool, wrap in cling film again and refrigerate for up to 2 days until ready to serve.

TO MAKE THE PARSNIP, truffle and walnut rémoulade, put all the ingredients into a large mixing bowl and toss together gently.

TO PREPARE THE GARNISH, heat a small heavy-based frying pan over a very high heat until smoking. Toss the pears in the sugar then place them carefully in the smoking pan and caramelise evenly on both sides. Add the butter to the pan, lower the heat and toss the pears around until they are nicely glazed. The whole process should take no more than 2 minutes, so your pears remain firm and do not overcook and become mushy. The pears should end up glazed a dark shiny brown.

WHEN READY TO SERVE slice the chilled tri tip into thin medallions then bring to room temperature. Divide the slices between each serving plate and top with a handful of parsnip, truffle and walnut remoulade. Arrange 3 halves of caramelised pear on each plate and scatter over the toasted walnuts, truffle slices and salad leaves. Drizzle with a little truffle vinaigrette and serve immediately.

Serves 4 as an entrée

PICKLED WAGYU *tongue*
with Mushrooms à la Grecque and Shaved Foie Gras

PICKLED WAGYU TONGUE

1 fresh Wagyu beef tongue

2 litres (4¼ pints) red wine

1 litre (2¼ pints) ruby port

100 g (3½ oz) salt

200 ml (7 fl oz) cabernet vinegar

200 ml (7 fl oz) sherry vinegar

1 head garlic

1 medium carrot

1 medium onion

2 sticks celery

4 sprigs rosemary

6 sprigs thyme

8 juniper berries, crushed

12 peppercorns

2 bay leaves

TO SERVE

handful frisée, golden leaves from the centre

Mushrooms à la Grecque (page 29)

200 g (7 oz) cooked foie gras, shaved

fleur de sel

freshly ground pepper

You need to pickle the tongue a few days before you want to serve it. The flavours develop dramatically over this time and you end up with a wonderful harmony between the rich, earthy flavour of the tongue and the sweet acidity of the pickling liquor.

TO PICKLE THE TONGUE, rinse it under cold running water then pat dry and set aside in a deep dish. Put all the remaining pickling ingredients into a large saucepan and bring to the boil over a high heat. Lower the heat and simmer gently for 5 minutes then lower the heat and allow to cool slightly. While the pickling liquor is still fairly hot, pour it over the tongue so that it is almost completely submerged. Cool to room temperature then cover with cling film and refrigerate for 2 days.

TO POACH THE TONGUE, put it into a large heavy-based saucepan together with the pickling liquor and all the aromatics. Bring to a gentle simmer then cover with a piece of greaseproof paper cut to the size of the pan. Poach very gently for 3 hours until the tongue is very tender. Remove the tongue from the poaching liquor and leave to cool. When cool enough to handle, peel away the skin and return it to the poaching liquor. Refrigerate until cold – the liquor will set into a jelly around it.

TO SERVE, slice the chilled tongue lengthwise into 10 even slices. Warm them through very gently in a little of the pickling liquor. Toss the frisée leaves with a few tablespoons of the mushrooms à la grecque dressing. Arrange the tongue slices on each serving plate and scatter over the mushrooms, shavings of foie gras and some frisée leaves. Season lightly and serve.

Serves 10 as an entrée

ROAST WAGYU SIRLOIN *bordelaise*
with Braised Brisket and Sauce Bercy

MARINATED AND BRAISED BRISKET

800 g (1 lb 8 oz) Wagyu beef brisket

1 medium onion, roughly chopped

1 large carrot, roughly chopped

2 sticks celery, roughly chopped

½ leek, roughly chopped

½ head garlic, roughly crushed

1.5 litres (3 pints) cabernet sauvignon

4 sprigs thyme

2 sprigs rosemary

1 bay leaf

4 white peppercorns

30 ml (1 fl oz) non-scented cooking oil

60 g (2 oz) unsalted butter

750 ml (1⅓ pints) Brown Veal Stock (page 256)

salt and freshly ground pepper

ROAST WAGYU SIRLOIN

600 g (20 oz) Wagyu sirloin

salt and freshly ground pepper

30 ml (1 fl oz) non-scented cooking oil

TO SERVE

2 pieces fresh bone marrow

fleur de sel

freshly ground pepper

8 Caramelised Shallots (page 281)

500 ml (18 fl oz) Sauce Bercy (page 263)

Bordelaise-style dishes originate from the Bordeaux region in France, which is renowned for its gastronomy and fine wines. Dishes that are cooked ' à la bordelaise' typically use bone marrow, shallots and wine – usually red wine for red meat and white wine for white meat and fish. Bordelaise sauce is the classic French accompaniment for grilled or roasted beef.

This is a wonderful hearty dish, full of rich flavours, and it beautifully showcases the range of textures and depth of flavour of Wagyu beef. As well as using the ever-popular sirloin, this dish also uses brisket, a secondary forequarter cut taken from the belly behind the foreshanks. Brisket is well-marbled with fat and is, along with the oyster blade, one of the best cuts for long, slow braising. Although the preparation is simple, the brisket does need at least 24 hours marinating before braising, to allow the flavours to penetrate the meat.

TO PREPARE THE BRISKET, cut it into 4 even pieces. Put them into a large heavy-based saucepan with the chopped vegetables and garlic. In another saucepan bring the wine to the boil with the herbs and peppercorns. Simmer until reduced to 1 litre (2¼ pints) then pour the hot marinade over the beef and vegetables. Leave to cool to room temperature then cover and refrigerate for 24 hours.

To braise the brisket, preheat the oven to 110°C (225°F) and remove the pieces of meat and all the vegetables and herbs from the marinade. Heat a large frying pan and add half the oil and butter. Fry the vegetables until golden brown and caramelised then transfer them to a casserole dish with the wine, herbs and the veal stock. Bring to a gentle simmer then skim well and season with salt and pepper.

Season the brisket pieces with salt and pepper. Heat the remaining oil and butter in a heavy-based frying pan and sear the meat until lightly browned all over. Add to the casserole dish and cover with a piece of greaseproof paper, cut to the size of the dish. Cover with a lid then cook in the oven for 4 hours. Check every 30 minutes or so and turn the meat around in the braising liquid. At the end of the cooking time the meat should be very soft and meltingly tender. Reserve until ready to serve.

continued …

continued

TO PREPARE THE SIRLOIN, preheat your oven to 225°C (425°F) and bring the meat to room temperature and season with salt and pepper. Heat an ovenproof frying pan over a high heat. Add the oil to the pan and sear the meat until lightly browned all over. Transfer the pan to the oven and roast for 12 minutes, turning regularly. Remove from the oven and leave to rest in a warm place for 6 minutes.

TO SERVE, cut the bone marrow into small medallions and season with fleur de sel and pepper. Warm in the oven for around 2 minutes until soft and juicy. Warm the caramelised shallots and the sauce bercy.

Carve the sirloin into 4 thick slices. Arrange on warm serving plates with the brisket pieces. Garnish with the bone marrow and caramelised shallots and spoon over a generous amount of sauce. Serve immediately.

Serves 4 as a main course

BALLOTTINE DE *queue de boeuf*

STUFFING

2 Savoy cabbage leaves

100 g (3½ oz) piece of pancetta

100 g (3½ oz) unsalted butter

100 g (3½ oz) button mushrooms, quartered

6 Roast Shallots (page 281)

salt and freshly ground pepper

WAGYU TAIL BRAISE

1 Wagyu Wagyu tail, bone in

500 ml (18 fl oz) red wine

150 ml (5 fl oz) non-scented cooking oil

1 head garlic, cloves roughly crushed

1 onion, cut into 2 cm (¾ in) dice

1 carrot, cut into 2 cm (¾ in) dice

½ leek, cut into 2 cm (¾ in) dice

1 stick celery, cut into 2 cm (¾ in) dice

225 g (7½ oz) unsalted butter

50 ml (1¾ fl oz) red wine vinegar

salt and freshly ground pepper

500 ml (18 fl oz) Brown Chicken Stock (page 254)

500 ml (18 fl oz) Brown Veal Stock (page 256)

SAUCE

100 g (3½ oz) button mushrooms, sliced

1 bay leaf

4 sprigs thyme

1 clove garlic, roughly crushed

150 ml (5 fl oz) red wine reduction

salt and freshly ground pepper

continued …

This is a recipe I learned using oxtail while working in England with Raymond Blanc at Le Manoir aux Quat' Saisons. Although it is time consuming and rather a difficult dish to perfect, it is more than worth the effort. The finished dish is an amazing combination of deep, robust flavours and the melting texture is bliss.

When you choose the Wagyu tail, make sure there are no bones piercing the flesh and that it has an even covering of meat and fat.

TO PREPARE THE STUFFING, blanch the cabbage leaves in boiling water for 30 seconds then refresh in iced water. Pat dry and set aside.

Trim the pancetta to a long strip around 1 cm (½ in) thick and the same length as the Wagyu tail. Melt half the butter in a heavy-based frying pan and sauté the pancetta until lightly caramelised. Remove from the pan and drain on kitchen paper. Melt the remaining butter in the pan and sauté the mushrooms until golden brown. Remove from the pan and drain on kitchen paper. Prepare the roast shallots (page 281).

TO BONE THE WAGYU TAIL, use a small sharp boning knife and make an incision along the underside, cutting from end to end. Start slicing the flesh away from the bone, along its length, keeping it in one piece attached to the skin. When you have eased half of it away, start working from the other side until you meet in the middle. Slice the meat away completely, being very careful not to pierce the skin. You should end up with a rectangular piece of skin, with meat attached. Reserve this and chop the bone into small pieces.

TO PREPARE THE WAGYU TAIL braise, put the red wine into a heavy-based saucepan and simmer until reduced by a third. Set aside 150 ml (5 fl oz) to finish the sauce later.

Heat a heavy-based frying pan over a high heat. Add 50 ml (1¾ fl oz) of the oil then the garlic and vegetables. Add 50 g (1¾ oz) of the butter and heat to a nut-brown foam. Cook for 6–8 minutes until the vegetables have caramelised a deep golden-brown. Tip into a colander to drain off any excess fat and reserve.

Heat a baking tray over a high heat. Add another 50 ml (1¾ fl oz) of the oil and sear the Wagyu tail bones. When they colour, add 75 g (2⅔ oz) of the butter and heat to a nut-brown foam. Lower the heat slightly and sauté the bones until they caramelise a deep golden-brown. Take care not to burn the butter. Tip the bones into a colander to drain off any excess fat and reserve.

Add 200 ml (7 fl oz) of the red wine reduction to the pan with the red wine vinegar and deglaze, making sure you scrape up all the sediment from the bottom. Simmer until reduced by half. Tip into a large casserole dish and add the reserved vegetables and half the bones. Set aside.

continued …

BALLOTTINE DE *queue de boeuf*

continued

TO STUFF THE WAGYU TAIL, place it skin side down on your work surface. Open it out flat and season with salt and pepper. Arrange the 2 blanched cabbage leaves on top of the meat and season again. Lay the pancetta down the middle of the Wagyu tail. Arrange a row of shallots down one side and a row of mushrooms down the other. Bring the cabbage leaves up and around the stuffing to form a big fat cigar, then bring the sides of the Wagyu tail up and secure firmly with string. The Wagyu tail needs to be tied firmly and securely along its length at 1 cm (½ in) intervals.

To braise the Wagyu tail, preheat your oven to 110°C (225°F). Heat the remaining 50 ml (1¾ fl oz) of the oil in a baking tray over a high heat. Season the stuffed Wagyu tail well and sear it all over in the baking tray until lightly coloured. Add the remaining 100 g (3½ oz) butter to the tray and heat to a nut-brown foam. Lower the heat slightly and sauté the Wagyu tail in the foam until caramelised a deep golden-brown.

Transfer the Wagyu tail to the large casserole dish with the deglazing liquor, vegetables and bones, and add the 2 stocks. Bring to a gentle simmer, skimming to remove any fat or scum that rises to the surface. Cover with a piece of greaseproof paper cut to the size of the dish. Cover with a tight-fitting lid and braise in the oven for 4–4½ hours. When cooked, the Wagyu tail should be very soft to the touch.

Remove the casserole from the oven and drain the Wagyu tail, reserving the braising liquor. When cool enough to handle, untie the string and wrap the Wagyu tail tightly in cling film to form a neat cylinder. When cold, transfer to the refrigerator until set firm.

To make the sauce, pass the reserved braising liquid through a chinois or fine sieve. Put into a saucepan and simmer rapidly until reduced to a sauce consistency. Add the reserved bones with the mushrooms, herbs and garlic and simmer gently for 3 minutes. Remove from the heat and infuse for 15–20 minutes.

Add the reserved 150 ml (5 fl oz) of red wine reduction and season lightly. Pass through a chinois or fine sieve and then a muslin cloth. Keep warm until required.

WHEN READY TO SERVE, cut the Wagyu tail into 4 thick medallions, still wrapped in the cling film. Warm through gently in a little of the sauce. Remove the cling film and arrange the medallions on warmed serving plates. Serve with the suggested garnishes.

Serves 4

Blood orange

JOE AND MARIA BARILA

Oranges have a rich and colourful past. Believed to have originated in China and South-East Asia more than twenty million years ago, the orange can be traced through history by examining the development of its name. The word 'orange' is derived from the Dravidian family of languages spoken in India, which was then translated into Sanskrit.

Arabs first brought oranges to Spain, and from there they spread throughout Europe. The first oranges are said to have been more bitter than the ones we know today as *Citrus sinensis* – close relatives of the Seville orange.

Cultivation of the orange is thought to have commenced before 4000 BC. Citrus fruits were in the Mediterranean region well before Christian times and by the fall of the Roman Empire oranges were thriving along what is now known as the Italian (or Apennine) Peninsula, with its warm climate and sandy soil.

Portuguese, Spanish, Arab and Dutch sailors all planted citrus trees along their trade routes once the health benefits of the orange were established, in an attempt to fend off scurvy. By law, each Spanish sailor travelling to the Americas had to carry with him 100 citrus seeds and by 1565 oranges were growing in Florida. Such conscientious transportation enabled oranges and other types of citrus fruits to flourish the world over. They now grow in all soils, favouring sandy, well-drained conditions. Orange trees are evergreen, which helps to protect the fruit from direct sunlight as it grows.

The blood orange, also known as a pigmented or Maltese orange, is distinguishable by its darker skin, but more notably its dark red flesh colour, which comes from the pigment anthocyanin, common in other red fruits and flowers but uncommon in citrus. It is native to Italy and has long been a European delicacy but is newer to Australian shores.

ARANCE *sanguine*

Australia's Riverina district has a climate perfect for citrus fruits. The long, hot summers, and porous, sandy soil provide ideal conditions for growing blood oranges. The Mildura region, in particular, is known for its fruit production, including navel and Valencia oranges, mandarins and wine and dried fruit grapes.

This agricultural centre was a popular post-war destination for Italian farming families wanting to make their fortune, and it was here that Joe Barila arrived as a seven-year-old. Money was scarce and Joe was put to work almost immediately. 'I didn't get the chance for a proper schooling, I went straight to work with fruit and vegetables, as that's what my father did,' Joe recalls. Today, Joe still keeps a

vegetable patch a few kilometres from his blood orange orchard.

Joe's wife Maria is also of Italian descent. Her parents arrived in Australia in the early-1950s and she was born a few years later. 'My father worked for years and finally saved enough to buy his own fruit block,' tells Maria. Joe and Maria both have vivid childhood memories of their parents talking fondly of their homeland, and of the beauty and taste of 'arance sanguine' – the blood orange. Joe and Maria married in 1975 and bought the farm where they now live – in Gol Gol, eight kilometres from Mildura. They have been growing blood oranges since 1989 and the trees now occupy two hectares of the 15-hectare property.

THE BLOOD ORANGE *orchard*

The skin of a blood orange can vary in colour from that of a navel orange to a bright crimson. The colour deepens as the fruit matures, and sunlight will bleach the colour from the skin of a mature blood orange. This happens especially in spring as picking time approaches and the trees are laden with fruit.

The price fetched by a blood orange is influenced by the colour of its flesh. At the farmer's orchard, a good quality blood orange with a rich, dark flesh will sell for twice that of another strain of orange, so getting the colour right is a priority for growers.

The Barilas grow a Sicilian strain, which has a distinct raspberry flavour, and when very ripe the flesh is almost black. The colour of the flesh begins to develop with a frost: cold weather brings out the colour in the blood orange and is welcomed – in moderation. Joe has noticed changes in the weather patterns around his property since he was a child. 'We used to have two or three frosts and then a good rain – ideal for growing blood oranges. Now we have more frosts,' he says. Too many frosts can be detrimental to the development of the fruit.

Picking begins in August and continues until October. From the two hectares devoted to blood oranges, the Barilas harvest between 25 and 30 tons of fruit each year. They hire four or five pickers every season, depending on ability. The preferred pickers are the nomads, who follow the harvesting seasons around Australia. Pickers are paid by the bin-load, each bin holding roughly half a ton.

Picking needs to be carried out under specific conditions. The day needs to have warmed, and dried any dew on the skins of the citrus. If picked when wet, the blood orange will show up handprints a few days later. The marks are caused by naturally occurring oils on the pickers' skin, and because of this curiosity picking starts as late as 11 a.m. on especially cold days.

The fruit is washed and packed on-site, then shipped, mostly to restaurants in Sydney and Melbourne, some to Brisbane. A small percentage is shipped abroad: America is the primary overseas customer for the Barilas' blood oranges, but it is still a small market.

The life cycle of the blood orange begins again in the spring. Buds bloom and then blossom. These blossoms will blow away in the spring breeze to reveal a young blood orange fruit.

SALAD OF RED PAPAYA, YOUNG COCONUT AND *blood orange*

with a Mandarin Granita

MANDARIN GRANITA

500 ml (18 fl oz) freshly squeezed
mandarin juice

80 ml (2¾ fl oz) white wine

150 ml (5 fl oz) Stock Syrup (page 258)

LEMON VERBENA SYRUP

100 ml (3½ fl oz) water

20 ml (⅔ fl oz) sweet white wine

100 g (3½ oz) sugar

2–3 lemon verbena stalks

few drops lime juice

SALAD

1 ripe red papaya

4 blood oranges

4 mandarins

1 young coconut

few leaves of lemon verbena,
cut to a fine chiffonnade

A lively fresh salad with a varying array of flavours and textures.

I love fresh, young coconuts – their delicate flavour and soft gelatinous texture is simply gorgeous, but they must be young and ripe.

The papaya used in this recipe is the red variety and preferred because of its unique floral aroma and sweet flavour, however it must be very ripe and aromatic.

The trick to recipes such as this is using fruit at its absolute peak and full ripeness – one cannot compromise! Mangoes, tangerines, lemonade fruit, passionfruit, melons and berries are just a few great additions or substitutions for this recipe.

TO PREPARE THE MANDARIN GRANITA, mix the mandarin juice with the wine and stock syrup. Stir well and adjust the sweetness to your liking. Pour into a square shallow tray and freeze for about 4 hours. Every 30 minutes scrape the surface to achieve a granular texture.

TO MAKE THE LEMON VERBENA SYRUP, put the water, wine and sugar into a heavy-based saucepan and heat slowly until the sugar has dissolved, stirring from time to time. Once the sugar has completely dissolved, bring the syrup to the boil and boil for 2 minutes. Remove from the heat and add the lemon verbena stalks. Leave to infuse for 20 minutes. Refrigerate and when cold add a squeeze of lime juice.

TO MAKE THE SALAD, peel the papaya, cut in half lengthwise and remove the seeds. Slice into neat wedges and place into a chilled mixing bowl. Peel the oranges and mandarins and use a very sharp knife to remove the pith then cut out the segments and add to the chilled bowl. Crack open the coconut and discard the juice. Use a spoon to scoop out the soft flesh and slice into neat julienne. Add to the bowl with the lemon verbena and chilled syrup and toss everything together gently.

TO SERVE, divide the salad and syrup between 6 chilled dessert bowls. Top with a scoop of granita and serve immediately.

Serves 6

BLOOD ORANGES MACERATED IN *Sauternes*

with Sauternes Jelly and Vietnamese Mint Sorbet

MACERATED BLOOD ORANGES

6 blood oranges

200 ml (7 fl oz) Sauternes

SAUTERNES JELLY

200 ml (7 fl oz) sauternes

100 ml (3½ fl oz) Stock Syrup (page 258)

60 ml (2 fl oz) water

few drops lemon juice

3 x 5 g (⅛ oz) gelatine leaves, softened in cold water

VIETNAMESE MINT SORBET

1 cup spearmint leaves

2 cups Vietnamese mint leaves

250 ml (8¾ fl oz) Stock Syrup (page 258)

200 ml (7 fl oz) water

TO MACERATE THE ORANGES, peel them and use a very sharp knife to remove the pith. Cut out the segments and put them in a bowl. Squeeze the juice from the remaining pieces of orange into the bowl. Add the Sauternes and mix well. Cover tightly with cling film and refrigerate for at least 3 hours.

TO MAKE THE JELLY, mix the Sauternes, syrup and water together and add a squeeze of lemon juice. Squeeze the excess water from the gelatine and put it in a small saucepan with a few spoonfuls of the wine mixture. Heat gently until the gelatine has dissolved then tip it into the rest of the wine mixture and stir well. Strain through a chinois or fine sieve into a shallow straight-sided container. Cover and refrigerate for 3 hours or until set.

TO MAKE THE SORBET, blanch the mint leaves in rapidly boiling water for 40 seconds. Refresh in iced water then drain well and squeeze out any excess water. Put the leaves into a blender with the syrup and water and blitz for 3 minutes until you have a very smooth, bright green purée. Strain through a chinois or fine sieve then transfer to an ice cream machine and churn according to the manufacturer's instructions.

TO SERVE, divide the macerated oranges between 6 chilled serving bowls and spoon over a generous amount of Sauternes. Dip the jelly container briefly in hot water to loosen. Cut into 1 cm (½ in) cubes and scatter among the orange segments. Use a dessertspoon to form small quenelles of sorbet and place one in the centre of each bowl. Serve immediately.

Serves 6

TERRINE AND SORBET OF *blood orange*

TERRINE

6 blood oranges

200 ml (7 fl oz) Stock Syrup (page 258)

100 ml (3½ fl oz) water

30 ml (1 fl oz) white wine

5 x 5 g (⅛ oz) gelatine leaves, softened in cold water

SORBET

400 ml (14 fl oz) freshly squeezed blood orange juice

200 ml (7 fl oz) Stock Syrup (page 258)

Orange segments, jelly and sorbet: three different textures from one amazing fruit.

At Bécasse we use a small hors d'oeuvres terrine mould to make the terrine, which is about 5 cm (2 in) high, 5.5 cm (2¼ in) wide and roughly 30 cm (12 in) long. Try to buy one with removable sides.

TO PREPARE THE TERRINE, peel the oranges and use a very sharp knife to remove the pith. Cut out the segments and lay them on a clean cloth to drain. Squeeze all the juice from the remaining orange pieces into a bowl. It should yield about 300 ml (10 fl oz) of juice, but make up any shortfall with an extra blood orange. Stir the syrup, water and wine into the juice.

Squeeze the excess water from the gelatine and put it in a small saucepan with a few spoonfuls of the orange mixture. Heat gently until the gelatine has dissolved then tip it into the rest of the orange mixture and stir well.

Double-line the terrine mould with cling film, leaving a generous overhang. Pour in a thin layer of jelly, around 1 cm (½ in) then top with a layer of orange segments. Refrigerate until set. Continue building layers of jelly and fruit until the mould is full. Reserve a few segments to garnish. Fold the cling film over the top and set in the refrigerator for at least 3 hours. Use a knife dipped in hot water to slice the terrine into 8 portions and keep chilled until ready to serve.

TO MAKE THE SORBET, mix the orange juice and syrup together then pour into an ice cream machine and churn according to the manufacturer's instructions.

TO SERVE, place a portion of terrine on chilled serving plates and arrange a couple of orange segments next to it. Scoop a large quenelle of sorbet and place one on top of the fruit. Serve straightaway.

Serves 8

CARAMELISED *blood oranges*
with White Chocolate Parfait

CARAMELISED BLOOD ORANGES

6 blood oranges

300 g (10 oz) sugar

WHITE CHOCOLATE PARFAIT

6 egg yolks

75 g (2²/₃ oz) sugar

100 g (3¹/₂ oz) white chocolate

375 ml (13 fl oz) thickened cream

TO SERVE

150 g (5 oz) white chocolate

Pouring hot caramel onto the oranges infuses them and releases all the flavour of the orange. As the caramel breaks down and mixes with the natural orange juices it thickens to a luscious citrus-caramel.

This is the perfect parfait: soft and rich without being too sweet and not icy or granular as some parfaits can be.

TO MAKE THE CARAMELISED ORANGES, peel them and use a very sharp knife to remove all the pith. Slice into thin rounds and lay them out on a stainless steel tray.

Put the sugar in a heavy-based saucepan and heat gently until it dissolves. Increase the heat and simmer until it caramelises a dark golden brown. Drizzle the hot caramel over the oranges then cover with cling film and refrigerate overnight.

TO MAKE THE PARFAIT, put the egg yolks and sugar into a bowl set over a saucepan of gently simmering water. Whisk briskly for about 10 minutes until the mixture bulks up and thickens to a pale, foamy sabayon. Remove from the heat and keep warm

Melt the chocolate over the same pan of simmering water and fold into the warm sabayon. Continue whisking until the sabayon is cool.

Whisk the cream to soft peaks and fold it gently into the sabayon. Tip into a plastic container and freeze until nearly set. Remove from the freezer and tip the parfait out onto a large piece of cling film. Roll to a neat log shape and wrap tightly in the cling film. Place back in the freezer to firm.

TO SERVE, melt the chocolate in a bowl set over a saucepan of gently simmering water. Pour over the back of a chilled stainless steel tray or a marble work surface and spread quickly to a thin layer. Allow to set then use a spatula to scrape into long curls.

Arrange the blood oranges on each plate in an overlapping circle. Use a knife dipped in hot water to cut the parfait into 8 slices and place one on each plate. Garnish with chocolate curls and a drizzle of caramel and serve straightaway.

Serves 8

CARAMELISED *blood orange tart*

with Crème Fraîche

BLOOD ORANGE FILLING

9 eggs

300 g (10 oz) sugar

zest of 3 blood oranges

200 ml (7 fl oz) blood orange juice

300 ml (10 fl oz) thickened cream

SWEET PASTRY

250 g (9 oz) plain flour

100 g (3½ oz) cold butter, diced

100 g (3½ oz) icing sugar, sifted

small pinch of salt

2 eggs, at room temperature

2 egg yolks, at room temperature

TO SERVE

200 ml (7 fl oz) crème fraîche

100 ml (3½ fl oz) thickened cream

1 teaspoon icing sugar

150 g (5 oz) castor sugar for caramelising

2 blood oranges, segments removed

This is my version of the classic caramelised lemon tart. It is not as sharp, but the blood orange has a delectable citrus tang and is very pretty.

Make the blood orange custard a day ahead to allow plenty of time for the flavours to develop.

TO MAKE THE BLOOD ORANGE FILLING, whisk the eggs and sugar together. Zest the oranges over the bowl to capture the aromatic oils with the zest. Add the juice and cream and whisk together. Refrigerate overnight to infuse.

TO MAKE THE SWEET PASTRY, sift the flour into a mound on your work surface and make a well in the middle. Add the butter and rub it in with your fingers until the consistency of fine breadcrumbs. Add the icing sugar and salt and mix well. Add the eggs and mix in quickly. Draw the flour into the mixture to form a rough ball. Knead briefly with the heel of your hand until smooth then shape into a ball, wrap in cling film and refrigerate for a minimum of 1 hour before rolling out.

Preheat your oven to 180°C (350°F). Butter a tart tin, around 4 cm (1½ in) deep and 24 cm (9½ in) in diameter, and place it on a baking tray. On a lightly floured work surface, roll the pastry out to 2 mm (⅛ in) thick and drape it over the tin. Ease the pastry into the side of the tin and pinch the overhang with your fingertips so that it stands up in a border above the tin. Refrigerate for 20 minutes.

Remove the tart from the refrigerator and line with greaseproof paper and baking beans. Bake for 10–15 minutes until golden. Turn the tin around a few times in the oven to ensure it cooks evenly. Remove the paper and beans and brush the pastry with the beaten egg yolks. Bake for another 2 minutes then remove from the oven and leave to cool a little.

TO BAKE THE TART, turn the oven down to 145°C (275°F). Strain the filling through a chinois or fine sieve into the tart shell. Bake for 45 minutes, or until the custard has just set. Remove from the oven and rest at room temperature for an hour or so to set before serving.

TO SERVE, put the two creams and the icing sugar in a mixing bowl and whip to firm peaks. Slice the tart into 12 portions. Dust the surface with sugar and caramelise with a cook's blowtorch.

Place a slice on each plate and serve with a quenelle of cream and a few segments of blood orange.

Serves 12

Basics

AND ACCOMPANIMENTS

Stocks

MUSHROOM STOCK

120 ml (4 fl oz) non-scented cooking oil

3 medium onions, finely sliced

2 kg (4 lb 4 oz) button mushrooms, finely sliced

salt and freshly ground pepper

250 g (9 oz) unsalted butter

300 ml (10½ fl oz) Madeira

1 head garlic, roughly crushed

3 sprigs thyme

2 bay leaves

2 litres (4½ pints) water

Heat 2 large heavy-based roasting trays over a medium heat. Divide the oil between the trays then add the onions and fry for 5 minutes until they begin to colour and soften.

Add the mushrooms to the trays and season well. Divide the butter between the 2 trays and heat to a nut-brown foam. Continue to cook over a medium heat until deep brown and caramelised, then drain off excess butter. Deglaze the trays with Madeira, being sure to scrape up all the sticky sediment from the bottoms of the trays, then add the garlic and herbs and stir well.

Cover with the water and bring to the boil. Tip all the onions and mushrooms with the water into a large casserole dish and bring back to the boil. Lower the heat and simmer gently, uncovered, for 40 minutes. Remove from the heat and leave to stand for 15 minutes. When slightly cooled, cover the pot tightly with cling film and leave to infuse for 2 hours, then pass through a chinois or fine sieve. Store in the refrigerator for 2 days or up to a month in the freezer.

Makes 2.5 litres (5 pints)

WHITE CHICKEN STOCK

3 kg (6 lb 6 oz) chicken carcasses

1 head garlic, cut in half crosswise

8 sprigs thyme

Roughly chop the chicken carcasses into small pieces. Put in a stockpot and add just enough water to cover. Bring to the boil slowly, skimming frequently. Add the garlic and the thyme, lower the heat and simmer gently for 2 hours.

Leave to cool slightly then pour through a chinois or fine sieve. Leave the stock to settle for around 2 hours then skim thoroughly and refrigerate. The stock will keep in the refrigerator for 2 days or up to a month in the freezer.

Makes 2.5 litres (5 pints)

BROWN CHICKEN STOCK

2 kg (4 lb 4 oz) meaty chicken wings

150 ml (5 fl oz) non-scented cooking oil

salt and freshly ground pepper

250 g (9 oz) unsalted butter, diced

500 g (18 oz) shallots, finely sliced

500 g (18 oz) button mushrooms, finely sliced

1 head garlic, cut in half crosswise

8 sprigs thyme

4 litres (8¼ pints) chilled White Chicken Stock (above)

It is important to add the white chicken stock straight from the fridge. As it heats, the proteins from the chicken will act as a raft, lifting any impurities to the surface. These need to be skimmed away, which results in a lovely clear stock.

Preheat your oven to 190°C (375°F). Roughly chop the chicken wings into small pieces. Heat a large baking tray in the oven then add the oil and chopped chicken pieces and season with salt and freshly ground pepper. Spread the bones out to ensure they colour evenly. Roast in the oven for 10–15 minutes, stirring regularly to prevent them sticking and burning.

When the bones are golden-brown, scatter over the diced butter and return to the oven. Once the butter heats to a nut-brown foam allow to caramelise for a further 5 minutes. Add the shallots, mushroom, garlic and thyme and cook for another 10 minutes until everything is caramelised a deep brown. Tip the contents into a colander to drain off the fat.

Deglaze the sticky sediment in the baking tray with a little water. Tip into a large stockpot with the roasted bones and vegetables then add the cold chicken stock. Bring to a boil, skimming to remove any fat or sediment that rises to the surface. Lower the heat and simmer gently for about 30 minutes, skimming frequently. Leave to cool slightly then pour through a chinois or fine sieve. Leave the stock to settle for around 2 hours then skim thoroughly and refrigerate. The stock will keep in the refrigerator for 2 days or up to a month in the freezer.

Makes around 3 litres (6½ pints)

BROWN PORK STOCK

8 kg (17 lb) meaty pork bones, chopped small

2 heads garlic, roughly crushed

12 sprigs thyme

3 onions, chopped

2 carrots, chopped

2 sticks celery, chopped

½ leek, chopped

150 ml (5 fl oz) non-scented cooking oil

80 g (2¾ oz) unsalted butter

Make sure you choose pork bones with a good covering of meat. This will result in a stock with a good colour and depth of flavour.

Put half the pork bones into a stockpot and cover with cold water. Bring to the boil and skim to remove all the impurities. Add 1 head of garlic, half the thyme and 1 of the chopped onions. Then add the carrots, celery and leek. Simmer for 2 hours, skimming from time to time. Drain the stock through a colander, discarding the bones and aromatics. Set this 'white' pork stock aside to cool.

Preheat your oven to 190°C (375°F). Heat a large roasting tray in the oven then add half the oil and remaining pork bones. Spread the bones out to ensure they colour evenly. Roast in the oven for about 30 minutes, stirring regularly to prevent them sticking and burning.

Meanwhile, heat the remaining oil in a stockpot then add the rest of the garlic and onions. Fry until the onions have begun to colour then add the butter and heat to a nut-brown foam. Reduce the heat slightly and add the rest of the thyme. Continue to cook until the onions have caramelised to a deep golden-brown.

Remove the roasted bones from the oven, tip them into a colander to drain off the fat then add them to the stockpot with the caramelised onions. Add the cold 'white' pork stock. Bring to a simmer, skimming to remove any fat or sediment that rises to the surface. Simmer for 1 hour, skimming frequently. Leave to cool slightly then pour through a chinois or fine sieve. Leave the stock to settle for around 2 hours then skim thoroughly and refrigerate. The stock will keep in the refrigerator for 2 days or up to a month in the freezer.

Makes 2 litres (4¼ pints)

BROWN LAMB STOCK

8 kg (17 lb) meaty lamb bones, chopped small

1 head garlic, cut in half crosswise

4 sprigs thyme

50 ml (1¾ fl oz) non-scented cooking oil

2 onions, chopped

2 large carrots, roughly chopped

3 sticks celery, roughly chopped

200 ml (7 fl oz) white wine

2 sprigs rosemary

Put half the lamb bones into a stockpot and cover with cold water. Bring to the boil and skim to remove all the impurities. Add half the garlic and 2 sprigs thyme. Simmer for 2 hours, skimming from time to time. Drain the stock through a colander, discarding the bones and aromatics. Set this 'white' lamb stock aside to cool.

Preheat your oven to 220°C (425°F). Heat a large baking tray in the oven then add the oil and remaining lamb bones. Spread the bones out to ensure they colour evenly. Roast in the oven for about 30 minutes, stirring regularly to prevent them sticking and burning. Add the chopped vegetables and the rest of the garlic. Roast for another 20 minutes until everything is caramelised a deep brown.

Tip the contents into a colander to drain off the fat then return to the baking tray and deglaze the pan with the white wine.

Tip into a stockpot and add the cold 'white' lamb stock. Bring to a simmer, skimming to remove any fat or sediment that rises to the surface. Add the remaining thyme and the rosemary and simmer for 2 hours, skimming frequently. Leave to cool slightly then pour through a chinois or fine sieve. Leave the stock to settle for around 2 hours then skim thoroughly and refrigerate. The stock will keep in the refrigerator for 2 days or up to a month in the freezer.

Makes 2 litres (4¼ pints)

BROWN VEAL STOCK

few tablespoons non-scented cooking oil
5 kg (11 lb) veal neck bones, chopped small
1 onion, quartered
1 carrot, halved lengthwise
¼ head celery, cut into large pieces
½ leek, halved lengthwise
½ head garlic, cut in half crosswise
1 bay leaf
4 white peppercorns
¼ cup thyme
100 g (3½ oz) fresh tomato paste
100 ml (3½ fl oz) red wine
½ calf's foot, split lengthwise

I use neck bones for this recipe as they have a good covering of meat and a great flavour. Ask your butcher to chop the bones into small pieces for you.

Preheat your oven to 220°C (425°F). Heat 2 large roasting trays in the oven until very hot then add a little oil to each. Divide the bones between the trays, spreading them out to ensure they colour evenly. Roast in the oven for about 30 minutes, stirring regularly to prevent them sticking and burning – even the slightest burn will taint the flavour of the stock. Remove the roasted bones from the oven and tip them into a colander to drain off the fat.

Spread the onions out on one baking tray and the carrots on the other. Return to the oven and roast until very dark. Divide the celery, leek, garlic, bay leaf and peppercorns between the trays and return to the oven. When all the vegetables are caramelised to a dark brown remove from the oven.

Add the tomato paste to both pans and return to the oven for a few moments then deglaze the pans with the red wine.

Put half the roasted bones into a large stockpot. Place the calf's foot on top followed by all the roasted vegetables and their tomato-flavoured pan juices. Cover with the remaining bones. It is important that the vegetables be kept submerged in the stock so they impart the maximum flavour. Fill the pot with enough cold water to cover the bones.

Bring to the boil, skimming to remove any fat or sediment that rises to the surface. Lower the heat and simmer gently for 8 hours, skimming frequently. Leave to cool slightly then pour through a chinois or fine sieve. Return the stock to the pan and simmer until reduced by around a third. Leave the stock to settle for around 2 hours then skim thoroughly and refrigerate. The stock will keep in the refrigerator for 4 days or up to a month in the freezer.

Makes 3 litres (6½ pints)

GAME STOCK

125 ml (4 fl oz) non-scented cooking oil
3 kg (6 lb 6 oz) game bones and carcasses, chopped small (use a selection of pigeon, pheasant, duck, partridge and guinea fowl)
8 shallots, finely sliced
250 g (9 oz) button mushrooms, finely sliced
½ head garlic, cut in half crosswise
6 sprigs thyme
2 bay leaves
200 g (7 oz) unsalted butter, diced
500 ml (18 fl oz) white wine
600 ml (20 fl oz) Madeira
3 litres (6½ pints) White Chicken Stock (page 254), chilled
1 litre (2¼ pints) Brown Veal Stock (above), chilled

Preheat your oven to 180°C (350°F). Heat 2 large roasting trays on the stove top until very hot then add some oil to each. Divide the bones between the trays and sear them quickly so they colour evenly. Scatter over the shallots and mushrooms then add the garlic, thyme and bay leaves. Transfer to the oven and roast for around 25 minutes until they are golden-brown and caramelised.

When the bones are golden-brown, scatter over the diced butter and return to the oven. Once the butter heats to a nut-brown foam cook for a further 20 minutes until everything is caramelised a deep brown. Tip the contents into a colander to drain off the fat. (Reserve this fat for vinaigrettes.)

Deglaze the sticky sediment in the trays with the white wine and reduce by half. Add the Madeira and bring to the boil.

Tip the juices from both baking trays into a large stockpot then add the roasted bones and the chilled stocks. Bring to a simmer slowly, skimming to remove any fat or sediment that rises to the surface. Lower the heat and simmer gently for 2 hours, skimming frequently. Leave to cool slightly then pour through a colander and then through a chinois or fine sieve lined with muslin. Leave the stock to settle for around 2 hours then skim thoroughly and refrigerate. The stock will keep in the refrigerator for 2 days or up to a month in the freezer.

Makes 2 litres (4¼ pints)

CLAM STOCK

30 ml (1 fl oz) non-scented cooking oil
6 shallots, finely sliced
3 cloves garlic, finely sliced
30 g (1 oz) fresh ginger, finely sliced
1 stalk lemongrass, finely sliced
1 teaspoon coriander seeds, crushed
1 kaffir lime leaf
300 ml (10 fl oz) white wine
1 kg (2 lb 2 oz) fresh clams
1 litre (2¼ pints) water
½ cup coriander stalks
pinch salt
freshly ground white pepper
few drops lemon juice

Heat a heavy-based saucepan over a medium-high heat. Add the oil then the shallots, garlic, ginger, lemongrass, coriander seeds and lime leaf. Sweat gently for 5 minutes until shallts are soft but not coloured. Add the white wine and simmer until reduced by two-thirds.

Meanwhile, put the clams into a double layer of plastic bags and seal. Smash with a rolling pin until thoroughly crushed, being careful not to let any juices escape. Add the smashed clams to the saucepan and add the water. Bring to the boil, then lower the heat and simmer gently for 5 minutes.

Remove the pan from the heat and add the coriander stalks, salt and pepper and lemon juice. Cover the pan tightly with cling film and leave to stand for 15 minutes to infuse. Pass through a chinois or fine sieve lined with muslin. Refrigerate and use within 2 days.

Makes 1 litre (2¼ pints)

MUSHROOM AND MADEIRA CONSOMMÉ

Consommés are clarified by cooking them very gently with a 'raft'. This is usually a thick paste made from minced meat, vegetables and egg whites. As the broth heats, the egg whites coagulate and the raft rises through the liquid to the surface, trapping any impurities on the way. It is important not to let the consommé boil or the raft will break up and the consommé will become cloudy.

200 g (7 oz) lean chicken breast, roughly chopped
1 carrot, chopped
1 onion, chopped
1 stick celery, chopped
1 clove garlic, roughly chopped
2 sprigs thyme
150 g (5 oz) egg whites (around 8)
2½ litres (5 pints) Mushroom Stock (page 254), cold
salt and freshly ground pepper
splash Madeira

To make the raft, put the chicken into a food processor and blitz until smooth. Tip into a mixing bowl. Put the vegetables, garlic and thyme in the processor and blitz to a rough purée then add to the bowl with the chicken. Add the egg whites and mix together well.

Put the cold stock into a large saucepan and whisk the raft in thoroughly. Heat very gently, whisking from time to time to prevent the solids from sticking and burning. As the stock comes to a simmer, the raft will begin to coagulate and rise to the surface. Once the raft has formed on the surface, make a little hole in it to allow the steam to escape and prevent it breaking up. Simmer very gently for 40 minutes then remove from the heat.

When cool, carefully ladle the consommé through a sieve lined with muslin. Taste and adjust the seasoning then stir in the Madeira. The consommé will keep in the refrigerator for 2 days or up to a month in the freezer.

Makes 2 litres (4¼ pints)

LAMB CONSOMMÉ

500 g (18 oz) lean lamb offcuts, trimmed of all fat and roughly chopped
1 carrot, chopped
½ onion, chopped
1 stick celery, chopped
½ leek, chopped
3 cloves garlic, roughly chopped
1 sprig rosemary
2 sprigs thyme
4 litres (8¼ pints) Brown Lamb Stock (page 255)
10 egg whites
salt and freshly ground pepper

To make the raft, put the lamb into a food processor and blitz until smooth. Tip into a mixing bowl. Put the vegetables, garlic and herbs in the processor and blitz to a rough purée then add to the bowl with the lamb.

Put the cold stock into a large saucepan and whisk in the purée and egg whites. Heat very gently, whisking from time to time to prevent the solids from sticking and burning. As the stock comes to a simmer, the raft will begin to coagulate and rise to the surface. Once the raft has formed on the surface, make a little hole in it to allow the steam to escape and prevent it breaking up. Simmer very gently for 50 minutes then remove from the heat.

When cool, carefully ladle the consommé through a sieve lined with muslin. Taste and season with salt and freshly ground pepper. The consommé will keep in the refrigerator for 4 days or up to a month in the freezer.

Makes 3 litres (6½ pints)

GAME CONSOMMÉ

200 g (7 oz) game meat offcuts, trimmed of fat and sinew and roughly chopped
1 carrot, chopped
1 onion, chopped
1 stick celery, chopped
1 clove garlic, roughly chopped
2 sprigs thyme
150 g (5 oz) egg whites (around 8)
2 litres (4¼ pints) Game Stock (page 256), cold
salt and freshly ground pepper
30 ml (1 fl oz) Madeira
20 ml (²/₃ fl oz) Armagnac

To make the raft, put the meat into a food processor and blitz until smooth. Tip into a mixing bowl. Put the vegetables, garlic and thyme in the processor and blitz to a rough purée then add to the bowl with the meat. Add the egg whites and mix together well.

Put the cold stock into a large saucepan and whisk the raft in thoroughly. Heat very gently, whisking from time to time to prevent the solids from sticking and burning. As the stock comes to a simmer, the raft will begin to coagulate and rise to the surface. Once the raft has formed on the surface, make a little hole in it to allow the steam to escape and prevent it breaking up. Simmer very gently for 40 minutes then remove from the heat.

When cool, carefully ladle the consommé through a sieve lined with muslin. Taste and adjust the seasoning then stir in the Madeira and Armagnac. The consommé will keep in the refrigerator for 4 days or up to a month in the freezer.

Makes 2 litres (4¼ pints)

GAME JELLY

1.5 litres (3 pints) Game Consommé (above)
8 x 5 g (⅛ oz) gelatine leaves, softened in cold water
20 ml (²/₃ fl oz) Madeira
salt and freshly ground pepper

Put 200 ml (7 fl oz) of the consommé in a small saucepan and bring to a simmer. Squeeze out the excess water from the gelatine and whisk it into the hot liquid until completely dissolved.

Put the remaining consommé into a large saucepan and warm through gently. Add the dissolved gelatine and stir well. Add the Madeira and season.

Remove the consommé from the heat and leave to cool slightly. Refrigerate until cold and set, which will take 2–3 hours. The jelly will keep in the fridge for up to 2 days. Serve it chilled.

Makes 1.5 litres (3 pints)

STOCK SYRUP

200 g (7 oz) sugar
200 ml (7 fl oz) water

This is an important dessert basic, used in everything from fruit salads, jellies and sorbets to sweet pastries. It is very versatile and can be flavoured with fresh herb leaves, vanilla pods or citrus zest.

The basic recipe is made from equal quantities of sugar and water boiled together for around 2 minutes, to make a syrup. You may prefer to make a larger quantity (as it keeps refrigerated for 2–3 weeks) in which case increase the quantities to 500 g (18 oz) sugar and 500 ml (18 fl oz) water and boil for 5 minutes.

Put the sugar and water into a heavy-based saucepan and heat slowly until the sugar has dissolved, stirring from time to time. Once the sugar has completely dissolved, bring the syrup to the boil and boil for 2 minutes. Remove from the heat and add the herbs or zest if using. Leave to infuse for 20 minutes. Refrigerate and when cold add a squeeze of lime juice if desired.

Makes around 200 ml (7 fl oz)

Sauces

ALMOND NAGE

ALMOND MILK

250 g (9 oz) almond meal

500 ml (18 fl oz) water

800 ml (1½ pints) milk

ALMOND NAGE

80 g (2¾ oz) unsalted butter

4 shallots, finely sliced

2 cloves garlic, finely sliced

80 g (2¾ oz) small button mushrooms, finely sliced

salt and freshly ground pepper

150 ml (5 fl oz) white wine

80 g (2¾ oz) flaked almonds, lightly toasted

300 ml (10 fl oz) Mushroom Stock (page245)

splash Madeira

squeeze lemon juice

To make the almond milk, put the almond meal into a mixing bowl. Put the water and milk into a saucepan and bring to the boil. Pour over the almond meal and stir well before leaving to cool. Refrigerate for 3 hours to infuse then pass through a chinois or fine sieve twice, and then pass through a muslin cloth.

To make the almond nage, heat a saucepan over a medium heat. Heat the butter and allow to foam but not colour. Add the shallots and garlic and sweat gently for 3 minutes until soft but not coloured. Add the mushrooms and season well. Sweat for another couple of minutes. Add the wine and simmer until reduced by two-thirds. Add the toasted almonds, mushroom stock and almond milk and bring to the boil. Season again then lower the heat and simmer gently for 15 minutes.

Remove from the heat and leave to cool slightly. Add the Madeira and lemon juice then tip into blender and blitz at full speed for 4 minutes until light and frothy. Pass through a chinois or fine sieve and serve.

Makes 500 ml (18 fl oz)

OYSTER AND GINGER NAGE

30 ml (1 fl oz) non-scented cooking oil

6 shallots, finely sliced

2 cloves garlic, finely sliced

50 g (1¾ oz) fresh ginger, finely sliced

2 sprigs thyme

200 ml (7 fl oz) white wine

200 ml (7 fl oz) Noilly Prat

400 ml (14 fl oz) Vegetable Nage (below)

400 ml (14 fl oz) oyster juice

salt and freshly ground white pepper

squeeze lemon juice

Heat a heavy-based saucepan over a medium-high heat. Add the oil then the shallots, garlic and ginger. Sweat gently for 10 minutes until soft but not coloured. Add the white wine and thyme and simmer until reduced by half.

Add the Noilly Prat and the vegetable nage. Bring back to the boil and simmer for 5 minutes. Add the oyster juice and remove from the heat. Season to taste with salt and pepper and lemon juice. Pass through a chinois or fine sieve lined with muslin. Refrigerate and use within 2 days.

Makes 1 litre (2¼ pints)

VEGETABLE NAGE

1 onion, finely sliced

2 carrots, finely sliced

½ leek, finely sliced

2 sticks celery, finely sliced

1 bulb fennel, finely sliced

4 cloves garlic, roughly crushed

3 sprigs thyme

4 white peppercorns

6 coriander seeds

3 star anise

1.5 litres (3 pints) water

salt

4 sprigs tarragon

6 sprigs chervil

2 sprigs coriander

Use this lovely aromatic stock as a vegetarian base for soups, purées and braised dishes. Its beauty is that it is fresh and delicate, so it has a very short shelf life, and should not be frozen.

Put the sliced vegetables into a large saucepan with the garlic, thyme and spices. Add the water and bring to the boil. Lower the heat and simmer gently for 5 mintues.

Remove from the heat and season with salt to taste. Add the fresh herbs and cover the pot tightly with cling film. Leave to infuse for 2 hours then pass through a chinois or fine sieve. Refrigerate and use within 24 hours.

Makes 1 litre (2¼ pints)

YABBY BISQUE

1 kg (2 lb 2 oz) yabby heads, claws and shells
50 ml (1¾ fl oz) non-scented cooking oil
2 carrots, roughly chopped
1 onion, roughly chopped
2 sticks celery, roughly chopped
½ leek, roughly chopped
4 cloves garlic, roughly crushed
60 g (2 oz) unsalted butter, roughly diced
2 tablespoons fresh tomato paste
100 ml (3½ fl oz) white wine
30 ml (1 fl oz) Cognac
3 sprigs thyme
2 stalks basil, roughly crushed

A bisque is an intensely flavoured soup or sauce made from the roasted shells of crustaceans. It is usually flavoured with tomato, white wine and Cognac or brandy. When made from freshwater crustaceans, it is known as sauce Nantua. You can substitute marrons for the yabbies to make a marron bisque.

Remove the innards from the yabby heads. Crush the heads, claws and shells with a heavy mallet. Heat a deep roasting tray over a medium-high heat. Add the oil and the crushed shells and heat until they change colour to a vibrant orange-pink.

Add the diced vegetables to the tray and mix in well. Scatter on the butter and heat to a very light brown foam. Continue to cook until the shells are deep red. Add the tomato paste and cook for another few minutes. Remove around one-third of the shells from the pan and set aside.

Add the white wine to the pan and deglaze. Add the Cognac and thyme then add enough water to just cover the shells. Bring to a gentle simmer and cook for 20 minutes without skimming. Pour through a colander and then a chinois or fine sieve.

Return the liquid to a clean saucepan and simmer rapidly until reduced to the consistency of a thin sauce. Add the reserved shells to the pan and cook for a few minutes to refresh the flavour. Remove the pan from the heat and add the basil. Leave to infuse for 2 minutes then pass through a chinois or fine sieve. The bisque will keep in the refrigerator for 2 days or up to a month in the freezer.

Makes 500 ml (18 fl oz)

PORK JUS

60 ml (2 fl oz) non-scented cooking oil
2 kg (4 lb 4 oz) pork shoulder, cut into 1 cm (½ in) dice
100 g (3½ oz) unsalted butter
10 shallots, finely sliced
6 cloves garlic, finely sliced
2 sticks celery, finely sliced
1 large Granny Smith apple, finely chopped
3 sprigs thyme
200 ml (7 fl oz) white wine
3 litres (6½ pints) Brown Pork Stock (page 255)
2 sprigs marjoram
salt and freshly ground pepper

Heat a large roasting tray over a high heat. Add the oil and then the pork and sear until lightly browned all over. Add the butter and heat to a nut-brown foam. Lower the heat and sauté for around 6 minutes, moving the pork around in the pan so that it caramelises a deep golden-brown all over.

Tip the contents into a colander to drain and reserve the fat. Put the meat into a large saucepan and tip the drained fat back into the baking tray. Add the shallots, garlic and celery and cook over a medium heat until they start to caramelise. Add the apple and thyme and cook until everything has caramelised a deep golden-brown. Carefully drain off any excess fat.

Deglaze the pan with the white wine, being sure to scrape up all the sticky sediment from the bottom of the pan. Simmer until reduced to a sticky syrup then tip everything into the saucepan with the pork.

Add the pork stock and bring to a simmer slowly, skimming to remove any fat or sediment that rises to the surface. Lower the heat and simmer gently for about 20 minutes, skimming frequently. Remove from the stove and add the marjoram. Leave to infuse for 5 minutes then pour through a chinois or fine sieve. Tap the sieve lightly; don't press the contents to extract more liquid as it will make the jus cloudy and grainy. This jus is at its best used on the same day, but will keep up to 2 days in the refrigerator or for a month in the freezer.

Makes 1.5 litres (3¼ pints)

LAMB JUS

30 ml (1 fl oz) non-scented cooking oil

500 g (18 oz) lamb neck and shoulder meat, cut to a small dice

6 shallots, finely sliced

30 g (1 oz) unsalted butter

500 ml (18 fl oz) white wine

2 cloves garlic , crushed

1 overripe tomato, roughly chopped

3 sprigs thyme

1 sprig rosemary

4 litres (8¼ pints) Brown Lamb Stock (page 255)

salt and freshly ground pepper

Heat a large heavy-based saucepan over a medium-high heat. Add the oil and then the lamb. Cook until the lamb has caramelised golden-brown. Add the shallots and the butter and heat to a nut-brown foam. Continue to cook over a medium heat until everything has caramelised a deep golden-brown.

Tip the contents into a colander to drain off the fat. Return the meat and onions to the pan and deglaze with the white wine, being sure to scrape up all the sticky sediment from the bottom of the pan. Add the garlic, tomato and herbs and simmer until reduced by half.

Add the lamb stock and bring to a simmer slowly, skimming to remove any fat or sediment that rises to the surface. Lower the heat and simmer gently for around 15 minutes until reduced to a sauce, skimming frequently. Don't over-reduce the stock or it will become overpoweringly strong. Taste and season with salt and pepper.

Leave to cool slightly then pour through a chinois or fine sieve. Tap the sieve lightly; don't press the contents to extract more liquid as it will make the jus cloudy and grainy. This jus is at its best used on the same day, but will keep up to 2 days in the refrigerator or for a month in the freezer.

Makes 2 litres (4¼ pints)

VEAL JUS

80 ml (2¾ fl oz) non-scented oil

1.5 kg (3 lb 5 oz) veal shoulder, diced to 2 cm (¾ in) cubes

150 g (5 oz) unsalted butter, diced

150 g (5 oz) shallots, finely sliced

150 g (5 oz) button mushrooms, finely sliced

200 ml (7 fl oz) white wine

80 ml (2¾ fl oz) Madeira

1.5 litres (3 pints) Brown Veal Stock (page256)

1 litre (2¼ pints) Brown Chicken Stock (page 254)

salt and freshly ground pepper

When properly made, this is the king of sauces! So many cooks miss the point with a simple jus such as this: caramelised meat juices. That's it. It's not difficult to achieve, but if the cook doesn't respect the caramelisation process and the delicate flavour of the young calf then the result will be simply a dull sauce lacking flavour and freshness.

Heat a large heavy-based saucepan over a high heat. Add the oil and then the veal in a single layer. It's important not to overcrowd the pan or the meat will stew rather than brown. Sear the veal all over then add the diced butter and heat to a light nut-brown foam. Lower the heat and caramelise gently, stirring from time to time. As you stir, scrape up the sticky sediment from the bottom of the pan and baste the veal. Cook for 5–10 minutes.

Add the shallots and mushrooms and cook for around 5 minutes until they have caramelised a deep golden-brown. They should smell pleasantly savoury – not at all bitter. Tip the contents into a colander to drain off the fat then return around two-thirds of the meat and vegetables to the pan. Deglaze with the white wine, being sure to scrape up all the sticky sediment from the bottom of the pan. When the wine has reduced to a sticky syrup, add the Madeira and bring back to the boil.

Tip into a large stockpot and add the veal and chicken stocks. Bring to a simmer slowly, skimming to remove any fat or sediment that rises to the surface. Lower the heat and simmer gently for 30 minutes, skimming frequently.

Pour through a chinois or fine sieve then return the liquid to a clean pan and bring to a boil. Boil to reduce by half, skimming frequently to remove any impurities. Add the reserved meat and vegetables to the pan, bring back to the boil then remove the pan from the stove and leave to infuse for 5 minutes.

Leave to cool slightly then pour through a chinois or fine sieve. Don't press the contents to extract more liquid as it will make the jus cloudy. Finish with an extra splash of Madeira and season with salt and pepper. The jus will keep in the refrigerator for 4 days or up to a month in the freezer.

Makes 1 litre (2¼ pints)

SQUAB OR GUINEA FOWL JUS GRAS

30 ml (1 fl oz) non-scented cooking oil

500 g (18 oz) game bones and carcasses, chopped small

200 g (7 oz) unsalted butter

5 shallots, finely sliced

150 g (5 oz) button mushrooms, finely sliced

3 cloves garlic, crushed

200 ml (7 fl oz) white wine

200 ml (7 fl oz) Madeira

1 litre (2¼ pints) Game Stock (page 256)

3 sprigs thyme

Gras is the French word for fat, and jus gras is a very tasty, rustic style of sauce where the fats released by the carcass during the roasting process are not drained away. This results in a thick layer of fat on top of the concentrated jus, which you whisk back in to emulsify the sauce before serving.

Heat a large heavy-based saucepan over a medium-high heat. Add the oil and then the game. Cook until the bones have caramelised a golden-brown all over. Add the butter and heat to a nut-brown foam. Add the shallots, mushrooms and garlic and continue to cook over a medium heat until everything has caramelised a deep golden-brown.

Deglaze the pan with the white wine, being sure to scrape up all the sticky sediment from the bottom of the pan. Reduce to a sticky syrup then add the Madeira, game stock and thyme. Bring to the boil then lower the heat and simmer gently for 20 minutes until reduced to a sauce. Don't over-reduce the stock or it will become overpoweringly strong.

Leave to cool slightly then pour through a chinois or fine sieve. Tap the sieve lightly; don't press the contents to extract more liquid as it will make the jus cloudy. This jus is at its best used on the same day, but will keep up to 2 days in the refrigerator or for a month in the freezer.

Makes 500 ml (18 fl oz)

ROUGET JUS

bones and heads of 3 red mullet

½ bulb baby fennel

½ stick celery, chopped into small dice

1 carrot, chopped into small dice

2 shallots, chopped into small dice

2 cloves garlic, crushed

2 star anise, roughly crushed

3 coriander seeds, roughly crushed

pinch saffron threads

1 small strip orange peel

dash Pernod

dash brandy

20 ml (⅔ fl oz) extra-virgin olive oil

20 ml (⅔ fl oz) virgin olive oil

30 g (1 oz) unsalted butter

2 overripe tomatoes, chopped

1 teaspoon fresh tomato purée

2 stalks basil, roughly crushed

extra-virgin olive oil

squeeze fresh orange juice

Remove the eyes from the red mullet and chop the bones and carcasses into small pieces. Put them into a large mixing bowl with the diced vegetables, spices, orange zest, Pernod, brandy and extra-virgin olive oil. Toss everything together well then cover the bowl with cling film and refrigerate for 2 hours to marinate.

Tip into a colander to drain, reserving the marinading liquid. Heat a saucepan over a high heat and add the olive oil. Add the fish bones, vegetables and spices and sauté gently. Add the butter and heat to a nut-brown foam. Continue to sauté until everything has caramelised a light golden-brown then add the tomatoes and tomato purée. Stir well and cook for another 3 minutes.

Remove around a third of the contents from the pan and reserve. Deglaze the pan with the reserved marinade then add just enough cold water to cover. Bring to a simmer and cook gently for 20 minutes. Pass through a chinois or fine sieve then return the liquid to a clean saucepan and bring to a simmer.

Simmer gently until reduced to a light sauce. Don't over-reduce the stock or it will become overpoweringly strong. Add the reserved bones to the pan, return to the boil then remove the pan from the heat. Add the basil stalks and leave to infuse for 2 minutes. Pour through a chinois or fine sieve then add a splash of extra-virgin olive oil and a squeeze of fresh orange juice. This jus will keep in the refrigerator for 2 days or up to a month in the freezer.

Makes 300 ml (10 fl oz)

RED WINE SAUCE

500 ml (18 fl oz) red wine

100 ml (3½ fl oz) ruby port

3 sprigs thyme

2 cloves garlic, crushed

¼ bay leaf

2 peppercorns

500 ml (18 fl oz) Veal Jus (page 261)

Put all the ingredients except for the veal jus into a heavy-based saucepan and bring to the boil over a high heat. Boil rapidly to reduce the alcohol, taking care as it may ignite.

When reduced to a thick syrup – about 60 ml (2 fl oz), add the veal jus. Lower the heat and simmer gently for 8 minutes, skimming frequently.

Remove from the heat and pour through a chinois or fine sieve. Don't press the contents to extract more liquid as it will make the sauce cloudy and grainy. Serve immediately.

Makes 500 ml (18 fl oz)

SAUCE ALBUFERA

1 kg (2 lb 2 oz) chicken wings, chopped small

1 litre (2¼ pints) White Chicken Stock (page 254)

1 litre (2¼ pints) pure cream

60 g (2 oz) unsalted butter

100 g (3½ oz) shallots, finely sliced

100 g (3½ oz) button mushrooms, finely sliced

3 cloves garlic, finely sliced

2 sprigs thyme

½ bay leaf

100 ml (3½ fl oz) white wine

50 ml (1¾ fl oz) Madeira

salt and freshly ground pepper

50 g (1¾ oz) Foie Gras Butter (page 265)

30 ml (1 fl oz) Armagnac

squeeze lemon juice

Put half the chopped chicken wings into a large saucepan and cover with the chicken stock. Bring to the boil, then lower the heat and simmer for 1 hour. Pour through a chinois or fine sieve and reserve.

In another saucepan simmer the cream until reduced by half.

In a heavy-based frying pan, heat the butter to a nut-brown foam. Add the shallots, mushrooms, garlic, thyme and bay leaf and sweat gently for 5 minutes until shallots are soft but not coloured. Add the remaining chicken wings and sweat for another minute then add the white wine and simmer vigorously until almost completely evaporated. Add the Madeira and bring to the boil, then add the reserved chicken stock and simmer until reduced by one-third.

Add the reduced cream and simmer for 4 minutes then taste and season with salt and pepper. Pour through a chinois or fine sieve and return to a clean saucepan. Use a hand-held blender to whisk in the foie gras butter and Armagnac and finish with a squeeze of lemon juice. Serve immediately.

Makes 600 ml (20 fl oz)

SAUCE BERCY

1 litre (2¼ pints) shallots, very finely sliced on a mandolin

6 sprigs thyme

4 cloves garlic

250 ml (8¾ fl oz) port

500 ml (18 fl oz) red wine

500 ml (18 fl oz) Veal Jus (page 261)

This sauce is named after a district of Paris famous for its wine market. The name Bercy is traditionally applied to a number of dishes served with a red wine sauce that is usually prepared with shallots.

Use a mandolin to slice the shallots as finely as possible. Put them into a mixing bowl with the thyme and garlic and toss gently to combine.

Put the port and red wine into a heavy-based saucepan and bring to the boil over a high heat. Boil for 2 minutes. Remove from the heat and allow to cool. When lukewarm, pour over the shallots, thyme and garlic and leave to marinate overnight.

The next day, tip the marinade and shallots into a heavy-based saucepan and bring to a simmer. Reduce until nearly all the liquid has evaporated and the shallots are almost dry. Add the veal jus to the pan and bring to a simmer. Cook for 15 minutes, skimming from time to time. Serve the sauce immediately, without passing through a sieve.

Makes 500 ml (18 fl oz)

CHARCUTIÈRE SAUCE

2 vine-ripened tomatoes

1 teaspoon tiny capers (preserved in salt), well rinsed

4 small cornichons, chopped into 2 mm (⅛ in) dice

6 baby pickled onions, chopped into 2 mm (⅛ in) dice

1 tablespoon finely chopped flat-leaf parsley

2 tablespoons Marinated Mustard Seeds (page 265)

200 ml (7 fl oz) Pork Jus (page 260)

Plunge the tomatoes in boiling water for a few minutes to loosen the skins, refresh in iced water, then peel. Cut the tomatoes into quarters and slice away the seeds and internal flesh to leave you with 8 flat 'petals'. Cut into very neat, small dice, about 2 mm (⅛ in) and set aside.

Put the rinsed capers into a small pan and cover with cold water. Bring to the boil then refresh the capers under cold running water for a minute – this will minimise the saltiness. Pat dry and set aside with the tomatoes and the other dry ingredients.

Put the pork jus into a small saucepan and heat to just below a simmer. Add all the other ingredients and warm briefly. Serve immediately.

Makes 400 ml (14 fl oz)

CAPER BEURRE NOISETTE

200 g (7 oz) unsalted butter
50 g (1¾ oz) baby capers
1 tablespoon rosemary leaves, chopped
1 tablespoon flat-leaf parsley, chopped
6 lemon segments, sliced into small pieces

Put the butter in a deep saucepan and heat to a nut-brown foam. Remove from the heat and allow to cool slightly. Pass through a fine sieve to remove any solids then add the remaining ingredients. Keep warm until ready to serve.

Makes 200 ml (7 fl oz)

GINGER BEURRE BLANC

50 g (1¾ oz) fresh ginger
200 ml (7 fl oz) white wine
200 ml (7 fl oz) white wine vinegar
1 clove garlic, crushed
½ bay leaf
2 sprigs thyme
50 ml (1¾ fl oz) pure cream
400 g (14 oz) chilled unsalted butter, diced
salt and freshly ground pepper
squeeze lemon juice

Peel the ginger and dice it finely. Put the peel and any trimmings into a small saucepan with the white wine, vinegar, garlic and herbs. Bring to the boil over a high heat and reduce rapidly by two-thirds. Remove from the heat and set aside.

Blanch the diced ginger in boiling water seasoned with a little salt, sugar and lemon. Refresh in iced water. Repeat 2–3 times, depending on the strength of the ginger. You want it to be aromatic with a hint of heat, but not overpowering. Drain and pat dry.

Put the reduction back on the heat, add the cream and bring to the boil. Lower the heat and allow to cool until it is warm, not hot. Slowly whisk in the butter, piece by piece, until all is incorporated. Keep the sauce at a constant temperature. If it gets too hot it may split, too cold and it will solidify.

Strain the sauce through a chinois or fine sieve and season with salt, pepper and a squeeze of lemon. Add the diced blanched ginger and keep warm until required.

Makes 400 ml (14 fl oz)

HOLLANDAISE SAUCE

1 shallot, finely sliced
1 clove garlic, finely sliced
1 sprig thyme
150 ml (5 fl oz) white wine
80 ml (2¾ fl oz) white wine vinegar
4 egg yolks
200 ml (7 fl oz) Clarified Butter (below), kept warm
salt and freshly ground pepper

To make a truffle hollandaise sauce, finely chop ½ Poached Truffle (page 50) and stir through the warm sauce after straining.

Put the shallot, garlic, thyme, white wine and vinegar in a pan and simmer until reduced by around two-thirds to a syrup. Tip though a fine sieve into a mixing bowl and allow to cool slightly. Add the egg yolks and whisk over a pan of simmering water until the mixture thickens to a pale, foamy sabayon. Continue whisking as you trickle in the clarified butter, still over heat. When all the butter has been incorporated you should have a bowl of thick, creamy sauce. Strain it through a chinois or fine sieve and season. Keep covered in a warm place until required.

Makes around 300 ml (10 fl oz)

Butters

CLARIFIED BUTTER

250 g (9 oz) unsalted butter

Clarified butter has had the milk solids removed, which means it can be heated to a higher temperature, without the risk of burning.

Put the butter into a small heavy-based saucepan and heat gently until completely melted. Keep at a constant temperature over a very low heat until the milk solids fall to the bottom of the pan. Ladle the clear liquid butter through a sieve lined with muslin and allow the clarified butter to set. Store in the refrigerator for up to 2 weeks.

Makes 100 ml (3½ fl oz)

GARLIC AND HERB BUTTER

250 g (9 oz) unsalted butter, diced
12 cloves garlic, roasted and puréed
2 cups flat-leaf parsley leaves, finely chopped
6 leaves tarragon, finely chopped
1 cup finely snipped chives
squeeze lemon juice
fleur de sel
freshly ground white pepper

When making this butter it is important to purée the herbs first as the heat from the friction of the blades allows the chlorophyll to leach out, resulting in a vibrant green colour.

Put the butter in a mixing bowl and allow to soften at room temperature.

Put the garlic and herbs into a blender with a tablespoon of butter and blitz until the chlorophyll is released from herbs and the mixture turns a vibrant green. Then add the remaining butter and whiz briefly to incorporate.

Add the lemon juice and season. This butter will keep for a week in the refrigerator or a month in the freezer.

Makes 350 g (12 oz)

FOIE GRAS BUTTER

100 g (3¹/₂ oz) unsalted butter, diced
100 g (3¹/₂ oz) cooked foie gras*, diced
1 tablespoon Armagnac
fleur de sel
freshly ground white pepper

Bring the butter and foie gras to room temperature then push them both through a drum sieve. Mix together until smooth then stir in the Armagnac and season to taste. This butter will keep for a week in the refrigerator or a month in the freezer.

Makes 200 g (7 oz).)

* Note: Raw foie gras is not available in Australia, but you can purchase good quality poached (mi-cuit) foie gras from specialist food stores. Pâté de foie gras is quite different and should not be substituted in this recipe.

Marinades

FOIE GRAS MARINADE

150 ml (5 fl oz) white port
150 ml (5 fl oz) Gewürztraminer
80 ml (2³/₄ fl oz) Sauternes
salt and freshly ground pepper
50 ml (1³/₄ fl oz) truffle oil

Put the port and wines in a heavy-based saucepan and bring to the boil. Lower the heat and simmer for 1 minute then add the salt and pepper. Whisk in the truffle oil and set aside. Pour over the foie gras while warm.

Makes enough to marinate 1 foie gras

GAME BIRD MARINADE

200 ml (7 fl oz) port
200 ml (7 fl oz) Madeira
100 ml (3¹/₂ fl oz) Cognac
salt and freshly ground pepper
50 ml (1³/₄ fl oz) truffle oil

Put the port and Madeira in a heavy-based saucepan and bring to the boil. Simmer until reduced by one-third. Add the Cognac and bring back to the boil for 1 minute then remove from the heat and season with salt and pepper. Whisk in the truffle oil and set aside and leave to cool slightly. Pour over game birds while warm.

Makes 400 ml (14 fl oz)

MARINATED MUSTARD SEEDS

50 g (1³/₄ oz) brown mustard seeds
50 g (1³/₄ oz) yellow mustard seeds
2 sprigs tarragon
300 ml (10 fl oz) water
50 ml (1³/₄ fl oz) chardonnay vinegar
1 teaspoon sugar
salt and freshly ground pepper

Put the mustard seeds into a small bowl with the tarragon and mix together.

Put the water, vinegar, sugar and salt and pepper into a heavy-based saucepan and bring to the boil. Pour the boiling solution over the mustard seeds and leave to cool. When cool, refrigerate overnight so the seeds marinate and soften. Store in the refrigerator for up to a week.

Makes 200 g (7 oz)

Dressings, oils and purées

LEMON VINAIGRETTE

80 ml (2³/₄ fl oz) freshly squeezed lemon juice

sugar

salt and freshly ground white pepper

120 ml (4 fl oz) extra-virgin olive oil

100 ml (3¹/₂ fl oz) virgin olive oil

Rub the inside of your mixing bowl with a clove of garlic before tossing the salad. It adds a gentle touch of garlic, without being overpowering.

Put the lemon juice into a mixing bowl with the sugar, salt and pepper. Whisk to dissolve then whisk in the two oils. Taste and adjust the balance of seasonings to your preference.

Makes 300 ml (10 fl oz)

TRUFFLE VINAIGRETTE

100 ml (3¹/₂ fl oz) Brown Veal Stock (page 256)

20 ml (²/₃ fl oz) sherry vinegar

2 tablespoons fresh black winter truffle, diced finely

100 ml (3¹/₂ fl oz) truffle oil

100 ml (3¹/₂ fl oz) grapeseed oil

salt and freshly ground pepper

If you want to make a more intensely flavoured vinaigrette, poach the truffle in the veal stock before you dice it.

Put the veal stock into a small saucepan and warm through gently. Whisk in the sherry vinegar and the diced truffle. It is important to do this while the stock is warm to release the maximum flavour from the truffle.

Whisk in the two oils and season to taste.

Makes 350 ml (12 fl oz)

VERBENA TEA VINAIGRETTE

¹/₂ cup lemon verbena leaves

2 stalks lemongrass, roughly chopped

zest of 1 lemon

3 sprigs lemon thyme

30 g (1 oz) fresh ginger, grated

1 teaspoon sugar

salt and freshly ground pepper

200 ml (7 fl oz) extra-virgin olive oil

70 ml (2¹/₂ fl oz) strong Marco Polo tea

30 ml (1 fl oz) chardonnay vinegar

juice of 1 lemon

Set aside 6 lemon verbena leaves for the garnish. Put the remaining lemon verbena, lemongrass, lemon zest, lemon thyme, ginger, sugar, salt and pepper into a large mortar and pound to form an aromatic paste. Divide between 2 small saucepans. Add the olive oil to one pan and add the tea, vinegar and lemon juice to the other. Heat both pans gently until just warm to the touch, about 50°C (120°F). Cover both pans with cling film and leave in a warm place to infuse for a couple of hours.

Strain the infusions through a piece of muslin then whisk the two together to make a vinaigrette. Taste and season with extra salt, pepper or lemon juice if necessary.

Finely slice the reserved lemon verbena leaves for garnish.

Makes 350 ml (12 fl oz)

BLACK OLIVE VINAIGRETTE

100 g (3¹/₂ oz) black olives

200 ml (7 fl oz) extra-virgin olive oil

3 sprigs thyme

¹/₂ bay leaf

4 cloves garlic, roughly crushed

30 ml (1 fl oz) sherry vinegar

salt and freshly ground pepper

Pit the olives and put the stones into a small saucepan with the olive oil, thyme, bay leaf and garlic. Heat gently to about 45°C (110°F) and leave to infuse for 2 hours. Strain the infused oil through a chinois or fine sieve.

Chop the olive flesh finely and put into a mixing bowl. Whisk in the vinegar, followed by the infused oil. Season to taste.

Makes 300 ml (10 fl oz)

WALNUT VINAIGRETTE

1 teaspoon Dijon mustard

80 ml (2³/₄ fl oz) sherry vinegar

100 ml (3¹/₂ fl oz) walnut oil

60 ml (2 fl oz) grapeseed oil

2 tablespoons walnuts, lightly toasted in a little walnut oil and finely chopped

salt and freshly ground pepper

Place the mustard in a mixing bowl and whisk while trickling in the vinegar until a smooth paste is formed. Continue whisking while you add the oils. Add the walnuts and season well.

Makes 250 ml (8³/₄ fl oz)

SAUCE GRIBICHE

At Bécasse we make two varieties of Sauce Gribiche: a traditional mayonnaise-based version and a more contemporary split-vinaigrette style. The basic ingredients remain the same. To vary the texture, try finely slicing the cornichons and pickled onions.

100 g (3½ oz) cornichons, finely chopped

100 g (3½ oz) pickled cocktail onions, finely chopped

1 tablespoon capers

½ cup fresh herbs (a selection of chervil, tarragon, chives, flat-leaf parsley), finely chopped

2 hard-boiled eggs, finely chopped

salt and freshly ground pepper

squeeze lemon juice

Put all the ingredients into a mixing bowl and stir to combine. Taste and adjust the balance of seasonings to your preference.

To make a mayonnaise-based dressing, mix all ingredients with 300 ml (10 fl oz) good quality mayonnaise.

To make a vinaigrette-style dressing, whisk the ingredients with 300 ml (10 fl oz) Lemon Vinaigrette (page 266).

Makes 500 ml (18 fl oz)

HERB FOAM

Foams have become very popular in recent years as they are light, flavoursome and very pretty. You will need to buy an espuma cream gun and gas canisters from a specialist cookery shop. You will need to buy an espuma cream gun and gas canisters from a specialist cookery shop.

20 ml (⅔ fl oz) non-scented cooking oil

1 onion, finely sliced

3 cloves garlic, finely sliced

1.5 litres (3 pints) pure cream

1 bay leaf

1 cup flat-leaf parsley leaves

½ cup chives

¼ cup tarragon leaves

½ cup chervil leaves

salt and freshly ground pepper

Heat the oil in a heavy-based saucepan. Add the onion and garlic and sweat gently for 5 minutes until onion is soft but not coloured. Add the cream and bay leaf and slowly bring to the boil. Simmer until reduced by two-thirds to about 500 ml (18 fl oz), stirring regularly to prevent the cream from burning on the bottom of the pan.

Meanwhile, blanch the herbs in rapidly boiling salted water for 20 seconds then refresh in iced water. When cold, drain well and gently pat them dry.

Remove the bay leaf from the reduced cream and pour cream into a blender. Add the blanched herbs and blitz on high until well blended and smooth. Taste and season well.

Strain through a chinois or fine sieve while still hot and transfer to an espuma cream gun. Use 3 canisters per 500 ml. Shake the can well and rest upside down for 15 minutes before use.

Makes 1 litre (2¼ pints)

VIETNAMESE DRESSING

Although I don't tend to use many Asian ingredients in my cooking, I love this wonderful vinaigrette, which is a Dietmar Sawyer recipe.

2 teaspoons grated ginger

1 teaspoon finely chopped garlic

1 teaspoon finely chopped chilli

2 tablespoons sesame oil

4 tablespoons peanut oil

2 tablespoons soy sauce

1 teaspoon finely chopped pickled ginger

1 teaspoon pickled ginger juice

pinch sugar

freshly squeezed lime juice to taste

few sprigs Vietnamese mint leaves, finely chopped

Put all the ingredients into a mixing bowl and whisk together. Taste and adjust the balance of seasonings to your preference.

Makes 250 ml (8¾ fl oz)

HERB OIL

1 cup flat-leaf parsley leaves
1/2 cup chives
1/4 cup tarragon leaves
1/2 cup basil leaves
salt and freshly ground pepper
200 ml (7 fl oz) grapeseed oil

Herb oils are extremely versatile: use them in dressings and vinaigrettes, in marinades or just as an attractive garnish. You can make a mixed-herb oil, as in the recipe that follows, or simply use one herb on its own for a purer flavour.

Blanch the herbs in rapidly boiling salted water for 30 seconds then refresh in iced water. When cold, squeeze out the excess water and chop them roughly.

Put into a blender and blitz on high to a deep green purée. Season with salt and pepper to taste. Set aside for 15 minutes to allow the chlorophyll particles to leach out into the oil. Pour into a muslin bag and hang for a couple of hours. Transfer the oil to an airtight jar and store in the refrigerator for up to 2 days.

Makes 200 ml (7 fl oz)

RAW TOMATO COULIS

300 g (10 oz) vine-ripened cherry tomatoes
sugar
salt and freshly ground pepper
squeeze lemon juice
extra-virgin olive oil

Halve the tomatoes and squeeze out the seeds and juice. Pass the seeds and juice through a chinois or fine sieve and reserve. Put the tomato flesh into a blender and blitz to a fine purée. Pass this through a chinois or fine sieve, adding a little of the reserved juice to thin it if necessary.

Add the remaining ingredients, then taste and adjust the balance of seasonings to your preference. This will largely depend on the quality, flavour and acidity of the tomatoes.

Makes 200 ml (7 fl oz)

PARSLEY COULIS

2 cups flat-leaf parsley leaves
1 teaspoon Dijon mustard
2 tablespoons roasted garlic purée (page 282)
200 ml (7 fl oz) grapeseed oil
40 ml (1 1/3 fl oz) hot water
salt and freshly ground pepper

This is a silky-smooth, vibrant green dressing that is perfect on charcuterie plates or as an accompaniment to beef or venison. It is also lovely with cold and smoked fish.

Pick the parsley leaves and wash and drain them well. Bring a large pan of salted water to the boil and blanch the parsley for a minute. Refresh in iced water then drain and squeeze out any excess water.

Roughly chop the parsley then put it in a blender. Add half the oil with the mustard and garlic and blitz on high to a fine purée. Add the hot water to emulsify, then slowly trickle in the remaining oil as if making a mayonnaise. Season with salt and pepper and pass the coulis through a chinois or fine sieve.

Makes 500 ml (18 fl oz)

CHLOROPHYLL

4 cups curly parsley leaves
1.5 litres (3 pints) water

A vibrant green paste that has myriad uses. Try it in sauces, soups, pasta or potato purée.

Pick the parsley leaves and wash and drain them well. Put in a blender with the water and blitz on high for a few minutes until you have a bright green water. Strain through a chinois or fine sieve into a heavy-based saucepan and heat gently. Stir continuously until the green particles of chlorophyll separate out from the water.

Remove the pan from the heat and tip into a plastic container. Add a large handful of ice and refrigerate.

When cold, pour the mixture through a thick tea towel. Discard the water. Scrape as much of the green paste as you can off the tea towel and store in an airtight container in the refrigerator for up to 1 week.

Makes 2 tablespoons

Mousses and dumplings

CHICKEN MOUSSE

300 g (10 oz) chicken breast, trimmed of all fat and sinew

10 g (²⁄₃ oz) salt

1 egg yolk

350 ml (12 fl oz) pure cream

salt and freshly ground pepper

Chill the bowl of your blender or food processor in the freezer.

Dice the chicken and put it in your processor with the salt. Whiz to a very smooth purée. Add the egg yolk and continue to purée. With the motor running, slowly pour in about 150 ml (5 fl oz) of the cream, to emulsify the mix to a velvet-smooth consistency.

Pass through a drum sieve and tip into a mixing bowl set over ice. Using a spatula, fold in the remaining cream and season well.

To test the flavour balance of the mousse, wrap a teaspoonful in cling film, secure tightly and poach for 2 minutes. Taste and adjust the seasonings if required.

Makes 600 g (20 oz)

SCALLOP MOUSSE

250 g (9 oz) scallops, cleaned of skirt, roe and muscle removed

10 g (²⁄₃ oz) salt

2 egg yolks

250 ml (9 fl oz) pure cream

salt and freshly ground pepper

squeeze lemon juice

Chill the bowl of your blender or food processor in the freezer.

Put the scallops in your processor with the salt and whiz for 2 minutes to a smooth paste. Add the egg yolk and continue to purée. With the motor running, slowly pour in about 150 ml (5 fl oz) of the cream, to emulsify the mix to a velvet-smooth consistency.

Pass through a drum sieve and tip into a mixing bowl set over ice in your sink. Using a spatula, fold in the remaining cream and season well with pepper and lemon juice.

To test the flavour balance of the mousse, wrap a teaspoonful in cling film, secure tightly and poach for 2 minutes. Taste and adjust the seasonings if required.

Makes 500 g (18 oz)

FOIE GRAS AND THYME DUMPLINGS

100 g (3¹⁄₂ oz) foie gras fat, scraped from the outside of a cooked lobe of foie gras

200 g (7 oz) plain flour, sifted

2 tablespoons thyme leaves

salt and freshly ground pepper

cold water

Finely chop the foie gras fat to small dice. Put into a mixing bowl with the flour, thyme, salt and pepper. Rub together until the fat is completely worked into the flour and it resembles very fine breadcrumbs. Add a few drops of cold water and bring together to form a dough. Roll into 8 neat balls and set aside until ready to cook.

Makes 12 small dumplings (3 per serve)

Pasta

PASTA DOUGH

500 g (18 oz) strong plain flour

1 teaspoon salt

290 ml (10 fl oz) egg mix (2 eggs mixed with egg yolks)

2 teaspoons extra-virgin olive oil

Mix the flour and salt and sift twice. Tip onto your work surface and make a well in the centre. In a separate bowl, whisk together the egg mix and oil. Pour into the flour and use your hands to gradually work the liquid into the flour to form a solid mass.

Knead for about 5 minutes until the dough is smooth and slightly springy. Divide into 3 even portions, wrap each in cling film and refrigerate for at least 30 minutes to allow the gluten to relax. This will prevent shrinkage later. Use within 2 days.

Makes 800 g (1 lb 8 oz)

MACARONI

100 g (3½ oz) Pasta Dough (page 269)
sifted plain flour
1 egg, beaten
non-scented cooking oil

To shape the macaroni you will need a macaroni rod – or a pencil or biro – around 1 cm (½ in) in diameter.

Bring the pasta dough to room temperature.

Roll it through your pasta machine, working down from the thickest setting to the third-finest setting. Roll through this setting twice.

Dust the pasta sheet generously with sifted flour and trim to a neat rectangle about the same width as your macaroni rod. Starting at one end of the sheet, roll the pasta around the rod so that there is a tiny overlap. Cut along the length of the rod, brush the seam with a little egg wash and press the sides together firmly.

Slide the macaroni rod out of the macaroni tube, and carefully transfer to a floured tray while you continue. The quantity of dough should make around 10 long macaroni tubes. Cut each one into thirds and leave at room temperature to dry for a couple of hours.

To cook the macaroni bring a large saucepan of heavily salted water to the boil and add a splash of oil. Stir the water to create a whirlpool and drop in the macaroni. Cook for 45 seconds then refresh in iced water. Leave in the water until cold then drain and toss in a little oil.

Serves 4–6

CANNELLONI

250 g (9 oz) Pasta Dough (page 269),
at room temperature
sifted plain flour
1 egg, beaten
non-scented cooking oil

To shape the cannelloni you will need a cannelloni rod – or a small piece of wooden dowel – around 3 cm (1¼ in) in diameter.

Roll the pasta dough through your pasta machine, working down from the thickest setting to the third-finest setting. Roll through this setting twice.

Dust the pasta sheet generously with sifted flour and trim to a neat rectangle about the same width as your cannelloni rod. Starting at one end of the sheet, roll the pasta around the rod so that there is a tiny overlap. Cut along the length of the rod, brush the seam with a little egg wash and press the sides together firmly.

Slide the cannelloni rod out of the cannelloni tube, and carefully transfer to a floured tray while you continue. The quantity of dough should make around 12 cannelloni tubes. Cut each one into thirds and leave at room temperature to dry for a couple of hours.

To cook the cannelloni bring a large saucepan of heavily salted water to the boil and add a splash of oil. Stir the water to create a whirlpool and drop in the cannelloni. Cook for 45 seconds then refresh in iced water. Leave in the water until cold then drain and toss in a little oil.

Makes 12

Offal and charcuterie

CALVES' AND LAMB SWEETBREADS

At Bécasse we only use calves' and lamb sweetbreads (glands) as these have a superior texture and flavour. Ask your butcher to make sure he only gives you pancreas glands, which are large and rounded. The thymus glands, which are located in the throat, are longer and tend to be stringy and tough. Sweetbreads need to be properly prepared – blanched, refreshed and peeled – before cooking.

Rinse the sweetbreads well under cold running water until the water runs clear. Place in a bowl and cover with cold water. Refrigerate and leave them to soak overnight, or for a minimum of 5 hours, changing the water several times.

Drain the sweetbreads and rinse again. Bring a large pan of lightly salted water to the boil and blanch the sweetbreads a few at a time for about 30 seconds. Remove the sweetbreads and refresh straight away in iced water. Drain on kitchen paper and when cool enough to handle, carefully peel away the membrane and any trace of bloody fibres.

Wrap loosely in cling film and refrigerate. Use within 3 days.

BRAISED TONGUE

1 litre (2¼ pints) red wine
1 litre (2¼ pints) port
½ head garlic
6 sprigs thyme
1 bay leaf
300 ml (10 fl oz) cabernet sauvignon vinegar
200 ml (7 fl oz) sherry vinegar
4 pig's or lamb's tongues
1 litre (2¼ pints) White Chicken Stock (page 254)

Put the red wine, port, garlic, thyme and bay leaf into a heavy-based saucepan. Bring to the boil and simmer until reduced by one third. Add both vinegars to the pan, bring back to the boil and remove from the heat.

Pour the liquid over the tongues while still hot so that the flavours can penetrate the meat. Allow to cool to room temperature then cover and place in the refrigerator to marinate for 12 hours.

Remove the tongues from the marinade and put them in a large heavy-based saucepan. Add the chicken stock and bring to a gentle simmer. Cover with a piece of greaseproof paper cut to fit the size of the pan and poach gently for about 3 hours, or until soft. The tongues are cooked when the skin will easily peel away from the flesh.

Makes 4 tongues

BRAISED LAMB NECK

1 x 600 g (20 oz) lamb neck, boned
50 g (1¾ oz) Aromatic Confit Salt (page 10)
20 ml (⅔ fl oz) non-scented cooking oil
1 medium onion, roughly chopped
1 small carrot, roughly chopped
1 stick celery, roughly chopped
½ leek, roughly chopped
½ head garlic, cloves separated
1 litre (2¼ pints) Brown Lamb Stock (page 255)
2 sprigs thyme
1 sprig rosemary
salt and freshly ground pepper

Rub the lamb neck all over with the aromatic salt, cover with cling film and refrigerate for 3 hours to marinate. Rinse off the salt and pat the neck dry.

Preheat your oven to 110°C (225°F). Heat a large casserole dish over a medium heat. Add the oil and then the lamb neck. Sear all over until caramelised a deep golden-brown. Remove from the pan and set aside.

Add the vegetables and garlic to the pan with the butter and heat to a nut-brown foam. Continue to cook at a steady temperature, until the vegetables have caramelised to a deep golden-brown. Put the lamb neck back in the pan and pour on the stock. Add the herbs and season well.

Cover with a piece of greaseproof paper cut to fit the pan. Cover with a lid and braise in the oven for 3 hours. Check every 30 minutes or so to turn the neck and to make sure the liquid is not boiling. When cooked the neck meat should be tender – you should be able to pierce the meat easily with a fork.

Makes 500 g (18 oz)

BRAISED PIG'S CHEEKS

100 g (3½ oz) Aromatic Confit Salt (page 10)
4 large pig's cheeks, fat and skin intact
salt and freshly ground pepper
1 tablespoon non-scented cooking oil
2 small carrots, roughly chopped
1 medium onion, roughly chopped
2 sticks celery, roughly chopped
½ medium leek, roughly chopped
½ head garlic, cloves separated and roughly crushed
60 g (2 oz) unsalted butter
100 ml (3½ fl oz) Madeira
2 litres (4¼ pints) Brown Pork Stock (page 255)
4 sprigs thyme
1 bay leaf

Rub the aromatic salt all over the cheeks and leave to marinate for about 8 hours. Rinse off the salt and pat the cheeks dry.

Preheat your oven to 110°C (225°F). Season the pig's cheeks with salt and pepper. Heat a large casserole dish over a medium heat. Add the oil and then the pig's cheeks, skin side down, and sauté until caramelised a deep golden-brown. Remove from the pan and set aside.

Add the vegetables and garlic to the pan with the butter and heat to a nut-brown foam. Continue to cook at a steady temperature, until the vegetables have caramelised to a deep golden-brown. Add the Madeira and simmer until reduced to a syrup. Put the pig's cheeks back in the pan and pour on the stock. Add the herbs and season well.

Cover with a piece of greaseproof paper cut to fit the pan. Cover with a lid and braise in the oven for 3 hours. Check every 30 minutes or so to turn the cheeks and to make sure the liquid is not boiling. When cooked the cheeks should be tender – you should be able to pierce the meat easily with a fork.

Makes 4 cheeks

BRAISED PIG'S TAILS OR EARS

6 large pig's tails or ears

1 tablespoon non-scented cooking oil

1 small carrot, roughly chopped

½ small onion, roughly chopped

1 stick celery, roughly chopped

½ medium leek, roughly chopped

½ head garlic, cloves separated and roughly crushed

60 g (2 oz) unsalted butter

80 ml (2¾ fl oz) Madeira

4 sprigs thyme

1 bay leaf

500 ml (18 fl oz) Brown Pork Stock (page 255)

salt and freshly ground pepper

Use this recipe to braise pig's tails and ears.

Preheat your oven to 110°C (225°F). Use a cook's blowtorch to singe away any hairs from the tails and set aside.

Heat a casserole dish over a medium heat. Add the oil and then the vegetables and garlic and sauté for a few moments until they begin to brown. Add the butter and heat to a nut-brown foam. Continue to cook at a steady temperature, until the vegetables have caramelised to a deep golden-brown. Add the Madeira and simmer until reduced to a syrup.

Add the pig's tails or ears, herbs and stock and cover with a piece of greaseproof paper cut to fit the pan. Cover with a lid and braise in the oven for 3 hours. Check every 30 minutes or so to turn the tails and to make sure the liquid is not boiling. When cooked they should be meltingly tender – you should be able to pierce the meat easily with your finger.

Makes 6 tails or ears

BRAISED BALLOTTINE OF PIG'S HEAD

1 large pig's head, ears and snout intact

150 g (5 oz) Aromatic Confit Salt (page 10)

1 head garlic, cloves separated

6 sprigs thyme

1 bay leaf

2 litres (4¼ pints) Brown Pork Stock (page 255)

2 litres (4¼ pints) Rendered Duck Fat (page 274)

This recipe is based upon a traditional English dish called bath chaps – it is just a little more complex and refined. When made properly the end result is a wonderful mosaic of different colours, textures and flavours from the component parts.

Check the pig's head carefully to make sure it is blemish-free and that none of the skin is torn or missing. The most challenging part of the dish is boning the pig's head – your butcher will probably do it for you, but really all you need is a very sharp knife, a steady hand and some confidence.

The boned head is braised in a mixture of stock and rendered duck fat – almost like a confit. It's a fabulous way of cooking as the fat floats on top of the flavoursome stock and you end up with the best of both worlds: a rich, tasty braise with the soft melting texture of a confit. To serve, cut into slices and sauté in a little butter and oil until golden-brown.

To bone the pig's head, sit it on a sturdy chopping board, so that it is facing you. Start by removing the ears and tongue and set them aside. You are aiming to remove all the meat from the cheeks, snout, and skull with the skin. Make an incision in the centre of the crown of the pig and run your knife down to the tip of the snout. Work your knife underneath the skin and work your way down the right-hand side of the pig's skull, carefully slicing the skin away from the skull. Manoeuvre carefully around the eye sockets, temple and snout, then run your knife along the jaw line and under the chin to the neck.

Repeat this process on the left-hand side. At the end of the boning process, you should be left with a large butterfly-shaped sheet of skin, with fat and meat attached. Sprinkle on the aromatic salt, then cover tightly and place in the refrigerator to marinate for about 6 hours.

Preheat your oven to 110°C (225°F). Remove the pig's head from the fridge, rinse off the salt and pat dry. Put it into a large braising pan with the reserved tongue and ears. Roughly crush the garlic cloves and add them to the pan with the herbs.

In another saucepan heat the stock and duck fat until just below a simmer, around 80°F (175°F). Pour onto the pig's head and cover with a piece of greaseproof paper cut to the size of the pan. Cover with a lid and cook in the oven for 4 hours, checking every 30 minutes to make sure the liquid is not boiling. When cooked the meat should be very tender.

Remove from the oven and drain the boned head, tongue and ears on a cooling rack. When cool enough to handle, place the head on your work surface and shape into a neat rectangle. Arrange the tongue and ears down the middle of the head and roll up very tightly in cling film. Secure well and hang in the refrigerator for a few hours to set firm. It will keep for up to 1 week.

Note: cut the ballottine straight from the refrigerator and still wrapped in cling film. Keep the cling film on while you fry the medallions to help them keep their shape – they are very delicate and easily disintegrate during the cooking process.

Serves 20 as an entrée

BOUDIN NOIR

Also known as black pudding, this is a savoury sausage consisting largely of seasoned pig's blood. In some countries, including Australia, you must have a licence to prepare smallgoods that use fresh blood. If you do want the sense of achievement and the pleasure of making your own, you'll need to use dried reconstituted blood or a jellied version. Alternatively you could try giving the recipe to your butcher to make for you.

1 pig's head, split and braised
50 ml (1¾ fl oz) non-scented cooking oil
1 large onion, cut into small dice
10 cloves garlic, cut into small dice
2 large Granny Smith apples, cut into small dice
1 teaspoon turmeric
2 teaspoons mace
1 teaspoon cinnamon powder
1 teaspoon clove powder
½ liquorice stick
½ teaspoon star anise powder
1 tablespoon Madras curry paste
300 g (10 oz) chilled pork back fat (lardo), diced small
200 g (7 oz) sultanas, soaked in 500 ml (18 fl oz) strong jasmine tea
1.5 litres (3 pints) fresh pigs' blood
2 teaspoons salt
1 teaspoon freshly ground white pepper
250 g (9 oz) thick sausage skins

Braise the pig's head in the same way as the pig's tails or ears (page 272).

Remove the braised pig's head from the cooking stock and dice all the meat and skin with a little of the fat. Set aside.

Heat a large heavy-based saucepan over a medium-high heat. Add the oil and the onions and garlic. Sauté until soft and caramelised. Add the apples, spices and curry paste and cook for another 15 minutes, stirring from time to time to stop the spices burning.

Tip into a large mixing bowl and leave to cool. Add the reserved pig's meat and back fat and mix well. Drain the sultanas and add them to the mixture.

Put the pig's blood into a blender and blitz for 20 minutes to aerate. This is important for a smooth, light sausage. Fold the blood gently into the sausage mixture and season well.

Put the sausage mixture into a piping bag and use to fill the sausage skins to make around 20 sausages. Be careful to ease the sausage-meat in without any air pockets and do not overfill the skins or they may expand and burst as you cook them.

Heat a large stockpot of water to 80°C (175°F). Add the sausages and cover with a plate to keep them submerged in the water. Poach gently at a steady temperature for 30 minutes. Make sure the temperature doesn't go above 80°C (175°F), or the sausages will burst and become grainy.

Remove the pan from the heat and leave the sausages to cool in the water. It is important that they are cooled slowly, as too abrupt a temperature change will also spoil their texture. Wrap them tightly and store in the refrigerator for up to 1 week.

Makes 20 boudins

SNAILS IN RED WINE

48 large snails

1 litre (2¼ pints) water

200 ml (7 fl oz) red wine

200 ml (7 fl oz) ruby port

80 ml (2¾ fl oz) cabernet sauvignon vinegar

½ head garlic

1 small carrot, roughly chopped

1 small celery stick, roughly chopped

½ small onion, roughly chopped

½ small leek, white part only, roughly chopped

6 sprigs thyme

6 white peppercorns

1 bay leaf

small handful mixed herb stalks (a selection of parsley, chervil and tarragon)

It is difficult to find fresh snails in Australia, although a few suppliers are beginning to farm them for the gourmet food market. Imported French snails in brine are readily available, although quality can vary. At Bécasse, we use Indonesian snails that are preserved in a traditional French brine (the duChef brand). In my opinion, these are excellent – the snails are large and plump with a delicate flavour and texture.

Make sure you rinse the snails thoroughly as the brine can have an unpleasant flavour.

Rinse the snails well under cold running water then leave to soak for an hour or so until any unpleasant odour has vanished.

Put all the remaining ingredients, except for the herb stalks, into a large saucepan and bring to the boil. Lower the heat and simmer gently for 5 minutes. Remove from the heat and leave to cool slightly.

Drain the snails and pat them dry. Put them into a shallow bowl with the herb stalks and pour on the warm marinade with all the aromatics. Cover with cling film and when cool refrigerate until required (at least overnight).

When ready to use, remove the snails from the marinade (which should then be discarded). Don't season the snails until the very last minute or they will become tough and chewy.

The snails will keep in the refrigerator, submerged in the marinade, for up to a week. The flavour will develop and improve over time.

Makes 48 snails

Confit dishes

RENDERED DUCK FAT

2 kg (4 lb 4 oz) raw duck fat

100 ml (3½ fl oz) water

6 sprigs thyme

2 sprigs rosemary

1 bay leaf

10 coriander seeds, coarsely ground

2 star anise, coarsely ground

4 white peppercorns, coarsely ground

1 head garlic, cloves peeled

The water is added to the pan to stop the fat from sticking and burning. As the fat renders down the water evaporates.

Put the duck fat in a heavy-based saucepan with the water, thyme, rosemary and bay leaf.

Put the coriander, star anise and peppercorns into a mortar and crush with the garlic. Add to the duck fat and heat very gently. Cook at a very low heat for about an hour, until the fat has rendered down to a clear liquid.

Strain through a chinois or fine sieve and refrigerate for up to 1 month.

Makes 1.5 litres (3 pints)

CONFIT DUCK LEGS

The confit method of preparing food comes from the French term meaning 'to preserve'. It is a method of slow-cooking in fat (rendered pork, duck or goose) or an aromatic oil and results in extremely tender meat, which flakes away from the bone easily. It is very important not to cook the legs too quickly as you risk overcooking them, which gives them a mushy texture, and they are also likely to become tough.

This recipe can also be used for other birds such as guinea fowl, pheasant, partridge and even chicken legs.

8 duck marylands

100 g (3¹/₂ oz) Aromatic Confit Salt (page 10)

2 litres (4¹/₄ pints) Rendered Duck Fat (page 274)

2 cloves garlic, roughly crushed

4 sprigs thyme

1 bay leaf

Rub the salt into the duck marylands, wrap them in cling film then refrigerate for 12 hours to marinate.

Preheat your oven to 110°C (225°F). Wash away the salt and pat the legs thoroughly dry.

Melt the rendered duck fat in a large ovenproof dish and heat to around 85°C (185°F). Add the garlic, thyme and bayleaf and then add the duck marylands, making sure they are completely submerged in the fat. Cover with a piece of greaseproof paper cut to the size of the dish. Cook in the oven for 3 hours until the meat is very tender and comes away from the bone. Drain the marylands in a colander and when cool enough to handle remove the meat and shred into small pieces. Keep the confit meat submerged in the fat. Cover tightly and keep in the fridge for up to 1 month.

Makes 8 duck marylands

CONFIT DUCK GIZZARDS

The gizzard is a small digestive pouch made of a thick muscle found in poultry and game birds. Gizzards can be roasted with the bird, minced and added to a stuffing or combined with the other giblets (heart, liver, kidneys, etc.) to make a ragoût. They are often preserved, especially in duck fat to make a confit.

6 large duck gizzards, rinsed well to remove any grit

80 g (2³/₄ oz) Aromatic Confit Salt (page 10)

800 ml (1¹/₂ pints) Rendered Duck Fat (page 274)

1 clove garlic, roughly crushed

2 sprigs thyme

Remove the 2 fleshy muscles from each side of the gizzard and trim off any sinew – you should end up with 12 pieces. Put them into a bowl and toss with the aromatic salt. Cover with cling film and refrigerate for 2 hours to marinate.

Preheat your oven to 110°C (225°F). Wash away the salt and pat the gizzards thoroughly dry.

Melt the rendered duck fat in a small braising pan and heat to around 85°C (185°F). Add the garlic and thyme and then add the gizzards, making sure they are completely submerged in the fat. Cover with a piece of greaseproof paper cut to the size of the dish. Cook in the oven for 3 hours, being careful not to let the temperature increase or the gizzards will toughen and shrink. Keep the confit gizzards submerged in the fat. Cover tightly and keep in the fridge for up to 1 month.

Makes 12 gizzards

CONFIT PORK NECK

1 x 600 g (20 oz) whole boned pork neck

150 g (5 oz) Aromatic Confit Salt (page 10)

2 litres (4¹/₄ pints) Rendered Duck Fat (page 274)

1 head garlic, cloves roughly crushed

4 sprigs thyme

1 sprig rosemary

1 bay leaf

Cut the neck into three even-sized pieces. Rub the aromatic salt in thoroughly then put the neck pieces in a shallow dish, cover with cling film and refrigerate for 6 hours.

Preheat your oven to 110°C (225°F). Wash away the salt and pat the neck pieces thoroughly dry.

Melt the rendered duck fat in a large ovenproof dish and heat to around 85°C (185°F). Add the garlic, thyme, rosemary and bay leaf and then add the neck pieces, making sure they are completely submerged in the fat. Cover with a piece of greaseproof paper cut to the size of the dish. Cook in the oven for 4 hours until the meat is very tender. Turn pork around in the fat every 30 minutes to ensure even cooking.

Drain the neck pieces in a colander and when cool enough to handle shred meat into small pieces. Keep the confit meat submerged in the fat. Cover tightly and keep in the fridge for up to 1 month.

Makes 1 neck

SPICED CONFIT PORK BELLY

100 g (3½ oz) Aromatic Confit Salt (page 10)

1 teaspoon five spice powder

500 g (18 oz) pork belly

30 ml (1 fl oz) non-scented cooking oil

2 medium onions, roughly chopped

1 head garlic, cloves separated and roughly crushed

6 sprigs thyme

1 bay leaf

4 star anise

10 coriander seeds, crushed

6 cloves, crushed

salt and freshly ground pepper

1.5 litres (3 pints) Brown Pork Stock (page255)

1.5 litres (3 pints) Rendered Duck Fat (page 274)

Mix the aromatic salt with the five spice powder and rub all over the pork belly, massaging it in well. Put the pork belly in a shallow dish, cover with cling film and refrigerate for 12–24 hours.

Preheat your oven to 120°C (245°F). Wash away the salt and pat the pork belly thoroughly dry. Heat a heavy-based saucepan over a medium heat. Add the oil, then the onions and garlic and sauté until caramelised a deep golden-brown. Add the herbs and spices, season with salt and pepper and set aside.

Put the pork stock and duck fat in a braising pan and heat gently until the fat has melted. Add the pork belly and the spiced onions. Cover with a piece of greaseproof paper cut to the size of the pan. Braise gently in the oven for 3 hours until the belly is very tender. Turn around in the braising liquor every 30 minutes to ensure even cooking.

Remove the belly from the braising liquor and leave to cool. The liquor can be used a couple of times and will keep for up to 10 days in the refrigerator.

Makes 500 g (18 oz)

CONFIT GLOBE ARTICHOKES

8 large globe artichokes

juice of 2 lemons mixed with 1 litre (2¼ pints) water

1 litre (2¼ pints) olive oil

4 cloves garlic, roughly crushed

2 sprigs thyme

1 bay leaf

salt and freshly ground pepper

Remove the outer leaves from the artichokes then use a sharp knife to trim around the artichoke hearts. Scoop out the chokes and discard them. Rub the artichokes all over with lemon juice then drop them into the acidulated water to stop them discolouring.

Put the oil in a large heavy-based saucepan and heat to around 85°C (185°F). Add the garlic, bayleaf and thyme. Drain the artichoke hearts and pat them thoroughly dry. Add them to the pan then place a plate on top to keep them submerged in the fat. Cover the pan and cook for around 30 minutes being careful to keep the temperature constant. Don't allow the fat to simmer – you should just see the odd bubble rising to the surface. Drain the artichokes, which should be tender but not mushy. Keep them in the fridge, submerged in the confit oil, for up to 2 weeks.

Makes 8 globe artichokes

CONFIT CELERIAC

2 medium celeriac

1 litre (2¼ pints) Rendered Duck Fat (page 274)

½ head garlic, cloves roughly crushed

3 sprigs thyme

1 bay leaf

salt and freshly ground pepper

Peel the celeriac then use a sharp knife to cut into 2 mm (⅛ in) slices. Put the rendered duck fat into a shallow braising dish and heat gently to about 75°C (165°F). Use the blade of a heavy knife or the palm of your hand to smash the garlic roughly and add it to the duck fat with thyme and bay leaf and season to taste.

Add the celeriac slices, and cover with a piece of greaseproof paper, cut to fit the dish. Place a plate on top to keep the vegetables submerged in the fat. Cover the pan and cook at a very low even temperature, 70–80°C (160–175°F), for around 30 minutes. Don't allow the fat to simmer – you should just see the odd bubble rising to the surface. Drain the celeriac, which should be tender but not mushy. Discard the aromatics and reserve the duck fat for another recipe.

Vegetable accompaniments

POTATO PURÉE

3 x 450g desirée or royal blue potatoes
salt
100 ml (3½ fl oz) milk
100 ml (3½ fl oz) pure cream
300 g (10 oz) cold butter, diced
salt and freshly ground pepper

Finding the correct potato to make the perfect purée can be tricky and will depend on the season. Generally I like to use desirée potatoes, but later in the season they can become a little watery and starchy. Royal blue and spunta potatoes are good alternatives, until desirée come back into peak condition. This is only a guideline, as each year and season is slightly different.

Peel the potatoes and cut them into even-sized pieces. Shape is not important but a consistent size is, to achieve a smooth, even-textured purée. Put the potatoes in a large saucepan, cover with cold water and season well with salt. Bring to the boil and then lower the heat and simmer gently for 12–15 minutes until tender. Drain in a colander and leave to steam-dry for 3–4 minutes.

Push the potatoes through a drum sieve while still hot. Try to push them through in one movement so as not to overwork the starch in the potatoes.

Put the milk, cream and a third of the butter in a saucepan and heat gently until the butter melts. Use a hand-blender to whisk to an emulsion. Fold it through the potato purée to slacken the mix then gradually mix in the rest of the butter. Taste and season according to your preference.

Serves 8 as an accompaniment

JERUSALEM ARTICHOKE PURÉE

500 g (18 oz) Jerusalem artichokes
juice of 2 lemons mixed with 500 ml (18 fl oz) water
120 g (4 oz) unsalted butter
1 onion, finely sliced
2 cloves garlic, finely sliced
2 sprigs thyme
squeeze lemon juice
salt and freshly ground pepper
300 ml (10 fl oz) White Chicken Stock (page 254)

You can adjust the thickness of the purée by adding more or less stock. For a vegetarian version, substitute Vegetable Nage (page 259) for the chicken stock.

Peel the artichokes and slice them thinly. Drop into the acidulated water to stop them discolouring.

Heat a heavy-based saucepan over a medium heat. Add two-thirds of the butter and heat until it starts to foam. Add the onion and garlic and sweat for 5 minutes until they soften but do not colour. Add the artichokes and the thyme and a squeeze of lemon juice. Season well with salt and pepper.

Add the chicken stock and cook for 25–30 minutes until artichokes are soft. Pour through a sieve, reserving the vegetables and hot stock separately. Tip the vegetables into a blender and blitz for 5 minutes, adding the hot stock a little at a time until you have a thick smooth purée. Whiz in the remaining butter until glossy. Taste and adjust seasoning if necessary. Push through a chinois or fine sieve and keep warm until ready to serve.

Serves 4–6 as an accompaniment

SAVOY CABBAGE PURÉE

150 g (5 oz) unsalted butter
1 medium onion, finely sliced
6 cloves garlic, finely sliced
1 small Savoy cabbage
4 sprigs thyme
1 bay leaf
500 ml (18 fl oz) White Chicken Stock (page 254)
salt and freshly ground pepper

For a vegetarian version, substitute the Vegetable Nage (page 259) for the chicken stock.

Heat a heavy-based saucepan over a medium heat. Add two-thirds of the butter and heat until it starts to foam. Add the onion and garlic and sweat for 5 minutes until they soften but do not colour.

Remove the dark outer leaves from the cabbage and set aside. Quarter cabbage and remove the core. Slice finely and add to the pan with the thyme and bay leaf and sweat for 5 minutes without colouring. Add the chicken stock and bring to a gentle simmer. Season well and cook for around 20 minutes, stirring from time to time.

Blanch the reserved cabbage leaves in boiling water for 3 minutes. Refresh in iced water then drain and pat dry. Chop roughly.

Tip the cooked cabbage into a blender and add the chopped blanched leaves. Blitz for 8 minutes, or until smooth and thick. Add the rest of the butter and whiz until a glossy, vibrant green purée. Taste and adjust seasoning if necessary. Push through a chinois or fine sieve and keep warm until ready to serve.

Serves 4–6 as an accompaniment

MUSHROOM PURÉE

30 ml (1 fl oz) non-scented cooking oil
1 medium onion, finely sliced
2 cloves garlic, finely sliced
50 g (1³/₄ oz) unsalted butter
200 g (7 oz) Swiss brown mushrooms, finely sliced
200 g (7 oz) button mushrooms, finely sliced
250 ml (8³/₄ fl oz) White Chicken Stock (page 254) or Mushroom Stock (page 254)
80 ml (2³/₄ fl oz) pure cream
few knobs butter
squeeze lemon juice
salt and freshly ground pepper
splash Madeira

Heat a heavy-based saucepan over a medium heat. Add the oil followed by the onion and garlic. Cook gently for 5 minutes until they start to colour, then add the butter and heat to a nut-brown foam. Add the mushrooms and continue to cook until they caramelise a deep golden-brown.

Add the stock and simmer for around 6–8 minutes, until reduced to a thick syrupy consistency. Add the cream and bring to the boil. Tip into a blender and blitz for 5 minutes until thick and smooth. Whiz in the remaining butter until glossy. Taste, add lemon juice and adjust seasoning if necessary. Push through a chinois or fine sieve, stir in the Madeira and keep warm until ready to serve.

Serves 4–6 as an accompaniment

BUTTERNUT PUMPKIN PURÉE

150 g (5 oz) unsalted butter
1 medium onion, finely sliced
1 head garlic, cloves peeled and finely sliced
1 small butternut pumpkin
500 ml (18 fl oz) White Chicken Stock (page 254)
5 sprigs thyme
1 bay leaf
salt and freshly ground pepper

You can adjust the thickness of the purée by adding more or less stock. And if you want a vegetarian version, substitute Vegetable Nage (page 259) for the chicken stock. Alternatively, make a little pumpkin stock from the pumpkin peel and trimmings.

Heat a heavy-based saucepan over a medium heat. Add two-thirds of the butter and heat until it starts to foam. Add the onion and garlic and sweat for 5 minutes until they soften but do not colour.

Peel the pumpkin and cut in half lengthwise. Scoop out the seeds and cut the pumpkin flesh into small, even-sized pieces. Add to the pan and continue to sweat, without colouring, for 10 minutes.

Add the chicken stock and bring to a gentle simmer. Add the thyme, bay leaf and seasoning to taste. Cover with a piece of greaseproof paper, cut to the size of the pan and simmer gently for about 20 minutes, or until the pumpkin is soft and the stock has thickened.

Tip into a blender and blitz for 5 minutes until smooth and thick. Add the rest of the butter and whiz to a glossy purée. Taste and adjust seasoning if necessary. Push through a chinois or fine sieve and keep warm until ready to serve.

Serves 8–10 as an accompaniment

TURNED POTATOES COOKED IN LAMB STOCK

16 small kipfler potatoes
500 ml (18 fl oz) Brown Lamb Stock (page 255)
2 cloves garlic
2 sprigs thyme
1 sprig rosemary
½ bay leaf
salt and freshly ground pepper

Wash the potatoes well then use a sharp turning knife to top and tail them. Work from top to bottom and cut the potatoes into seven-sided barrels. Keep covered in water until ready to cook.

Put the potatoes into a saucepan with the stock and herbs and bring to a gentle simmer. Season well then simmer gently for 8–10 minutes, or until the potatoes are tender. If not using straightaway, leave to cool in the lamb stock.

Serves 3–4 as an accompaniment

HERB CRUSHED POTATOES

71 kg (2 lb 2 oz) medium nicola potatoes, very well washed
sea salt
120 ml (4 fl oz) extra-virgin olive oil
fleur de sel
freshly ground white pepper
squeeze lemon juice
6 tablespoons mixed herbs, finely chopped (a selection of parsley, chervil, chives and tarragon)

I like to use nicola potatoes for this recipe as they have a soft buttery texture and sweet earthy flavour. Alternatively, use kipfler or Dutch cream potatoes.

It is important not to boil the potatoes or they will split and absorb too much water. This will ruin both the flavour and texture of the potatoes.

Put the potatoes into a large saucepan and cover with water. Season with salt and bring to a light simmer, but do not allow to boil. Simmer very gently for 45 minutes, or until tender.

Drain the potatoes and peel when cool enough to handle. Put them into a large mixing bowl and use your hands or a fork to crush roughly. Add the oil, season and add a squeeze of lemon juice. Just before you serve, mix in the fresh herbs.

Serves 12 as an accompaniment

SWEDE AND CARROT DAUPHINOISE

250 ml (8¾ fl oz) pure cream
75 ml (2⅔ fl oz) milk
¼ head garlic, cloves roughly crushed
2 sprigs thyme
2 medium-large desirée potatoes, peeled
3 large carrots, peeled
1 medium swede, peeled
butter
30 g (1 oz) grated gruyère cheese
30 g (1 oz) grated parmesan cheese
salt and freshly ground pepper

Preheat your oven to 190°C (375°F). Put the cream and milk in a heavy-based saucepan with the garlic and thyme. Bring to a simmer, then lower the heat and simmer very gently for 20 minutes to infuse. Strain through a chinois or fine sieve and set aside.

Cut the potatoes, carrots and swede into 3 mm (⅓ in) slices using a mandolin or very sharp knife.

Grease a deep, rectangular ovenproof dish with a little butter and line the bottom with greaseproof paper. Place an overlapping layer of potatoes in the dish then ladle over some of the infused cream. Sprinkle with a little of each cheese and season well. Repeat with a layer of carrot and then swede and continue to the top of the dish, reserving a little of the cheese.

Cover the dish with aluminium foil and bake for 2 hours or until the vegetables are tender. Remove the foil and sprinkle on the remaining cheese. Return to the oven for 15 minutes to brown the top.

Cool to room temperature then cover with greaseproof paper, weight down and refrigerate until cold. Turn out onto a tray and cut into portions. To serve, either warm through in the oven or fry in a little butter.

Serves 8–10 as an accompaniment

CREAMED SWISS CHARD

6 stalks Swiss chard (silverbeet)

juice of 1 lemon mixed with 500 ml (18 fl oz) water

250 ml (8³/4 fl oz) pure cream

2 cloves garlic

1 bay leaf

3 sprigs thyme

3 sprigs rosemary

salt and freshly ground pepper

To prepare the creamed Swiss chard, peel the stringy outer layer from the stalks, cut into long batons and put them into acidulated water to prevent discolouration. Heat the cream, garlic and herbs in a heavy-based saucepan. Bring to a gentle simmer and season with salt and pepper. Drain the chard and pat thoroughly dry. Add to the hot cream and cook for 12–15 minutes until tender. Keep warm.

Serves 4 as an accompaniment

GLAZED SALSIFY

400 g (14 oz) salsify

juice of 1 lemon mixed with 500 ml (18 fl oz) water

130 g (4¹/2 oz) unsalted butter

3 shallots, finely sliced

100 g (3¹/2 oz) leek, white part only, finely sliced

100 g (3¹/2 oz) celery, finely sliced

3 cloves garlic, finely sliced

150 ml (5 fl oz) white wine

juice of 1 lemon

3 sprigs thyme

1 bay leaf

salt and freshly ground pepper

200 ml (7 fl oz) White Chicken Stock (page 254)

Wash the salsify well then peel and put straight into the acidulated water to stop it discolouring. Trim each one to neat 5 cm (2 in) batons and keep in the water until ready to cook.

Heat a heavy-based saucepan over a medium heat. Add about a third of the butter and heat until it foams. Add the vegetables, except salsify, and garlic and sweat gently until soft but not coloured. Add the white wine and lemon juice and simmer gently until the liquid has reduced by two-thirds.

Add the salsify to the pan with the herbs, seasoning and remaining butter. Toss gently and add enough stock to just cover the vegetables. Simmer gently for 20 minutes, uncovered. Remove from the heat and leave the vegetables to cool in the stock.

To serve, either reheat the salsify in a little of the cooking stock or drain and caramelise it in a little butter, finished with a splash of red wine jus.

Serves 4 as an accompaniment

BRAISED BABY TURNIPS

12 baby turnips

juice of 1 lemon mixed with 500 ml (18 fl oz) water

300 ml (10 fl oz) White Chicken Stock (page 254)

splash chardonnay vinegar

2 cloves garlic

2 sprigs thyme

¹/2 bay leaf

1 teaspoon sugar

salt and freshly ground pepper

Trim away the long roots from the baby turnips. Trim the stalks, leaving about 1 cm (¹/2 in) still attached, and carefully scrape around the base of the stalks to remove any dirt. Rinse well then peel as neatly as possible to preserve the natural round shape. Drop into acidulated water to stop them discolouring.

Put the baby turnips into a small heavy-based saucepan and cover with the chicken stock. Add the remaining ingredients and simmer gently for 15 minutes or until tender. Use straightaway, or refrigerate and keep submerged in the braising stock for up to 2 days.

Serves 4 as an accompaniment

BRAISED BABY ONIONS OR SHALLOTS

12 baby onions or shallots

20 g (²/3 oz) butter

2 cloves garlic, crushed

4 sprigs thyme

¹/2 bay leaf

1 litre (2¹/4 pints) White Chicken Stock (page 254)

salt and freshly ground pepper

Pre-heat your oven to 110°C (225°F). Peel the onions or shallots, being careful to leave the roots intact so they will hold together while braising.

Heat a heavy-based saucepan over a medium heat then add the butter, garlic and onions. Sweat gently for 2 minutes then add the remaining ingredients and bring to a gentle simmer. Cover with a piece of greaseproof paper cut to the size of the pan. Braise very gently for 45 minutes, or until the onions are tender. Be careful not to let the stock boil, as the onions are likely to lose their shape or even disintegrate. Use straightaway, or refrigerate and keep submerged in the braising stock for up to 2 days.

Serves 4 as an accompaniment

ROAST SHALLOTS

12 large shallots
20 ml (²/₃ fl oz) non-scented cooking oil
salt and freshly ground pepper
60 g (2 oz) unsalted butter
30 ml (1 fl oz) sherry vinegar
100 ml (3¹/₂ fl oz) Veal Jus (page 261)
2 cloves garlic, crushed
3 sprigs thyme
1 bay leaf

Preheat your oven to 160°C (320°F). Peel the shallots, being careful to leave the roots intact so they will hold together while roasting.

Heat a small baking tray over a medium-high heat. Add the oil and then the shallots and sauté gently until they begin to colour. Season well then add the butter and heat to a nut-brown foam. Continue to sauté until shallots have caramelised a deep golden-brown.

Add the vinegar to the pan and simmer briskly until reduced to a syrupy glaze. Add the veal jus to the pan and swirl around to mix everything together well. Add the garlic and herbs, transfer to the oven and roast for 20–30 minutes, or until the shallots are tender. Remove from the oven and leave to cool slightly before serving.

Serves 4 as an accompaniment

CARAMELISED SHALLOTS

8 large shallots
¹/₂ tablespoon non-scented cooking oil
100 g (3¹/₂ oz) unsalted butter
salt and freshly ground pepper
50 ml (1³/₄ fl oz) Madeira
sea salt

Preheat your oven to 160°C (320°F). Brush the shallots clean but do not peel them, then cut them in half crosswise.

Heat a small baking tray over a low heat and add just enough oil to moisten. Add the shallots to the pan, cut side down, and arrange them so they sit snugly together. Leave for around 10 minutes so that the natural sugars are released and they start to caramelise.

Add the butter and increase the heat so that it melts to a nut-brown foam. Season generously and baste the shallots. Transfer to the oven and cook for 20 minutes. Check from time to time to make sure the butter doesn't burn.

Remove from the oven and season again. Add the Madeira and swirl around in the pan juices.

Carefully squeeze the shallots out of their skins and serve at once with the pan juices and a light sprinkling of sea salt.

Serves 4 as an accompaniment

LYONNAISE ONIONS

4 onions
50 ml (1³/₄ fl oz) Rendered Duck Fat (page 274)
4 sprigs thyme, leaves picked from the stalks
2 cloves garlic, peeled
salt and freshly ground pepper

Cut the onions in half lengthwise then trim the root and remove the papery skin. Use a sharp knife to slice the onions very finely.

Heat a heavy-based saucepan over a medium-high heat and add the rendered duck fat followed by the sliced onions. Sauté for 8–10 minutes stirring from time to time, until the onions soften down to a golden-brown tangle. They will reduce considerably, so transfer to a smaller saucepan and return to the heat.

Lower the heat and add the thyme leaves and garlic cloves and season lightly. Cook very gently, uncovered, for 2–3 hours, stirring from time to time to make sure the onions don't burn. Add a little more duck fat if need be. After 2–3 hours the onions should be a dark golden-brown with a lovely rich caramel flavour. Serve straightaway or refrigerate for up to 1 week.

Serves 4 as an accompaniment

ROAST GARLIC

1 head garlic
3 sprigs thyme
1 sprig rosemary
1 bay leaf
30 ml (1 fl oz) olive oil
salt and freshly ground pepper

Serve the peeled roasted garlic cloves whole as a garnish, or pound them gently in a mortar to make a garlic purée.

Preheat your oven to 160°C (320°F). Break the head of garlic into individual cloves leaving the skins intact.

Heat an ovenproof frying pan until very hot. Add the garlic cloves with the herbs, oil and seasoning and toss together well. Transfer to the oven and roast for 40 minutes until the garlic cloves are golden-brown and very soft.

Remove from the oven, peel the garlic cloves and serve immediately.

Serves 4 as a garnish

CHOUCROUTE

15 juniper berries
10 black peppercorns
3 star anise
1 cinnamon stick
3 cloves garlic
8 sprigs thyme
1 bay leaf
100 g (3½ oz) Wet Salt (page 9)
1 large Savoy cabbage, cored and very finely sliced
300 ml (10 fl oz) Rendered Duck Fat (page 274)
2 large onions, very finely sliced
300 g (10 oz) pancetta, cut into a few big chunks
750 ml (1⅓ pints) riesling

This is the French word for sauerkraut, meaning 'bitter herb', and is a specialty of Alsace, Lorraine and parts of Germany. The dish is finely sliced white cabbage that is then salted and fermented. Traditionally it accompanies smoked pork or sausages.

Crush the juniper berries, peppercorns, star anise and cinnamon in a mortar then add the garlic, thyme and bay leaf and pound to a fragrant paste. Scrape into a large mixing bowl, add the salt and mix together well. Add the cabbage to the bowl and mix together thoroughly. Cover with cling film and leave in a warm place for 24–48 hours to ferment. The longer you leave it, the stronger the flavour will be. Tip into a colander and rinse well under running water to remove the salt.

Preheat your oven to 100°C (210°F). Heat a large casserole dish and add the duck fat and onions. Sweat for about 10 minutes until soft. Add the cabbage to the pan with the pancetta and riesling. Cover with a piece of greaseproof paper cut to the size of the casserole dish. Cover tightly and braise in the oven for 4 hours. Stir every 30 minutes to make sure the cabbage cooks evenly and doesn't burn.

Remove from the oven and leave to cool. Tip onto a flat tray and pick out any large pieces of spice.

Serves 12 as an accompaniment

HORSERADISH CHANTILLY

200 ml (7 fl oz) pure cream
1 fresh horseradish, grated
1 teaspoon Dijon mustard
salt and freshly ground pepper
squeeze lemon juice

Use as an accompaniment to joints of roast beef and pork, on charcuterie plates or in sandwiches.

Put the cream into a mixing bowl and add the grated horseradish. Leave to infuse for at least 12 hours to extract the maximum flavour.

Whisk in the mustard, followed by the salt, pepper and lemon juice to taste. Whisk to medium-firm peaks and set aside until ready to use.

Makes 300 ml (10 fl oz)

ARTICHOKES OR ASPARAGUS BARIGOULE

12 globe artichokes or 20 spears white asparagus, medium thick

1 medium onion

300 ml (10 fl oz) olive oil

1 medium carrot, finely sliced

6 cloves garlic, finely sliced

salt and freshly ground pepper

300 ml (10 fl oz) white wine

50 ml (1³/4 fl oz) white wine vinegar

6 sprigs thyme

12 coriander seeds, crushed and tied in a muslin square

500 ml (18 fl oz) White Chicken Stock (page 254) or Vegetable Nage (page 259)

squeeze lemon juice

generous handful fresh herbs, a selection of coriander, basil, flat leaf parsley and tarragon

Artichokes à la barigoule is a famous Provençal recipe with numerous variations. Larger artichokes, for instance, may be stuffed with bacon, mushrooms and breadcrumbs while smaller artichokes are braised unstuffed in a wine-based, vegetable braise.

The name of the dish is thought to derive from the Provençal word for the milk-cap mushroom, and originally the artichokes were cooked like mushrooms, cut flat at the base and grilled or braised in an aromatic oil. I also like to prepare asparagus in this way – especially white asparagus.

If preparing artichokes, remove the outer leaves then use a sharp knife to trim around the artichoke hearts. Scoop out the chokes and discard them. Rub the artichokes all over with lemon juice then drop them into acidulated water to stop them discolouring.

If preparing asparagus, peel them and snap off the woody ends.

Cut the onion in half lengthwise. Remove the core and use a sharp knife to slice as finely as possible.

Heat a heavy-based saucepan then add the oil followed by the onions, carrot and garlic. Season generously and sweat for about 5 minutes until the vegetables are soft but not coloured.

Add the white wine, vinegar, thyme and the muslin bag of coriander seeds. Simmer on a high heat to reduce the liquid by two-thirds. Add the artichokes or asparagus and toss well. Add the stock and bring to a simmer and cook for 1 minute.

Taste and adjust the seasoning balance to your preference. Add a squeeze of lemon juice to freshen the flavour then add the fresh herbs and stir well. Cover with cling film and leave to infuse at room temperature. Refrigerate overnight to allow the flavours to develop.

Serve the artichokes or asparagus with the braising vegetables and liquor. Alternatively, serve them on their own, in which case you can purée the braising liquor and vegetables to make a tasty soup. Pass through a chinois or fine sieve and serve chilled on a hot day.

Serves 4 as an accompaniment

Deep-fried garnishes

DEEP-FRIED PARSLEY LEAVES

2 cups flat-leaf parsley leaves

300 ml (10 fl oz) non-scented cooking oil

salt and freshly ground pepper

Use this method for deep-frying all kinds of leaves to use as fragrant crisp garnish. I particularly like lemon verbena, Vietnamese mint and basil.

Put the oil into a small deep saucepan and heat to 180°C (350°F).

Drop the parsley leaves into the oil one at a time. Be careful as the oil is likely to spit. Deep-fry each leaf for a few seconds until crisp and bright green. Remove from the oil with a slotted spoon and drain on kitchen paper. Season with salt and freshly ground pepper, keep warm and use within an hour or so.

Serves 12 as a garnish

EGGPLANT CRISPS

2 Japanese eggplant
300 ml (10 fl oz) non-scented cooking oil
salt and freshly ground pepper

Heat the oil in a small deep saucepan to 160°C (320°F).

While the oil is heating, use a mandolin or very sharp knife to slice the eggplants thinly. Deep-fry the eggplant slices a few at a time, stirring them in the oil to ensure they colour evenly. Remove from the oil and drain on kitchen paper. Season with salt and freshly ground pepper, keep warm and use within an hour or so.

Serves 4 as a garnish

DEEP-FRIED GINGER

100 g (3½ oz) fresh ginger
300 ml (10 fl oz) non-scented cooking oil
salt and freshly ground pepper
squeeze lemon juice

Peel the ginger and slice it finely. Blanch in boiling water seasoned with a little salt, sugar and lemon. Refresh in iced water. Repeat 2–3 times, depending on the strength of the ginger. You want it to be aromatic with a hint of heat, but not overpowering. Drain and pat dry.

Heat the oil in a small deep pan to 180°C (350°F). Deep-fry the ginger slices for a couple of minutes, until golden and crisp, turning them in the oil to ensure they colour evenly. Remove from the oil and drain on kitchen paper. Season with salt and freshly ground pepper, add lemon juice, and keep warm and use within an hour or so.

Serves 4 as a garnish

DEEP-FRIED SHALLOT RINGS

1 litre (2¼ pints) non-scented cooking oil
6 shallots, sliced crosswise into rings
300 ml (10 fl oz) milk
100 g (3½ oz) plain flour, sieved and seasoned with salt and pepper
salt and freshly ground pepper

Put the oil into a small deep saucepan and heat to 180°C (350°F).

Separate the shallot rings and soak in milk for a few minutes to soften the flavour. Drain well and pat dry. Toss the shallot rings in the seasoned flour, shaking off any excess.

Deep-fry the shallots a few at a time until golden-brown. Keep them moving around in the oil so that they colour evenly. Remove from the oil with a slotted spoon and drain on kitchen paper. Season with salt and freshly ground pepper, keep warm and use within an hour or so.

Serves 4

Glossary
OF TERMS AND INGREDIENTS

AROMATIC Fragrant plants used to add to dishes. They are an indispensable addition to many dishes, and can be leaves, seeds, fruits, stalks or bulbs. They are distinguished from spices largely in that they contribute fragrance to a dish, whereas spices contribute flavour.

BAIN-MARIE A double boiler or hot water bath used to keep sauces, soups or dishes warm, for melting delicate ingredients such as chocolate, or for cooking dishes very slowly. At home, a makeshift bain-marie can be made by suspending a bowl over a saucepan of gently simmering water. The important thing is not to let the bottom of the bowl touch the water and not to let the water boil as condensation will spoil the preparation.

BALLOTTINE A French dish that is usually (but not exclusively) applied to game birds and poultry. These are boned out, stuffed and rolled to form a cylindrical shape. They are often wrapped in muslin or crepinette and are poached or braised before being sliced.

BARIGOULE Traditionally a method for preparing artichokes ('à la barigoule'), thought to derive from the Provençal name for the milk cap mushroom. Originally the artichokes were cooked like mushrooms, cut flat at the base and grilled or braised in an aromatic oil. Other vegetables, such as asparagus, may also be cooked in this way.

BASTE To spoon pan juices over a dish to add flavour and keep the food moist during the cooking process.

BEURRE NOISETTE Literally, 'hazelnut butter', made by heating butter past the melting stage until it turns deep brown and smells nutty, but before it burns. Beurre noisette can be used to baste food during cooking or as a simple sauce, especially for fish.

BLANCH To immerse food in rapidly boiling, seasoned water before refreshing it in iced water. This method is used to par-cook ingredients – especially vegetables, to preserve the colour, and to loosen the skins of tomatoes, almonds etc.

BLIND-BAKE To pre-bake a lined pastry tart shell before it is filled. This is done to ensure the pastry is thoroughly cooked and to help prevent wet fillings soaking into the pastry and making it soggy.

BONITO FLAKES Bonito fish are steamed, dried and then shaved into paper-thin flakes. They are most often used with konbu (dried sea kelp) to make dashi broth.

BRAISING DISH A heavy-duty two-handled cooking pan, which has tremendous heat-retaining qualities. Braising dishes are excellent for long slow cooking (braising) as the dish will maintain an even, low temperature for a long period of time.

BRINE A salt solution used to preserve meat, vegetables and fish. It generally consists of water, salt, sugar, red or white wine and sometimes aromatics and spices.

BRUNOISE A French term applied to a perfect tiny dice of an ingredient, usually vegetables. Traditionally brunoise are cut to 2 mm (1/8 in) dice.

CÈPE Also known as porcini, this is a large boletus mushroom with a dark brown cap and a bulbous swollen stalk. Incredibly flavoursome, the cèpe is one of the most highly prized mushrooms of Europe.

CHANTERELLE A very tasty, fragile, orange-yellow, funnel-shaped mushroom.

CHANTILLY A flavoured cream, lightly beaten to the consistency of a mousse. Chantilly cream is often lightly sweetened and is mainly used in desserts and pastries.

CHIFFONNADE The preparation of leafy herbs or vegetables, typically lettuce and flat-leaf parsley, which are stacked together and very finely shredded.

CHINOIS A conical strainer, usually made out of fine metallic mesh, used to pass sauces, stocks and purées, resulting in a very fine, smooth finish.

CHLOROPHYLL The pigment in green vegetables and herbs that is responsible for capturing the light energy needed for photosynthesis.

CIVET Traditionally, a game stew, made from wild rabbit, hare, venison, boar and sometimes, seafood. The sauce is usually made with wine and thickened with the animal's own blood, which gives it a distinctive reddish colour. The name is derived from the French word *cive* – spring onion – which is a traditional flavouring.

CLARIFIED BUTTER Clarified butter is a pure, clear fat that has had the milk solids removed. This means it can be heated to a higher temperature, without the risk of burning. It is made by gently heating butter until the milk solids fall to the bottom of the saucepan.

COLANDER A large, flat-bottomed perforated bowl used for draining liquids from coarse solids or for washing.

CONFIT From the French word meaning 'to preserve' this is one of the oldest ways of preparing and conserving food. It is a method of slow-cooking in fat (rendered pork, duck or goose) or an aromatic oil and results in extremely tender meat, which flakes away from the bone easily. Confit foods are stored in a pot, covered in the same fat.

CREPINETTE Also known as *crépine* or caul, it is a fatty membrane that lines the stomach of animals, and in cooking it is usually obtained from pigs. Dishes prepared 'en crepinette' are encased in caul before cooking. The caul melts during the cooking process, keeping its contents moist and intact. Always order young crepinette as it has a fine, even membrane, which is stronger and contains fewer holes.

CURING This is one of the oldest preserving processes known to man, in which the food product (meat or fish) is completely covered in a dry salt mix or a liquid brine for a period of time. This process reduces the moisture content and kills bacteria (which can lead to spoilage), and thus allows food to be preserved. Curing is often used in the process before smoking.

DASHI Essential in Japanese cooking, this is an all-purpose broth made from konbu (dried kelp) and bonito (dried fish flakes).

DODINE This is a technique for poultry or game birds (often duck) which are boned out and stuffed with a mixture of the breast meat, confit leg meat and offal. The birds are rolled in crepinette and braised.

DRUM SIEVE Also known as a tammy, this is a flat, round sieve made with a fine metallic mesh. It is used for passing mousses, purées and so on, to remove any lumps or foreign matter.

DUXELLE A basic preparation of sautéed mushrooms which are finely chopped. Often mixed with shallots and chopped herbs, duxelle is used as a stuffing, garnish or in sauces.

EMULSION A way of mixing one ingredient into another with which it does not mix. Typically, emulsions consist of a fatty substance (such as an oil or butter) dispersed in water, vinegar or lemon juice. Emulsions, such as vinaigrettes, can be held briefly by briskly whisking the oil into the acid, but to hold an emulsion stable, for sauces like hollandaise for instance, it needs to be bound by an emulsifier, usually egg yolk.

ESCABÈCHE Escabèche is a traditional Spanish marinade, particularly used for fish or small game birds. The fish or birds are fried, then covered with a hot spicy marinade. They are left to cool in the marinade for 24 hours or so and then served at room temperature.

FRICASSÉE A way of preparing chicken, meat and sometimes fish, in a white sauce or velouté. The ingredients are cut into small pieces and dusted in flour before being sautéed without browning. White stock is added and the dish is cooked in the thickening liquid.

FRISÉE Also known as curly endive, this is a salad leaf with an appealing bitter flavour. The outer leaves are dark, tough and inedible, but they protect a delicate heart of pale golden leaves.

INFUSE To steep herbs, spices and other flavourings in a hot liquid to impart a delicate fragrance. The resulting liquid is called an infusion.

INTERCOSTAL Also known as the rib fingers, this intensely marbled section of meat lies between the ribs of the Wagyu cattle.

JULIENNE A method of cutting a vegetable into thin slices and then into thin strips resembling a matchstick. Traditionally, julienne strips are around 3 cm (1¼ in) long and around 2 mm (⅛ in) thick.

JUS A French word translating roughly to 'juice', but with a specific culinary meaning. A *jus* is used primarily as a gravy for roast meats and is made by diluting the pan juices with stock and then boiling and reducing it, until the goodness from the roasting pan has been absorbed. The word 'jus' is also applied to raw vegetable and fruit juices.

KONBU Sea kelp harvested from the cold waters north of Japan. It is sold dried and is essential in making dashi.

MÂCHE Also known as lamb's lettuce, it has a young delicate rounded leaf.

MANDOLIN An extremely sharp vegetable slicer with two adjustable blades: one plane for slicing fine ribbons, the other grooved for linguine.

MILLE FEUILLE Literally 1000 leaves or layers. Traditionally, this is a pastry dish, consisting of thin layers of puff pastry that are sandwiched with cream, jam or confectioner's custard. The term is also loosely applied to other multi-layered dishes.

MIREPOIX A mixture of coarsely chopped vegetables used as a base for making stocks, bouillons, braises and stews. It usually comprises onion, carrot, celery and leek. For a white mirepoix, the carrot is omitted.

MIRIN A sweet rice wine used in Japanese cooking. Japanese brands are usually the best quality.

MOREL Known as *morille* in French, this is a very rare but tasty mushroom found in the springtime. Its rich brown conical cap is deeply furrowed in a honeycomb pattern. Morels are one of the great mushrooms of Europe.

MORTAR AND PESTLE A mortar is a bowl, the pestle a pounding stick. They are commonly made of marble, sometimes earthenware and, occasionally, wood. Originating in ancient times they are used to pound pastes, powders, herbs and spices and are an essential piece of kitchen equipment.

MOULI/DAIKON A long, thick white radish which is very popular in Japanese cuisine.

NAGE A nage is a delicately flavoured, aromatic broth in which shellfish and crustacea are lightly poached and served. It is often finished with a dash of cream and fresh herbs. Dishes prepared in this way are described as *à la nage* (literally, 'swimming').

PANCETTA Cured, smoked and aged belly of pork.

PARMIGIANO REGGIANO A superior Italian Parmesan cheese that is aged for three years.

PICKLING This is a technique for preserving food – typically vegetables and fruits – in a lightly spiced vinegar. The acid permeates the food and kills most of the bacteria and also somewhat softens their texture. Pork and beef are pickled in brine to which saltpetre has been added.

QUENELLE A presentation method for creams, ice creams, sorbets and mousses. Quenelles are shaped into little smooth 'dumplings' between two spoons, or by a dragging and curling an oval spoon across the surface of the mixture. The spoons should be warmed slightly to ensure the quenelle is smooth and to prevent it sticking.

REDUCE To boil a liquid uncovered over a high heat, to reduce the quantity and concentrate the flavour and consistency.

REFRESH To plunge a blanched vegetable, herb or pasta into iced water to immediately stop the cooking process and retain flavour, texture and colour.

RENDER To gently melt and clarify solid fat into a liquid, often using a little water and various aromatics.

SAKE A clear Japanese wine made from fermented rice.

SAUTÉ To cook small pieces of meat, fish or vegetables in a frying pan or saucepan over a moderately high heat. Stirring or gently shaking the pan will aid the even distribution of heat and assist in an even browning.

SEAR To quickly colour meat, fish, poultry or game in a very hot frying pan with a little non-scented oil. This method prevents the juices from running, browns the food nicely (if required) and reduces the cooking time.

SKIM To ladle off any impurities in stocks and sauces as they rise to the surface during the cooking process. Skimming is essential to obtain a fresh clear stock.

STOCK A flavoured liquid base used for making sauces, soups, stews and braises. They are based on meat, poultry or seafood bones and off cuts or vegetables and flavoured with herbs. For brown stocks, these base ingredients are browned in fat and roasted in the oven, which darkens the colour and deepens the flavour. Stocks are an essential ingredient in cooking.

SUGAR SYRUP Also known as stock syrup or gomme, stock syrup is an important dessert basic, and used in everything from fruit salads, jellies and sorbets to sweet pastries. It is a solution of equal parts sugar and water boiled together to make a syrup and can be flavoured with vanilla pods, citrus zest or fresh herb leaves.

SWEAT Generally applied to vegetables when they are cooked in a small amount of fat over a gentle heat, sufficient to soften, but not to colour them.

TERRINE Traditionally, a deep earthenware dish with straight sides and a tight-fitting lid. Nowadays, terrines are produced in a varying array of shapes, sizes and materials. Dishes that are cooked, served or pressed in such a mould are known as terrines. They are usually made from mixed meats, but can also be made with poultry, seafood and vegetables. They are often set in aspic jelly.

TORO A Japanese term applied to bluefin tuna, meaning 'belly', which has varying degrees of fat content and marbling. It is highly prized by the Japanese for sushi and sashimi. (*Shimo turi* – meaning 'marbling'; *Akami* – the loin; *Chu toro* – the highly marbled middle section of the belly; *Oh toro* – pale coloured, the most intensely marbled tip of the belly)

TROMPETTES Also known as *trompette-de-la-mortes*, horn of plenty and trumpet of death. These are common French woodland mushrooms resembling a black funnel or trumpet.

WAKAME A dark, nutritious Japanese seaweed usually bought dry in tiny pieces. It should be soaked in warm water for 15 minutes before use.

Index

Acknowledgements

A special thank you to the people who let us into their homes and lives. Sharing your incredible stories, wisdom, methods and motivation made it a unique and exciting experience for us all.

Liam – It was when I met you at Cassis in '94 that everything started to fall into place. You have taught me a hell of a lot over the past twelve years, most importantly to keep striving for perfection at whatever cost and to never give up. You are a true inspiration and a great friend.

David Price – Thank you for getting me started and for sending me on my way.

Graham – Thank you for believing in us and for giving us that foot-up we so desperately needed. Your trust is everything to us.

It takes many people to create a book such as this. I was fortunate enough to put together a team of very special and extremely talented young professionals, who together worked tirelessly on this project from start to finish. I value the special moments, trips, fun and memories we all had in producing this work. I wish to thank those who have played a special part:

Kirsty de Garis – Thank you for your amazing words, your uncompromising professionalism and your never-ending support throughout this project. Thank you for putting up with my million and one questions, my constant changes of mind. You have been a pillar of support.

James Metcalfe – After opening the original Bécasse in Surry Hills with me, and now as head chef, your complete dedication to the restaurant is unwavering. A bloody workhorse, your enthusiasm for this project has been highly contagious to all. You have been extremely loyal and are a great friend – thank you.

Steve Brown – You really do possess those very rare qualities of a great photographer – a gifted eye, a special feeling of 'the right moment'. A true dream and an honour to work with. And also a splendid bloke.

Cassandra Warner of Scribble Design and Hamish Freeman and Klarissa Pfisterer of Pfisterer + Freeman – Thank you for your fantastic designs and unique concepts. Your professionalism and creativity have been tremendous. You took our words, our recipes and our photos and made them into something very special. Thanks a million.

Toru Kiuchi – Thank you for your commitment to Bécasse, your interest in the book and, above all, for all the laughs.

Also to Mary Small and the team at Hardie Grant for believing in this project and supporting my work. With your expertise and experience this book has been taken to the next level. Sandy, Jane, Julie and Fran – thanks heaps. Thanks also to Lucy Malouf for the final recipe edit.

Angela Bowne – Your support, direction and legal advice is most appreciated.

Thanks to those special friends I have worked with and known for many years – Alex Mackay, David Goodridge, Matt Kemp, Warren Turnbull, Sean Connelly, Colin Fassnidge, Brett Graham, Robin Zavou, Anthony Puharich – you are all a constant source of inspiration.

A heartfelt thanks to all the staff at Bécasse for your continued support, dedication and loyalty. It is great to share our vision with such a wonderful and talented bunch of people.

To the special guests and loyal customers who have supported Bécasse for many years, and the growers, farmers and suppliers, who have been an integral part of our success – thank you.

And above all to my beautiful and loving wife Georgia.

Producers

SALT
Sunsalt
www.sunsalt.com.au

MUSHROOM
Noel Arrold
tel. (02) 4871 2879

TRUFFLE
Tim Terry/Tasmanian Truffle Enterprises
www.tastruffles.com.au

GOAT'S CHEESE
Woodside Cheese Wrights
www.coriole.com/i.cfm/63/

SHELLFISH
Salty Seas
tel: (03) 6376 1252

CRUSTACEA
Mulataga
www.mulataga.com

TUNA, MULLOWAY AND KINGFISH
The Stehr Group
www.stehrgroup.com

OCEAN TROUT AND SALTWATER CHAR
Petuna Seafood
www.petuna.com

SQUAB PIGEON
Glenloth Game
tel: (03) 5493 7383

PORK
Bangalow Sweet Pork
www.sweetpork.com.au

LAMB
Castricum Brothers
www.castricum.com.au

WAGYU BEEF
David Blackmore
www.blackmorewagyu.com.au

BLOOD ORANGE
Joe and Maria Barila
tel: (03) 5024 8528